PORTRAIT OF DORSET

Portrait of
DORSET

by

RALPH WIGHTMAN

This edition edited by

ROLAND GANT

ILLUSTRATED
AND WITH MAP

ROBERT HALE . LONDON

© *Ralph Wightman* 1965, 1968, 1977 and 1983

First published in Great Britain 1965

Reprinted 1966
Second Edition 1968
Reprinted 1972
Reprinted 1974
Third edition 1977
Fourth edition 1983

Robert Hale Limited
Clerkenwell House
Clerkenwell Green
London EC1R 0HT

ISBN 0 7090 0844 9

Printed in Great Britain by
St Edmundsbury Press, Bury St Edmunds, Suffolk
and bound by Hunter & Foulis

CONTENTS

I	THE SHAPE OF THE LAND	9
II	THE HEATH	22
III	THE HEATH VILLAGES	42
IV	THE CHALK FRINGE	59
V	THE CHALK—TYPICAL UPLANDS	79
VI	THE DRY UPLANDS	117
VII	THE BLACKMORE VALE	129
VIII	WEST DORSET	150
IX	THE COAST	162
	Index	186

EDITOR'S NOTE

Since 1971, the year in which Ralph Wightman died, there have been changes in Dorset as everywhere else. Geoffrey N. Wright, Editor of the 1977 edition of this book, referred to the 1974 county boundary revisions and made a number of important changes to the original text. The further changes which I have made are limited to those passages which, if left unaltered, would misinform, baffle or send adrift those who are not already intimately familiar with the county. In no respect does this revision of information affect the flavour and opinions of this affectionate and highly personal portrait of his native county by a great man of Dorset.

January 1983   R.G.
Armswell, Dorset

ILLUSTRATIONS

1	The Great Heath	*facing page* 16
2	Lyme Regis High Street	17
3	Brownsea Island across Poole Harbour	32
4	St. Martin's church, Wareham	33
5	The River Frome by Wareham Bridge	48
6	Bere Regis church roof	49
7	Bulbarrow Hill	64
8	The Frome, Lower Bockhampton	65
9	Ramparts of Maiden Castle	80
10	Dorchester	81
11	The Cerne Giant	96
12	Piddletrenthide	*between pages*
13	Wynford Eagle church	96 *and* 97
14	Milton Abbas village	
15	Gold Hill, Shaftesbury	*facing page* 97
16	The Northern edge of Cranborne Chase	112
17	Sherborne Abbey	113
18	The church tower, Beaminster	128
19	West Bay, near Bridport	129
20	Golden Cap from Thorncombe Beacon	144
21	Chesil Beach	145
22	The sea is beyond the Chesil Beach across the Fleet and Portland is on the horizon	160
23	Old waterfront and harbour, Weymouth	161
24	Pack Horse Bridge, Fifehead Neville	176
25	Bridge over the River Stour at Sturminster Newton	176
26	Corfe Castle	177

MAP

Dorset	*pages* 12–13

ACKNOWLEDGEMENTS

The photographs reproduced in this book are the copy-
right of the following: Mr. Leslie D. Frisby of Dorchester, nos. 1, 5 and 6; Mr. Geoffrey N. Wright, nos. 2, 14,
16, 19, 20 and 26; Mr. R. Winstone of Bristol, 3, 4, 8, 11
and 15; Mr. Will F. Taylor of Reigate, 7, 9, 17 and 21;
The Mustograph Agency, 10, 18 and 23; Roland Gant,
nos. 12, 13, 22, 24 and 25.

I

THE SHAPE OF THE LAND

DORSET has no high mountains and no coal. Everything else of beauty and almost everything of utility can be found within its borders.

In the absence of coal, industry has not blasted the countryside, but manufactures have had their influence on the life of the county. Bridport has made ropes and nets for more than eight centuries. Today fishermen from the ends of the earth still use Bridport nets. The Tudor industry of making West Country cloth has not survived, but we are left with the pleasant houses of prosperous merchants in Beaminster. Long before the age of oil there was prospecting in the shale of Kimmeridge. Industry shaped the small towns more than agricultural markets and fairs, in fact weekly livestock markets were largely a Victorian development usually connected with the railways. The great annual fairs were not necessarily closely associated with towns at all, and much of the trade at them was done by travelling hucksters. Woodbury Hill Fair, for instance, was held on a bare hill about a mile from the relatively small village of Bere Regis. A similar function was held at Toller Down Gate, three miles from Beaminster. Neither had any influence on Dorset towns, which all had perfectly plain industrial or ecclesiastical reasons for existence. The thought of towns trading with rural areas has been much developed in recent years. The old contact—except for the immediate fields—was confined to annual sales of corn, wool and cheese. Dorset industry has always provided most of the living of the towns; their situation was also fixed partly for defence, as at Wareham, and partly through the growth of extremely rich abbeys.

The shape of the countryside arose from the underlying rocks. I am using the word "rock" in its geological sense, meaning stone, sand, clay and chalk. It is the immense difference in the strata of Dorset that gives the county its infinite variety of scenery. A geological map shows all the rocks of Eastern England coming down into Dorset like the ribs of an open fan. The result is a miniature of almost every kind of scenery.

For instance, a model of the Weald of Sussex can be found in Purbeck, with North and South Downs and a valley of Wealden Clay. The heaths of Surrey are basically the same as that collection of Dorset Commons which Thomas Hardy called Egdon Heath. The chalk is nobly represented from the Hampshire/Wiltshire border to the great cliffs near Weymouth, and to the towering Stone Age fort at Eggardon. We have the Midland Plain in Blackmore Vale, the red soil of the Cotswolds reduced to a narrow ridge, and in West Dorset the tumbled hills which motorists always imagine to be in Devon. The mighty rock of Portland is wholly Dorset and is like nothing else on earth.

These underlying rocks shape the land in the sense that chalk and hard stone are largely flat. The action of falling rain and running water has brought out the character of these widely varied foundations of the land. Chalk gives rounded slopes with steep-sided narrow valleys between rolling plateaux. Limestone hills usually have flat tops with sides which are almost cliffs. The sandstone hills are conical to the point of looking almost artificial. They owe their shape to a small cap of stone.

The only two rock formations which are at all extensive in Dorset are the chalk and the many coloured sands and clays of the heathland. They occupy most of the east of the county and give the widest areas of consistent scenery. Much of the rest of Dorset changes so quickly that it is confusing even for natives. There is a feeling that in the countryside of the chalk and the heath there is an understandable plan, but that the rest of the county was made by young and playful gods.

Several rivers cross the heath land and produce a predictable pattern. Writing about similar country in the New Forest of Hampshire in his *Rural Rides* of 1825, William Cobbett described the soil as "spewy sand". This somewhat inelegant description conveys a real meaning to a farmer. Professor John Perceval of Reading University, writing in 1905, uses the scientific name Bagshot Beds for the underlying strata of the Dorset Heaths. He says, "The Bagshot Beds are composed of a series of sands of various colours, black, red, white and yellow, with thin irregular seams of pipe clay in places. The sands occupy the extensive waste land in the south-east corner of the county round Poole and Wareham. The district grows little but heather, gorse and sedge. A few plantations of pines and fir trees are scattered here and there. A large part of the land is undrained bog, and is little cultivated." My own experience of heath is that after rain the water will lie on the surface for hours in clear but slightly peat-stained pools. Yet digging seems to uncover nothing except a coarse dry sand, into which one would expect rain to sink as fast as it disappears into the sands of the sea shore. To a cultivator there is something mysterious about an extremely porous soil which is none the less waterlogged. This condition exists on all the heath with the extreme of blowing sand in summer and standing water after every heavy shower. Rivers flowing through the sands and gravels of the heath do not cut deep channels as one might expect. Instead there is a tendency for flooding over wide valleys with the dropping of a great deal of mud. Throughout the ages the river valleys have made fertile plains, especially where the streams have previously flowed for much of their length through chalky soils. The mud from the chalk is alkaline and counteracts the very sour soil of the heath. Such chalky streams are the Frome and Piddle which have made fertile meadows inland from Wareham, and the much bigger Stour River. The Stour gives the wide fertile stretch from Corfe Mullen, through Wimborne to Hampreston, Long Ham and West Parley. Here it crosses the county border, but continues with a similar productive border across the Bournemouth heaths to Christchurch. The only other stream of any size on the heath has an edging of meadows, but these are small and not very good. The reason may be that the Moors River does not flow through chalk, but is acid from its birth. It has not brought down any fertile silt, and in fact on occasions has done more harm than good. The strange sands under these heaths are sometimes capable of flowing like the material in an hour glass. I have seen minor excavations tap running sand, which has flowed along with the stream covering the neighbouring meadows in inches of barren white sand which has buried the grass. Similar, but underground, movement of sand has produced deep conical pits in the heath, of which more later. The essential look of the south-eastern heath is low lying country, largely barren, but crossed by fertile river valleys.

Between the heather and the chalk a narrow belt of woodland crosses the county from Cranborne through Kingston Lacy to Bere Regis and to Puddletown. It is never a mile wide but the trees can be seen, always about one field in, on the main road from Puddletown to Wimborne, and again from Wimborne to Cranborne. This strip of naturally wooded land is on Reading Beds and London clay.

On the left of the road is the chalk which is generally treeless, except where men have planted beeches to make avenues, clumps and vistas. The natural trees on the chalk are on the silt of the narrow river valleys, where tall elms are common, or on some of the flat hill tops where clay is found over the chalk. This "clay with flint" is mainly at the northern

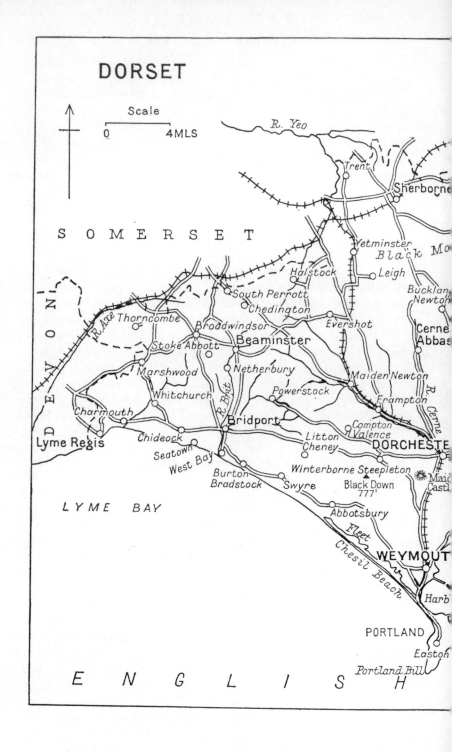

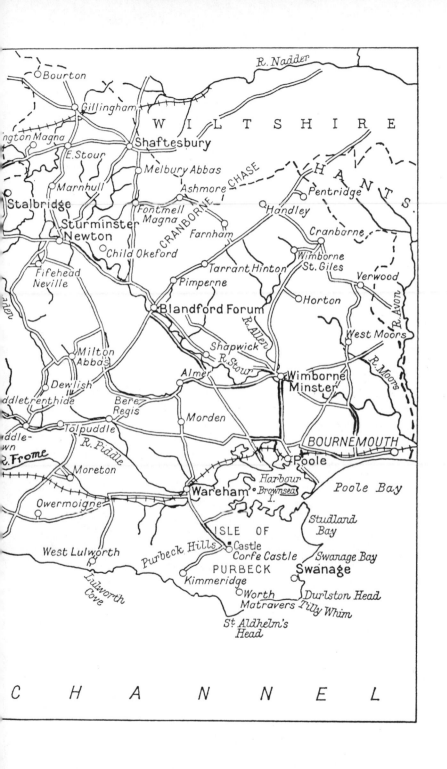

end of the chalk formation at Ashmore, Tarrant Gunville and Farnham in Cranborne Chase. The clay varies in depth from one to six feet or more and gives a sticky red soil very different from the thin grey earth which covers most of the chalk. Some of the woodlands in the Chase may well be utterly unchanged from the Stone Age, but where smaller patches of clay occur through the chalk area it is usual to find plantations of hazel and ash. These may not be more than 150 years old, and were coppiced about every ten years for wattle hurdles and hay cribs.

The chalk landscape runs from the Wiltshire border diagonally to the south-west. It is about ten miles wide and is easily the biggest single type of country in Dorset. From the Puddletown/Wimborne road, where the chalk dips under the trees bordering the heath, the general slope of the land is upwards towards the sudden escarpment which runs from Melbury Down near Shaftesbury to Iwerne, Hilton, Minterne and Corscombe. There are a few passes through this noble line of hills, but the general impression from Bulbarrow Hill and Batcombe Down is of a wall cutting the county in two. It is not quite a cliff although Thomas Hardy used the thought when he spoke of the green sea of Blackmore Vale washing up to the foot of the bare chalk uplands. The hills are rather a wall in the sense that the mighty earthworks of Maiden Castle are walls. They are very steep, but rounded, and clothed in short, sweet turf. You look down 400 feet to small fields, tree-lined hedges, and apparently endless grass. Behind you the chalk falls away for ten miles in rolling country which seems completely empty. It is a strangely pleasant emptiness because large fields of corn speak of care and cultivation. There must be people to tend this fruitful earth but their dwellings are hidden. The fact is that the rain of the ages has cut narrow valleys in the chalk. These are roughly parallel with each other and often about three miles apart. There is thus a plateau of swelling but reasonably flat fields intersected by deep little valleys, each with a stream, or a line of winter springs—"winterbornes"—twisting through it. All the houses and all the cowsheds had to be near drinking water, until iron pipes became common about fifty years ago. In the bottom of the valleys there was room for a watercourse and a road bordered by a row of houses. Villages straggled for two miles and almost joined each other. There are a dozen Winterborne villages, four Tarrants, more than half a dozen Piddles or Puddles, and three Cernes. Yet from the hill tops all the valleys are invisible. You look over them, with only an occasional old cottage to mark a forgotten form of farming.

Looking down from the escarpment Blackmore Vale gives no impression of loneliness. Many farms and villages are hidden in trees, but the land looks rich and is obviously inhabited. Hardy called it "The Vale of Little Dairies", and it is true that the small farms are dotted about in a way which is quite different from the chalk. Almost always on the chalk every house for humans and for cows was built in the valleys by the water. Dry land remote from rivers was used for crops or for keeping sheep which can get most of their water needs from dewy herbage or succulent turnips. On the clay there was usually plenty of water for animals. Often it was not the best of water but the soil was impervious, and it was easy to dig a hole which immediately became a pond. There was none of the trouble encountered on the chalk hills of having to line the pit with clay brought from a considerable distance. There was no danger of cows treading through the clay lining, nor of the whole thing drying out and cracking. Any pit in the clay was a pond and could have a farm arranged round it. Remember that cows have to be milked twice daily, and therefore must not have to walk too far from grazing fields to milking shed. On the natural pasture of the days before scientific agriculture, it took about 2½ acres of fairly good grass to provide hay and grazing for each cow. Thus a forty-cow dairy would need 100 acres. With the farm house in the middle the land would stretch out for a half mile or a little more in each direction, say three eight-acre fields in depth round the yard and buildings. Before the days of machine milking, three milkers were needed for forty cows and this often meant the farmer's family plus one employed man. A group of buildings thus might consist of a farm house, one cottage, a large cowstall, a stable and piggery and a stackyard for hay.

Thomas Hardy looked down from the chalk escarpment and saw these little farms dotted all over the Vale. Sometimes roads wind to find them, but quite often they stand back a couple of fields down their own lanes. The casual visitor sees the Vale as a stretch of uniform country with at least as definite a character as the chalk hills. Hardy knew its rich variation. The only constant thing about this part of Dorset is that the farming is still very largely a matter of green pastures and milk. In other parts of England the limestone belts which cross the Vale would give rise to large fields of reddish soil. There would be quarries, stone walls instead of hedges, and large arable fields. Miniatures of this sort of countryside can be found in the Vale, but on the whole the form of farming is based on grassland and dairies of forty to sixty cows. The reason is that the bands of changing rock are so narrow that they are always influenced by the adjoining wider strips of clay. For instance, the greensand at the very foot of the chalk hills runs from Shaftesbury to Cattistock but is never more than a mile wide. The Oxford Clay from Stalbridge to Batcombe is four or five miles wide but the Corallian limestone to the south-east is less than a mile, and the Cornbrash limestone on the other side of the clay seldom more than two fields. Thus the wide strips of Oxford Clay and Kimmeridge Clay dominate the farming of the much narrower areas of more kindly land adjoining. Most farms have a fair proportion of clay which is naturally suited to grass, and the result is that all the area tends to be devoted to dairying. Only during the war years, when ploughing was enforced, did a patchwork of arable appear in the Vale. The plough returned to fields with a very old reputation for arable, and most of it was on the limestone or greensand. Today grass has returned to most of the Vale, but one influence of the underlying rock remains. The greensand and the limestone provide dry ground for building and springs of drinking water. Almost every village in the Vale is on greensand or limestone. These villages run across this apparently similar countryside almost touching each other. On the clay between the drier land there are only isolated farms and rather forbidding names have a habit of appearing. There is a reference to clay, bad drainage and mud in names such as Marsh Farm, Lowbrook, Knackers Hole, Puxey Farm, Deadmoor Common and Ryewater.

On the very narrow strips of drier land with drinking water, the villages are thick and produce a church every three miles or so. For instance, on the greensand, which is seldom a mile wide and often only a few hundred yards, this is the tally. On the county border with Wiltshire there is Shaftesbury and Melbury Abbas followed by Compton Abbas, Fontmell Magna, Sutton Waldron, Iwerne Minster, Iwerne Courtney, Childe Okeford, Shillingstone, Okeford Fitzpaine, Belchalwell, Ibberton, Woolland, Stoke Wake, Hilton, Melcombe Bingham, Melcombe Horsey, Buckland Newton, Minterne Magna, Hilfield, Batcombe, Evershot, Frome St. Quinton, Cattistock, Wraxall, Rampisham, Corscombe, and Chedington. Some of these villages have only tiny patches of greensand, as at Stoke Wake where the farming is entirely dominated by the adjacent clay. Those in the north below Shaftesbury may have enough sand to give several farms with a fair amount of arable. A few at the end of the list, such as Minterne, get most of their living from the adjacent chalk hills. Corscombe has chalk hills above and clay vale below. The general plan of

The Great Heath

the countryside is that they all lie quite close to the chalk escarpment and their reason for existence is the springs in the greensand. This is not a river valley like the narrow cuttings through the chalk. It is a line of springs about thirty miles long coming out of the chalk ridge, and mainly draining in rivulets into the River Stour.

West of the greensand in the Vale is a belt of clay about three miles wide. This is Kimmeridge Clay, which takes its name from an isolated outcrop which can be seen in the cliffs of Purbeck, twenty miles to the south. It gives a wet but fairly fertile soil suitable for permanent pasture. The only villages are situated where the clay has been modified by deposits of gravel or alluvium. Hammoon, for instance, is on silt from the River Stour, and has the best permanent pasture in Dorset. West Orchard has gravel and some of the rock which occurs in layers through the Kimmeridge Clay. These layers can be seen in the cliffs at Purbeck. The village of Motcombe and much of the small town of Gillingham are also on the better drained parts of the Kimmeridge Clay belt. The only other village is Manston. The total on Kimmeridge Clay is five as opposed to twenty-nine churches on the much smaller area of the greensand.

Next comes a strip of limestone called Corallian which gives more rolling country than the clay, although this is not noticeable when looking down from the chalk hills. This limestone is never more than two miles wide but is thick with villages—Silton, Milton, Buckhorn Weston, Kington Magna, West Stour, East Stour, Fifehead Magdalen, Stour Provost, Todber, Marnhull, Hinton St. Mary, Sturminster Newton, Fifehead Neville, Hazelbury Bryan, Mappowder and Wootton Glanville. Where ploughed fields occur the soil is usually pleasantly red in colour, which is often a sign of a limestone soil, especially where flat stones abound. Other indications are the building stone quarries at Marnhull, and the low but distinct escarpment where the main A30 road drops off the Corallian at West Stour.

The next belt is the widest and flattest part of the Vale. The Oxford Clay gives a strip four to five miles across and only where there are gravel patches do villages occur. These villages usually have a small centre with a large number of scattered farms on the lines of those previously described as typical of cow country. Many of the farmers in the numerous Corallian parishes have fields on the clay. The only villages actually on this formation are Lydlinch, Stock Gaylard, Pulham, Holnest, Leigh and Chetnole. Hermitage and Batcombe are very near the edge. A feature of the Oxford Clay is the very wide lanes, at

Lyme Regis High Street

least the distance between the hedges is wide. The actual tarred road may be too narrow for two cars to pass. Presumably the lanes were made very wide because in the old days they must have been exceedingly muddy. Later, when stone was put down, it was only necessary to metal the middle of the track. A good example of this type of road can be seen between Pulham and Holwell. The ancient bridges are extremely narrow, but otherwise the distance between hedges is enough for four lines of traffic, with the tarred road almost single track.

Another characteristic of the Oxford Clay is the almost complete absence of ploughland, and often a tendency for the land to be so flat that drainage is difficult. Good pastures, once famous for cheese, abound at Chetnole, Leigh and Holnest. At Middlemarsh there is some sad, wet woodland and rushy pasture, while Lydlinch Common is typical of the worst of this soil.

The Oxford Clay is bounded on the north-west by a very narrow ridge of limestone called Corn Brash which is only a few fields wide but which is crowded with villages. It runs through Stalbridge, Stourton Caundle, Bishop's Caundle, Haydon, North Wootton, Folke, Long Burton, Yetminster, Ryme Intrinsica, Melbury Osmond, Melbury Bubb and Melbury Sampford.

Beyond the ridge of Corn Brash are no less than three major changes in soil in the five miles to the county border at Trent. First comes a stiff brown clay soil on a geological formation known as Forest Marble. Lillington and Leweston are on this soil which runs as an escarpment to Purse Caundle on the borders of Stalbridge. Then there are the soils of the Inferior Oolite centred on Sherborne and including Oborne and Bradford Abbas. Here the underlying rock is either limestone giving flat-topped hills or a yellow sand with layers of sandstone rock. This gives rounded hills and very deep lanes. The sides of the lanes are cliffs, and a good example of this can be seen where the A30 road drops from Sherborne into Yeovil. Finally, in this corner of Dorset the village of Trent rests on Middle and Upper Lias. This yields some of the deepest and most fertile land in Dorset.

So far we have dealt with the shape of some four-fifths of the land of Dorset, from the heath at Studland Bay, then north of a line through East Lulworth to Kingston Russell, and east of a line at right-angles to this finishing at Yeovil in Somerset. There remains first the far west of the county, second the coastal strip south of Bridport, Portesham, Bincombe, Poxwell and West Lulworth, third, the Isle of Portland and fourth, Purbeck. It is still true, of course, that the underlying "rock" determines the shape of the land, but in most of West Dorset and in the coastal strip west of Lulworth the changes in rock occur with amazing frequency. The result is tumbled country which gives a strange feeling of chaos. Instead of one geological formation following another in orderly sequence, we get patches of greensand rock capping hills at Pilsdon Pen and Stonebarrow Hill, or stretches of Oxford Clay in the Vale between Broadwey and the Abbotsbury Swannery. Many of the formations we have already found in Blackmore Vale occur in wild confusion. The sands of the Inferior Oolite give round knolls such as the one looking down on Bridport's main street. They also yield many more instances of the type of deep lanes found near Yeovil. At Loders the lanes are almost tunnels, with wide flat-topped hills immediately adjoining.

The only sizeable patch of unchanging soil in the far west is one not yet encountered in Dorset. Marshwood Vale is almost a basin, the flat bottom of which is Lower Lias. In some western counties this gives extremely fertile soil but in Marshwood it is mainly a blue clay of a very impervious nature. The elevated ground encircling this Vale is Middle or Upper Lias, similar to the very good land at Trent.

The varied geology of the far west and the coastal strip east of Bridport shapes the amazing coastline. At Lyme Regis greensand and Lias Clay gives cliffs liable to slip. Then greensand, limestone rock and clay produces wonderfully coloured cliffs of which Golden Cap—600 feet— is the queen. East of Bridport Harbour—West Bay—the sandstone cliffs, familiar as deep lanes inland, are fronting the sea but protected by the beginning of a ridge of pebbles which stretches from Bridport for nearly twenty miles to Portland Bill. This ridge—the Chesil Beach —is the only example of a different power than geology influencing the shape of the land. The pebbles were thrown up by the tides, and they form an unbroken bank which curves so smoothly that it looks artificial. The sea has been known to come over it occasionally in the centuries, but there has been no permanent breach. As a result the perpendicular sandy cliffs of West Bay still stand. They would have gone long ago and taken the golf course with them without the rampart of the pebbles. The clayey Fullers Earth and Forest Marble behind the beach from Burton Bradstock to Abbotsbury would also have gone, so would Abbotsbury village, leaving St. Catherine's Chapel as an island. The Chesil protects all the clay land south of the great ridge from Abbotsbury Camp to the high cliffs east of Weymouth. In 1824 the waves broke through or over to flood Abbotsbury meadows to a depth of twenty-two feet, and at Fleet, near Weymouth, the village was swept away, leaving only the chancel of the church. A complete break would leave Portland as a real island, but at the moment there is a bridge and this is the only practical connection with the mainland. The words "real island" are used because Portland is joined to the mainland by the Chesil Beach. At Abbotsbury the beach forsakes the land and sweeps across to Portland with a sluggish half-salt lagoon behind it. There are eight miles of this utterly bare ridge with the sea on one side and the brackish waters of the Fleet on the other. It is possible to walk eight miles on loose pebbles but not easy. It has been done often enough but the "practical" entrance to Portland is the bridge at Wyke from which a road and formerly the railway beside it ran along the last mile of the Chesil.

This shape of the land on the coast was made by the sea which also graded the pebbles from the size of a duck's egg and bigger at Portland down to near a coarse rounded sand at Bridport. Portland itself returns to the tradition of the geology fixing the landscape. This is an enormous block of stone known as Portland and Purbeck beds. It sticks out into the sea like the beak of a huge bird at the end of the long neck of the Chesil ridge. On any map it is the most conspicuous point on the south coast of England, and for this reason weather forecasters always use it for the diagonal lines they draw across England. They then discuss the outlook for the west and for the east, leaving Dorset with no weather at all.

The south-east corner of the county is more variable than anything else. It not only has a miniature of the Weald of Sussex all in one mile south of Creech Barrow; there is also Kimmeridge Clay at Kimmeridge and both Portland and Purbeck beds at St. Aldhelm's Head. These beds can yield sand, clay, two building limestones and marble. It is not surprising that the contours in this bit of country are as near together as the changes in strata, but it has not the feeling of chaos encountered in the unpredictable hills and vales of West Dorset. Purbeck has a definite shape. A barrier of chalk hills runs from the sea at Arish Mell, south of East Lulworth, to the sea at Ballard Down, between Studland and Swanage. The wall of chalk is almost straight, about 500 feet high, and unbroken except for the narrow gap at Corfe Castle. Immediately south is a valley half a mile wide of Wealden Clay. This runs from Tyneham through Steeple and Church Knowle to the sea at Swanage Bay. South again is the coastal ridge of Portland and Purbeck stone, from Worbarrow Bay to Peveril Point in Swanage. Finally there is the patch of heavy land with low cliffs from Kimmeridge Bay to Egmont Point.

The county is unique in the variations it offers in underlying rock, every one of which gives different scenery. There is scientific justification for claiming that three-quarters of England can be seen in a county less than sixty miles long and forty miles wide. A claim can be made that the typical beauties of the various formations are better seen in Dorset than anywhere else. For instance, Salisbury Plain is probably the biggest area of rolling chalk upland in England. In Dorset we have the same loveliness of open fields and the smooth curves of clean, small hills, plus the great cliff of White Nothe rising straight from the sea. If it be claimed that equally beautiful and more famous chalk cliffs can be seen at Dover, a Dorset man can still retort that we can give a miniature of the great Midland Plain in sight of salt water. We provide Surrey heaths without the bungalows, in spite of recent heath land encroachments round Poole. The small county is a jewelled miniature of "this sceptered isle".

II

THE HEATH

"THE shape of the countryside arose from the underlying rock." I trust that this statement has been justified, and that geologists will bear with my science. Much of the farming also is governed by the underlying rock because it is from this that the top soil was made. The exception is when soil has been transported from a distance, as for instance when silt has been dropped by flooding rivers. The position of villages was determined by geology, partly through supplies of drinking water, and partly through sound foundations for houses. The materials for old houses came from the rock and soil beneath the surface. In Dorset this was influenced by the fact that there are so many different strata close together. For a church or a large house it was easy to obtain stone within a few miles. Only cottages and barns tended to be built of very local material. There are oak-framed brick cottages on the London Clay near Holt, cob and thatch are common through the chalk belt, with a flint facing on slightly better houses, and on the limestone at Yetminster some barns and cottages might have come from the Cotswolds. Everywhere, of course, red brick and slate are usual for the period from the coming of the railways to 1950. Since 1950 there has been some realisation that the building stone of Dorset is within easy reach and since it is good enough to be exported across the Atlantic it might well be used at home. There has been a welcome increase in stone building.

With these facts in mind the barren sand of the heath might be expected to have a purely negative influence. It is fundamentally useless for agriculture, although modern science can produce expensive improvements. Springs and wells are often unpalatable and unreliable. It contains no building material and building sites may be liable to subside, or develop into bogs. To a considerable extent the heath was utterly barren and empty. To an appreciable degree it still is, yet it has affected the life of Dorset more than any other part of the county.

The whole story of the heath is full of paradox. In the first place no one ever thought of it as an entity until Thomas Hardy coined the name Egdon Heath. There were no agricultural villages on the stretch of land which I have copied Hardy in lumping together as "the Heath". All the villages round its borders had their own stretch of open heather much of which is now enclosed and planted with conifers. These patches of land bear the name of the neighbouring village for the most part—Puddletown Heath, Bere Heath, Winfrith, Bloxworth and so on. Only near the Hampshire border does the word "common" occasionally appear as with Cranborne Common and Verwood Common. This is significant because quite frequently the heaths are not commons. There was never much common grazing as on similar land in the New Forest. Generally speaking the commons of Dorset are on far better land, such as St. James Common near Shaftesbury. The heaths were used as sources of furze in the old days when bakers burnt the stuff in bread ovens. Before the 1914 War cottagers on the edge of the Heath cut thin "turves" of peat for fuel. I do not know any real beds of peat such as those of the Somerset Moors which still have a commercial value. The peat of the Dorset heaths is thin, poor stuff and the right to cut it was never highly esteemed. In fact there may have been no right to cut. Certainly there seems to have been little comment on the planting of heaths with trees by private owners, or by the Forestry Commission. Such planting must have nullified any turf and grazing rights.

Forestry has transformed vast stretches of heath. Agriculture has crept in to a much smaller extent, except where the sand has been overlaid with alluvium or gravel. We have noted the fertile silt valleys of the Frome, Piddle and Stour, but the patches of gravel may not be very obvious as far as herbage is concerned. Frequently they grow heather or bracken similar to that on the original barren sand. In recent years, however, areas on this gravel have been turned into good arable land. Some outstanding work was done by Mr. Noel Paul, south of the railway between Moreton Station and Dorchester. During the 1939 war much of his reclaimed land became part of the grass airfield at Woodsford. It was amazing how quickly and strongly gorse returned in those odd corners which were not kept clear. Soon after the end of the war the land was returned to Mr. Paul and provided what must have been one of the largest wheat fields in England. From the middle of this flat land the tall grain seemed to run almost to the horizon. In the same area near Moreton Station the gravel overlying the sand has been widely worked and this working is still going on. In most cases only heather land is involved, but a few cultivated fields have vanished.

A very similar state of affairs occurs north of the main Purbeck Ridge, but here the extraction is of ball clay. Since the war open-cast coal mining in parts of England has involved restoration of the top soil, but the gravel and ball clay workings of Dorset do not seem to attempt much in this line. The result after gravel working is a fantasy of barren hills and hollows. After the clay workings at Furzebrook there are a few derelict mines, but much more often deep still pools. One of these lakes became so popular as a beauty spot that it was fenced in and provided with a car park and tea room. Surely this is a most unusual sequel to industrial activity? The Blue Pool is a beauty spot and it is blue, at least it is intensely blue in sunshine, but green in shadow. There is an acre or two of water, which is fifty feet deep in places. This is surrounded by pleasant beaches and by sandy cliffs or by forests of pines growing on steep banks. It is a very miniature lake-land scene, and yet it has a strange power of giving the impression of solitude and mystery. The restaurant is just round the corner but the Blue Pool is lost in a primeval wilderness.

Within a mile or so there are many other pools with no car parks and no turnstile. None are so large as the Blue Pool but one, covered in water lilies, is worth finding. It adjoins the road from East Creech to Stoborough but is completely hidden in the trees and shrubs. In this area you may find miniature railways twisting through the waste to open workings or winding gear controlling tracks disappearing down steep inclines into the bowels of the earth. One of these mines is at the foot of the zig-zag road from the top of the Purbeck Ridge to East Creech. This was a small pasture field of three or four acres when I first knew it before 1939. Today it is covered in spoil and will never again be of agricultural use. Possibly part of it will be a pool, some of it will certainly be a bog, and weedy bushes will hide the scars. This is not industry in the sense of the mining areas of Durham. When I last called at Creech in 1963 one man was working the winding gear and two men were underground cutting the clay. Incidentally the local saying used to be that a piece of china clay the size of a penny was worth a penny, and since this was said before the war it must now be worth even more.

Both clay workings and gravel pits on the Heath are seldom destroying good land in Dorset. Farmers and farm workers have few strong feelings about them. The churning up of barren heather, gorse and bracken destroys little which they regard as valuable. Even when good fields are obliterated, as the one at East Creech, it is regarded as exceptional. Since ball clay and gravel must be obtained, it is fortunate that they occur mainly on worthless soils. "If it must be done this is the best place for it."

Such a reaction was fairly general about two activities on the Heath which have changed it more fundamentally. A gravel pit or clay working merely altered the shape of the surface to a slight extent, and may have substituted brambles for heather, ragwort for stunted pines, and rhododendrons for bracken. When the Army came to Bovington Heath in the 1914–18 War, or the Atomic Research Station to Winfrith Heath after the 1939 War, the results involved more than the destruction of heather.

The camp at Bovington started as the usual collection of temporary army huts. The tanks exercising on the Heath destroyed the heather. It is a characteristic of this curious soil that weeds do not grow very freely. Once the heather was destroyed it was very slow to return even when the tank exercise area was reduced. The soil remained bare for many years after 1945 on Southover Heath, south of Tolpuddle, when the tanks were withdrawn to Bovington and Wool Heaths, nearer the camp. The sands seem to be not only poverty stricken but poisonous. This can also be seen on the railways through true heath land where the edges of the cuttings do not grow any tall grass and very little herbage of any kind after more than a hundred years. Once the covering and root mat of the heather has gone the soil remains bare, and is very liable to erode in deep gullies. Future generations will find strange trenches, with no apparent plan, on the land which the tanks have churned up in the last fifty years.

I do not regard this marking of the heath as a "fundamental change" any more than the gravel workings or forestry plantations. This soil has produced self-sown pine woods in the past, plus many strange stirrings of the surface. Previously mention was made of running sand which could cause soil subsidence. The western heaths at Puddletown, Affpuddle and Turnerspuddle have many conical pits, some of which are so deep that full-sized trees, growing in the bottom, do not reach the level of the surrounding land. The most famous is Culpeppers Dish by the roadside on Briantspuddle Heath. This deep pit, similar to a volcanic cone, is alleged to be named after Culpepper, the famous herbalist. With its tree in the middle it represented, presumably, a vast pestle and mortar. Local legends attribute the pits to the devil; learned men of Victorian days had theories of temples from prehistoric times. Two of the difficulties of explaining them in terms of human activity

are the absence of any banks of spoil, and the fact that there is no sign
of any sort of track from the bottom to the top. We have circular pits
in chalk fields of similar depth but there is always a winding path up
which donkeys with panniers brought the chalk to spread it over the
fields. The heath pits are perfectly conical. Without much doubt their
formation is natural, although it is possible for those who like mysteries
to consider visitors from outer space. Two pits have actually formed in
my memory, one on the farm of Mr. Noel Paul of Woodsford and
one on Mr. Stanley Osmond's land at West Stafford. Both came into
existence before we had heard of flying saucers. I think they are due to
an underground stream tapping a layer of running sand. The subsidence is very much the shape of an eddy in running water, and when
sand flows it behaves very like moving water.

By "fundamental change" I am not thinking of an altered surface
in an already haphazard countryside, nor of plantations which forest
fires can destroy all too easily. Bovington Camp is a town which has
lost most of its temporary buildings. Very obviously the Dorset County
Council regard it as permanent. The new school between Bovington
and Wool is sufficiently large and expensive to show that this land is
not expected to return to lonely heather. Even more firmly permanent
is the United Kingdom Atomic Energy Research Establishment. This
is on the other bank of the Frome some two miles from Bovington.
It did not go through any phase of cheap temporary hutments; it was
planned from the start on most modern lines. From the railway between Wool and Moreton the traveller sees a completely new factory
layout on what used to be empty, uninteresting heath. Many of the
buildings look like ordinary offices or laboratories. There is one strange
seaside ice-cream kiosk with an incongruous spire which may have
some very sinister purpose, but the atomic furnaces—if that is the word
—are not obvious. The structures seen from the train could be offices,
flats, schools, pubs and churches from Crawley New Town, or from
some other modern settlement where all buildings look alike. The only
mystery is that kiosk with the spire, but it is so near the boundary fence
that it may be no more than a kennel for guard dogs.

At this point I must add that I have no knowledge of any guard
dogs at Winfrith. Public Relations Officers may object to unfounded
unfunny jokes. There is certainly a fence at Winfrith and a gate where
passes are required. It is, however, fairly easy to get a pass and to be
shown much of the work in progress. I have happy memories of a tour
with local farmers and of a pleasant lunch in the canteen. Efforts are

being made to hide the new buildings behind shelter belts of trees—a
return to landscape gardening. Inside the perimeter lawns have been
successfully grown on this very unresponsive soil. My reaction is still
that if tanks and atomic energy research are inevitable this was the right
soil to select. Neither Camp nor Establishment are enormous blots on
the landscape although they have permanently altered the heath. The
objection is to their influence outside the immediate site.

On this score the Research Station has led to some improvement in
local roads, and to an increase in house building in local towns and
villages. This is no more than would have resulted from starting any
form of industry in the neighbourhood. Many local people regard this
development as essential. For years they have longed for light industry,
and stressed the fact that our boroughs such as Dorchester and Wareham are too small to retain their identity under modern conditions of
Local Government. This may be true but the new suburbs round every
town and village are sadly uniform. In my youth Dorchester had
spread very little beyond its famous Walks. These avenues were
planted on the lines of the old Roman walls. Wareham, in 1914, had
scarcely any houses outside the ancient earthworks which were town
walls before the Romans came. Inside their boundaries the two towns
were highly individual. Each had been scarred by many fires but there
were fragments from more than a thousand years of history. No two
houses in their High Streets were alike. There were buildings dating
from Wareham's Saxon Chapel of St. Martin, through Norman times,
to Gothic churches, from Tudor cottages to Queen Anne houses and
to pleasant Georgian shops. Fortunately the town centres have not been
wholly destroyed, although multiple shops have a habit of using one plan
for all their branches. It is the new buildings outside the walls which are
entirely lacking in individual character. At Wareham the town is
almost encircled by marshy meadows so that the new suburbs are completely separate physically from the old town. In Dorchester the
housing estates have grown out from the centre to the west, but are
separated by a small green belt on the south-east. The important separa-
tion, however, is not so much physical as cultural. These hundreds of
acres of small light convenient houses could be anywhere. They are
much the same in Dorchester, Wareham, Charminster and Croydon.
These centres contain a few shops, but seldom a pub, and there is little
to bind the inhabitants to the town. It is too far to go into town in the
evening, or rather if an outing is desired it is almost as easy to get to
the professional, sophisticated pleasures of Bournemouth as to travel to

local entertainments. The Atomic Research Station and Bovington Camp have increased the demand for houses which are not part of local villages and towns. This is a modern trend which is unavoidable and, at the time of writing, it is the only influence of the U.K.A.E.E. on the life and look of Dorset. Much more blame must be accepted by Bovington.

It is in the nature of modern weapons that their range is always increasing. Atom bombs require oceans or hundreds of miles of deserts for their tests. On a smaller scale tank guns need much larger ranges than they did in 1918. Once a permanent camp had been built there was no hope of getting it moved to an emptier part of Britain. The only alternative was to take more land in Dorset, first as a temporary 1939–45 War measure, and now permanently. One of the loveliest and least touched villages on the coast Tyneham, has been evacuated. However since the recommendations of the Nugent report in 1974 the Army now allow a great increase in public access. Range Walks are open for block periods of nine to eighteen days during public holidays, and for about seven weeks from the end of July to mid-September. In addition, there is public access every Saturday and Sunday outside these periods, apart from about six weekends in the year. The East Lulworth to West Holme road is sometimes closed when certain firing points are being used, and the East Lulworth to Steeple road is closed when there is range firing. The view from this Purbeck ridge is something out of this world, with the bays, cliffs and valleys of Purbeck on one side, and on the other is the flat heathland. In the distance is the blue vastness of Poole harbour and the chalk hills of Dorset and the Isle of Wight.

Thus for about 140 days a year the rare charms of Worbarrow and Mupe Bays are available to the public, who can enjoy the scenic coast path, even at Arish Mell and Gold Down, where walks are fenced on both sides to prevent people straying on uncleared land—before every public access period all roads and paths have to be cleared of unexploded shells.

To an amazing extent the Dorset coast is "undeveloped". Poole, Studland, Swanage, Lulworth Cove, Weymouth, Bridport and Lyme Regis are the major exceptions and of these only Poole and Weymouth are of any size. There are twenty miles between Bridport and Portland Bill without a bathing hut for hire. I do not think there is a tea shop unless it is at Osmington Mills. There are few beach amenities from Lulworth Cove to Swanage. Compare this with the almost continuous development of the coast from Kent to Poole, and of the commercialisation of every beach in south Devon. It seems almost miraculous that Dorset should have remained so little changed. Without much doubt the reason was the survival of great estates whose owners would not allow building, roads, car parks and camping sites. Very possibly their reasons were selfish. They may have been thinking of keeping out the common people for very private reasons not connected with the preservation of beauty. At one time I can remember being annoyed because the local lord had barred the way to what was known as Encombe Glen or the Golden Valley near Chapman's Pool in Purbeck. Since then I have blessed him, having seen what can happen at Preston near Weymouth.

Unfortunately great landowners are not immortal and the pressure of immensely inflated land values goes beyond anything most of us can imagine. In an ordinary inland village land which has planning permission for building can be worth thousands an acre, when it is worth hundreds for farming, and could have been bought in 1939 for £20. Even to a rich man these figures present an enormous temptation. Think of it in this way. A man may have inherited a thousand acres of land before the war. If he can sell seven acres for building he will have all the rest of it still, and yet will have received what the whole was worth to his father. In such circumstances there must be some doubt as to the future security of lovely country based on large family estates. The beauty could go and the bulk of the estate could remain in the same hands. It is also difficult to have complete confidence in Town and Country Planning, or in the security conferred by a district becoming designated as of "natural beauty". The time may come when we bless Bovington Camp for its barbed wire and for the "Keep Out" notices on the Purbeck Ridge and the lonely coast. Tanks may become as obsolete as long bows, and we may get the range back, even more lonely than it was when Tyneham's little church served the tiny settlement under the hill.

The other way in which the barren heath land has influenced Dorset is more the effect of the sea than of the desolate sandy soil. Poole Harbour on the eastern boundary of Dorset is entirely surrounded by the heath. The important point about this stretch of water is that the entrance from the sea in Studland Bay is only a few hundred yards across. Poole Harbour is almost an inland sea whose indented shores stretch for one hundred miles. There is a car ferry across the entrance but no bridge, so that there is a very real barrier to traffic from the east. To get from the town of Poole to the heath across the harbour you wait for the ferry or drive twenty-six miles round via Wareham. In a strange way this stretch of water stopped the "development" of the whole of Dorset. Poole has dramatically extended eastwards as a very large residential and holiday town covering all the heath between the harbour and the Bournemouth border. On the western side of the water there is hardly a house to be seen on the heather and bog land between the water and the Purbeck hills. The effect of the water barrier is much more than local. All the roads from London, from the vast holiday towns of the south coast such as Brighton, and from the great industrial development of the Portsmouth/Southampton area have to keep north of Poole Harbour. The millions of people who seek holidays in the West Country beyond Dorset are diverted into traffic streams to the north of the county. The flow of cars rushing to Devon and Cornwall tend to travel through Salisbury and not to touch Dorset except on the borders at Shaftesbury and Sherborne. Those travellers from the east who come through Dorchester catch their first glimpse of the sea on the hills above Bridport. The impetus of their progress slows, and a few stop in Chideock, Charmouth and Lyme Regis under the impression that they are already in Devon. Many swing inland beyond Charmouth, on the easier road, and go through Axminster and Honiton to the crowded gateway to Devon and Cornwall on the Exeter bypass. Dorset should be grateful to Poole Harbour with its edging of barren heath.

Apart from Bovington Camp, Poole itself is the only town wholly on the heath. In fact it must be repeated that there are no villages on the heath, except where river valleys have modified the sterile soil. It is another paradox of the heath that this land which cannot support a small farm should carry by far the largest town in Dorset. The reason is that Poole was founded in ancient times on the trade of the sea and has grown in very recent years as a residential centre and by catering for the holiday industry. In addition there are local light industries including a pottery of international reputation. It is significant that when the system of manors was developing in Saxon days there was no manor of Poole. It formed part of the manor of Canford, a village six miles inland, on the good alluvial soil of the Stour valley. The settlement at Poole was on a small patch of land, almost an island, by the side of the water. This is the site of the old town with a history which certainly goes back to the time when the Danish raiders swept in from the sea. The present town includes Hamworthy which the Romans used as port, but it is probably more accurate to think of the beginning of the real Poole as being "almost as an isle in the haven". This we are told "hangith by N.E. to the mayne land by the space almost of a flite shot". Poole got its first charter from the manor of Canford in 1248. This does lead to one reference to the heath. In the thirteenth century the six burgesses appointed to look after the liberties of Poole were granted "peaceful pasturage" for their cattle. This is one case where a heath became a common. There would have been no point in recording this grazing right if common grazing already existed on the Canford Heath.

The mariners of Poole have always been associated with good seamanship, and it must be admitted with piracy. This was not at all unusual in early days and especially when Elizabeth was on the throne. Some of the exploits of Drake and Raleigh make strange reading. British admirals have become much more respectable since those days. Harry Page was Poole's most famous raider and he became such a nuisance in the Channel that foreign royalty were involved. In 1406 the kings of France and Spain combined to send an expedition to burn the town, but the pirate captain escaped into the wild heath.

By the quayside in the old town of Poole there is a feeling of permanence. Poole was important from the days of King Alfred and his first English fleet. It is still important. This waterfront has known many great men. Possibly Canute the Dane was the first king to land on the quay but that was as a raider before he conquered Wessex. Probably Richard the Lionheart left here for the Crusade. Certainly Charles II was entertained lavishly by the mayor. It may be that this entertainment was intended to blunt the royal memory of the fact that Poole had been very active on the side of Parliament, a few years earlier during the reign of the king's father, Charles I. The tradition of important visitors continued in the 1939 War. Poole was a terminus for flying boats from the ends of the earth. On at least one occasion the Dorset police were heavily reinforced when Winston Churchill landed after a conference with Roosevelt which had shaped the course of the world.

The trade of the port has not grown with the passing of the centuries, but it has not died in the way that Wareham and Lyme Regis are no longer used by ocean going ships. Much of Poole's waterfront is occupied by the warehouses of agricultural merchants. These have been called the Poole Pirates in farming circles so there is a distinct link with the past. In fact there are links with other activities. Without any doubt the great expanse and lonely shores of Poole Harbour once provided an ideal base for smuggling. As recently as the end of the last war a very daring attempt was made in the same sort of "free trading". It only failed through sheer bad luck.

Then in one respectable manner history seems likely to repeat itself. The first Queen Elizabeth created Poole a county with its own Sheriff, Recorder and Quarter Sessions. Later the borough became part of the County of Dorset, but for a long time Poole has wanted to be a county borough. It may well be that the reign of Queen Elizabeth II will see this change take place. To the outsider unused to the workings of local government, it would seem that any alteration should be the merging of Poole with Bournemouth. They are physically merged already. My personal impression is that Poole would sooner stay with Dorset than join their upstart neighbours. In Dorset they are by far the greatest power on the County Council; with Bournemouth they might be a junior partner. Obviously the town wants to be a County on its own, but if this is banned they might stay with Dorset. I hope this happens, both as a Dorset ratepayer and as a Dorset native proud of our greatest town. [Poole is now a District with a Council.]

I use the word "great" with size in mind, although Poole could lay claim to the description on other scores. As a yachting paradise it has no equal. On the one hand are dozens of deserted inlets, little lost beaches at Arne, Middlebere, Wytch, and Ower, inhabited and uninhabited islands, and the narrow twisting channel to Wareham. On the other shore are the luxuries of good hotels available all the year, and miles of golden sands with summer holiday attractions. Presumably there are people who detest all contact with civilisation, just as others are happy in crowds and rather frightened in solitude. Most of us enjoy the freedom of quiet places—rules and regulations are inseparable from crowds. Yet every now and then we enjoy equally the party atmosphere of the fairground, or the luxury of civilised entertainment which can only be obtained in prosperous cities. Poole offers the best of all worlds in the time taken to cross a few hundred yards of water.

Of the islands in Poole Harbour, Brownsea is not only the biggest but the most famous. It has recently attracted shoals of trippers from Sandbanks, probably because until recently it has been forbidden ground. For many years the owner, an elderly lady, kept it absolutely private and allowed no boats to land. In addition she did not allow birds and animals to be killed, even to the extent of keeping a few very old cows producing nothing. If these cows had been kept to yield milk, it would naturally have been necessary to get them in calf once a year.

Brownsea Island across Poole Harbour

This would have meant the killing of most of the calves, which is a fact some vegetarians do not appreciate. With milking cows on the island the only way to stop slaughter was to stop breeding. This eventually meant the end of milk secretion, and to the cows leading an entirely unproductive life, whilst they waited for natural death. Since the island did not grow enough grass for hay it meant that winter fodder had to be imported from the mainland. It may be understandable that during the 1939 War there were people who thought that the use of hay for unproductive animals should not be allowed. How such people justified the feeding of their own pet dogs I do not know. The Dorset War Agricultural Executive Committee were quite content to let the old lady alone with her square mile of poor soil and useless cows, even if she was wasting a little indifferent hay. However, the local jealousy over this very private island found other reasons for interference. Brownsea was alleged to be swarming with rats, which invaded the mainland. Rats were pests which the W.A.E.C. were charged to control. It was said that the island had once been cultivated, and ploughing should be enforced. This was supported by a statement that valuable machinery was lying idle, notably a threshing machine, then badly needed for food production. This again was very much the responsibility of the W.A.E.C., and a visitation had to be made. The whole story is the reverse of the usual popular idea of a committee being a collection of officious busybodies. There was no plague of rats on the island, the machinery was built-in and could not have been made portable, the potential plough land would have tied up much more labour than it was worth, the amount of hay going to the old cows was small, and their value as human meat was nil.

After Mrs Christie's death in 1961 Brownsea passed to the National Trust and is now one of their most visited properties. There is limited public access to the 200-acre Nature Reserve, and there has been a return to an earlier claim to fame. The first Boy Scout camp was held on Brownsea and Scouts have now returned to find more blood-sucking flies than anywhere else in Britain. Henry VIII built a fort here to defend the entrance to Poole, which was used later in 1589 to enforce a toll on shipping entering the harbour. The present castle is merely the restored form of a nineteenth-century building which was destroyed by fire in 1896. The war-time story of the previous cultivation of the island was a matter of living memory. Much of it had been ploughed, and an early attempt was made to establish the very modern horticultural industry of bulb growing. It is possible that modern scientific knowledge would have made this venture a success. Unfortunately it came too soon, before the days of chemical fertilisers, when the only common soil improvers were lime and dung. Both of these were cut off from Brownsea, and expensive to import. The soil here is heath or alluvial sand. The waste quickly reoccupied the land, when it became once more the Hermitage it had been in the Middle Ages. Today the trip across the harbour to Brownsea is extremely pleasant, but I am not sure that it is any better than the old trip around it without landing. The swamp of the Nature Reserve is very like the shady New Forest bogs as far as insect life is concerned. It is not true that there are gad flies as big as vampire bats—they are less than half as big.

Having listed Bovington Camp and Poole as the only towns on the Heath where the soil is unchanged, barren sand I now have a feeling of doubt. Wimborne certainly is in a river valley on good alluvial soil, but Wareham is almost the reverse. It is on a narrow spit of heathland with alluvial valleys on two sides and Poole Harbour on the third. The soil does not give the impression of being heath because the small area of the town has been lived upon for so long. It is very usual for agriculturists to talk of alluvium, silt, gravel, or glacial debris being deposited over the basic rock and altering the whole nature of the soil. I have done it frequently in this book when writing about the heath and about the clay of Blackmore Vale. What is mentioned less frequently is the much smaller area covered by deposits from inhabited places. For instance, my house on the chalk was built in 1573, almost certainly on the site of an older dwelling. The soil in my garden is a black powdery loam, eighteen inches deep and free from stones. In the neighbouring fields the soil is four inches deep and full of flints. Through the centuries the ashes, refuse and sewage of the house have made the eighteen inches of soil in my garden. The same thing, on a bigger scale, happened at Wareham. This spit of land was protected on three sides by the marshy rivers and the tidal harbour. It was an obvious place for defence. The present walls are earthworks of largely Roman origin, but these were probably on a Bronze Age site. At the very least men have lived here for two thousand years. It is not surprising that the soil of Wareham gardens has little resemblance to the original sterile sand of the Heath.

For me Wareham has a fascination which never grows stale. It has been swept by fire so often that few complete ancient buildings remain,

yet the feeling of an abiding place is very strong. The earthworks of
the town wall are old enough but not very impressive. The straight
causeway over the river marshes on either side of the town ramparts
is certainly Roman, or earlier, but there is nothing grand about it.
There was a Norman castle in the south-west of the town but not a
very big one. Sir Frederick Treves in his *Highways and Byways in
Dorset* accepts the theory that it was destroyed in the reign of King
John. Wareham was prosperous in its time, with two mints, but that
sort of thing led only to the solid houses of merchants and not to the
great house of a noble. Churches it certainly had in plenty. The
Dorset County Guide published in 1956 gives the number as eleven.
Sir Frederick Treves mentions eight and this figure is agreed by the
Dorset County Handbook. The present population of the town is nearly
5,000, and at first sight eight churches seems a very large number,
even if we assume that the population was at least double in Tudor
times. The same state of affairs occurs with most very old towns,
especially where they were connected with important religious foundations. Shaftesbury, which is about the same size as Wareham had
twelve churches. The monastic houses of course had their own churches,
but we are still left with the feeling that there must have been a super-
fluity for the ordinary citizens. In wandering round Wareham, however, I realised that there was a factor I had forgotten. Not only was
church-going universal when the original buildings were erected, but
there was only one organised church. In my familiar market town of
Dorchester church-going was fairly usual for most people fifty years
ago when I was a boy. Dorchester then had about 10,000 inhabitants.
There were five Anglican churches, one Roman Catholic, a Wesleyan,
a Congregational, a Baptist, a Mission Hall, a Salvation Army Barracks,
one chapel of unknown denomination turned into a pub, and another
into a Masonic Hall. The first ten on this list were well attended so
the Wareham churches do not seem so wildly unnecessary for the age
before the Reformation.

The temptation must be resisted to say that Wareham had eight
(or eleven) churches and now it only has three. It has three very old
churches and a number of more modern buildings used for differing
forms of worship.

Of the three old churches, St. Martin's, the Chapel on the Wall,
has already been mentioned. When Treves wrote in 1906 it was apparently deserted. In fact he said then—"The voice of the preacher has
not been heard for 170 years". Today it is well tended once more,

and it has collected a very modern memorial to add to its Saxon and Norman stones. An effigy of T. E. Shaw, Lawrence of Arabia, has been erected. He died nearby on the Heath, in 1935, when serving as an aircraftman under the name of Shaw. The resurgence of St. Martin's may hold hopes for Holy Trinity in South·Street. This was once the principal church of the town but after having fallen on evil days in recent years it became a school and a Mission Hall. After the tower was restored from decay further energetic steps were taken to save the building particularly its leaning south wall and it has acquired a new lease of life as an Art Gallery.

It is the church of Our Lady St. Mary which dominates the quay and is the most striking building in the town. This was the site of a heathen Roman temple, followed by a Saxon nunnery, and traces of each can be seen. Here the body of the Saxon King Edward was brought after his murder by his stepmother Elfrida at Corfe Castle. The body was transferred to a nunnery at Shaftesbury where the martyr was made a saint and developed a reputation for miracles. It brought Shaftesbury a considerable income from pilgrims which could well have gone to Wareham.

The tide still laps the quay by Wareham bridge but the only ships are yachts and small pleasure craft from Poole. It is said that the channel silted as long ago as Norman times and allowed Poole to take Wareham's seaborne trade. Probably the decay was very slow. Wareham provided three ships for Edward III in his French invasion. Even in this century coal and grain ships have come up on the tide to warehouses on the quay. Today I suggest hiring a rowing boat and paddling up above the bridge with the rising water and dropping back when the tide turns. If timing makes this impossible then drop downstream through the tall reeds past Redcliff to the open water of Poole Harbour, returning once more on the rising tide. Remember the tidal water above the bridge is preferable since you will meet only rowing boats. The lower reach may have quite a few small motor boats and possibly fairly large pleasure craft, and the channel is very narrow.

Wareham has always been the gateway to Purbeck with its causeways through the marshes and its old bridge. Just as Poole Harbour has diverted holiday traffic and residential development further west into Devon, so Wareham checks some of the local flow of trippers making for Swanage, Studland, Corfe and Purbeck. The streets are wide and the river bridge satisfactory, the barrier is the level crossing

just out of the town. On a Sunday evening in August I have known a
queue of cars to be stationary for six miles, and I have been more than
an hour travelling the four miles from Corfe. It is brisk walking pace,
but maddening in a machine capable of doing the journey in four
minutes. This is one of the few main roads in Dorset on which local
knowledge is unable to find much of a by-pass. Every minor road to
the right of the Corfe/Wareham highway leads through heath to the
shores of Poole Harbour. The turnings on the left to Church Knowle
or to East Holme still have to cross the railway by level crossings. The
main line is crossed by a bridge about one mile from Wareham on the
Dorchester road but this does not lead to any obvious circular route for
the bulk of the traffic for Poole and Bournemouth. Indeed a very good
road—recently a gravel track—is signposted "Worgret Heath" which
gives no promise of getting to Poole via Bere Regis. In any case it is
a very long detour and to reach the bridge it is necessary to turn left
in Wareham only one mile from the crossing at the station which
causes all the trouble. Since the homecoming traffic has already crawled
from Corfe, there is no great point in going ten miles out of the way
to move the last mile. Purbeck is worth exploring but there is a heavy
price in frustration if you want to return between six and eight o'clock
on holiday week-ends. [The Wareham–Swanage line is now closed.]

Wareham grew on a ridge of heath land because it was obviously
defendable. Its commercial value came not from agriculture but from
sea-borne trade, and from the fact that it controlled the only easy route
into Purbeck. When the Romans took over the old settlement they
found no obstacle in laying out their favourite town plan of four
streets meeting in the centre. The rivers were outside the town and
helped its defences by forming marshes. Inside there was a flat space
which allowed a copy of the Roman layout from the Pretorian Camp
in Rome. Wimborne is quite different. The Romans had villas there
but it is difficult to see any trace of a Roman plan. Wareham was protected by rivers, but made by man from the heath. Wimborne was
made by rivers and man had to fit in as best he could. It is in no sense
a heath town, the rivers changed all that by laying down broad plains
of fertile silt. The Stour flows in from the west and the Allen from the
north. Actually it is hardly true to say that Wimborne is on the Stour.
The river curves round the town on the south and sets a firm boundary
to expansion in that direction. We cross a major road bridge in entering
Wimborne from Dorchester, and another on leaving towards Poole.
In fact the Poole bridge marks the boundary between the town of

Wimborne and the District of Poole. This is a little surprising since
the centre of Wimborne is a few hundred yards away, and the centre
of old Poole more than five miles.

The stream whose meanderings dictated the internal shape of Wimborne is the Allen. Modern planners find it as difficult to arrange a free
flow of traffic inside the town as the Romans would have done in
laying out their idea of a model settlement. Outside the town the wide
flood meadows of both rivers have provided main road authorities
with endless problems in planning a by-pass. There are two schools of
thought, one wants to go north of the town and the other south.
There is quite a fair hope that things are so nicely balanced that we shall
be spared a racetrack for people with no more sense than to wish to
avoid Wimborne.

The town is completely dominated by the old church. In 1857
excavations at the Minster are reported to have uncovered "bases of
columns at regular intervals, a considerable length of very early tessellated pavement, and a large stone pediment clearly indicating the site
of a Roman temple". There is nothing unusual in Christian churches
being built on the site of pagan shrines, and it is very likely to have
happened in Wimborne, where the area of dry land is very limited.
What many of us tend to forget is that this does not necessarily involve
any conscious continuity. Our school history books jumped from the
Romans to the Saxons and Danes in one paragraph, and most of us
never realise the long barbarian centuries which followed the departure
of the legions. By the time the Saxons had become Christian and
civilised, the grass had grown over almost every sign of Rome. Long
before there was central government under a Wessex king, or an art
of building in stone, every memory of tessellated paving had been lost.
For hundreds of years, almost completely without written records, men
"saw with heavy eyes and broke with heavy hands".

The oldest obvious parts of the present church are Norman but there
had been religious communities in Wimborne since about A.D. 705.
This is as big a gulf from the Romans as the age which separates us
from the Tudors. In writing this book about my native county I find
it difficult to avoid spending far too much time on the soil and the
history. Other people may have little interest in either, and are apt
to be excessively bored by mention of Norman arches or fifteenth-
century Continental glass. It is a fact though that almost always the
most impressive building by any standard in any town or village is
the church, and it is impossible to write about any place without

mention of the churches. In Wimborne Minster there is something of
interest for every possible taste. If you are not moved by the sight of
250 chained books, there is the fascinating astronomical clock made
in 1320. For human interest the effigy of a grandson of John of Gaunt
is shown in full armour but with one glove removed to hold the hand
of his wife. Above all the honest agnostic must feel the majesty and
dignity of this ancient place. The atheist may find no god, but the
common men who raised this wonder had no doubt about the image
in which they had been made.

For a history of Wimborne I recommend a book by A. Lindsay
Clegg, *A History of Wimborne Minster and District*. He points out that
Wimborne has always been a royal manor and that this has influenced
the town almost to the present day. The first monastery was built
about A.D. 705 on land belonging to a Saxon king and he made his
sister the first abbess. She was Cuthburga who was later to be known
as St. Cuthburga. Apparently this was a double monastery of monks
and nuns which was a fairly common arrangement in Saxon times.
The men and women were in completely separate buildings and not
even the king was allowed to enter the nunnery. The only man
admitted was the priest who conducted Holy Communion. This early
abbey seems to have survived the peak of the Danish raids of the next
two centuries, but to have been utterly destroyed about the year
A.D. 1000. Past historians have blamed the destruction on the Danes
but Lindsay Clegg suggests that it might have happened in the civil
war of Wessex, when Earl Godwin and his son Harold were in revolt
against King Edward the Confessor. Remember Wimborne was a
royal manor and the abbey was a royal foundation, and therefore fair
game for rebels. This would place the destruction in 1052, but in any
case it had gone and been replaced by the date of the Conquest in 1066.
The replacement was by a royal college founded by King Edward the
Confessor and enjoying amazing freedom from the bishop of Salisbury.
Later Edward II called it the "King's Free College" and exempted it
from the jurisdiction of the bishop. Thus for five hundred years until
the dissolution in 1547 Wimborne had an astonishing degree of freedom directly under the monarch. It was also a centre of learning from
the earliest times and had established a free grammar school before
1500, well before the dissolution of the college. Very soon after the
dissolution Queen Elizabeth I gave a grant of former college property
to support a master at £10 2s. 11d. per annum, with a proviso that the
school should be named "The Free Grammar School of Queen Eliza-

beth". In my youth the school was carrying on very much in the same way as other local grammar schools in Dorset. Small fees were paid by pupils and some assistance was received from the County Council. At its best, after 1936, the Council help doubled the fees paid by the pupils and paid the salaries of the teachers. But the Education Act, 1944, made it apparent that the school could not continue to be even semi-independent. Today it is a mixed school, very much larger than it has ever been before, and because of its size, forced to move from the shadow of the Minster.

Apart from the Minster there is nothing obvious in the town to attract the tourist. The shops are pleasant, the hotels hospitable without being especially noteworthy, and the car parking facilities are merely fair. Sir Frederick Treves said it was a "characterless place, that, having set its face against any show of individuality, has become successfully mediocre". This harsh description is unfair, and is the sort of superficial judgement which occasionally mars his great book. The men whose fathers have lived for much more than a thousand years on a royal manor, in the shelter of a mighty church free from episcopal jurisdiction, with a school more than four centuries old, are individual enough when you get to know them. As a young man—in the early 1930s—I attended regularly the corn and cattle markets of Dorset. The shopkeepers and farmers of Wimborne were outstandingly likeable. The townsmen had the sure knowledge of being "citizens of no mean city", and the farmers were established for the most part on good land. Even in the black depression of 1920–39 they were better off than most Dorset agriculturists. At first sight this may seem strange since the Heath almost surrounds the town, from Corfe Mullen to Canford, and from Hampreston to Holt. The first explanation is that all the cultivated land in these villages and in Wimborne itself is on rich river alluvium. Even more important, the very large population of Christchurch, Bournemouth and Poole provided a ready market. The sea to the south of these towns gave the agriculture of Wimborne district a monopoly of supplies of fresh milk and vegetables. The result was a higher price for milk in those days before the Milk Marketing Board had pooled and levelled returns to all farmers. In addition market gardening was prosperous at Longham and Hampreston, and glasshouse culture at Leigh, just off the Ringwood road.

At Wimborne market there was none of the snobbish atmosphere which farmers from very large farms have produced in neighbouring counties. Instead there was a spirit of friendly independence, a lack of servility, and a welcome free from patronising condescension. This attitude to life still persists, and may explain why Wimborne shows no alarm at the presence of Poole on its doorstep. A lesser town might fear this mighty and restless neighbour. Wimborne, in spite of Sir Frederick Treves, retains a sturdy, unfussed individuality.

III

THE HEATH VILLAGES

THERE are no settlements on the heath arising from the natural agricultural use of the soil. Poole and Wareham were founded on sea trade, Bovington is entirely military and Winfrith the last word in scientific experimental stations. Wimborne is almost surrounded by barren land but is on London Clay or fertile alluvium. Every village giving its name to a common or heath will be found to have similar reasons for existence, residential or industrial, or getting its living from immediately adjacent fertile soil of a completely different character. A journey round Poole Harbour stresses the essential barrenness of the heath.

Starting at Studland it is at once obvious that the village first got its living as well as its shelter from the great chalk hill of Ballard Down. Its golden sands have attracted visitors and led to a golf course, a good inn and one superb hotel. Thanks to the Bankes, an old land-owning family, there was no sprawl of development in the bad days before Town and Country Planning, and Poole Harbour helped by stopping any easy spread along the coast from the east. Studland has its day trippers, some campers, and full car parks for a few months in summer. Even in summer it is possible to find relatively quiet sands if you are prepared to walk. For the rest of the year a deep peace settles on this incredibly beautiful land. St. Aldhelm built Studland church in Saxon times; much of the present building is Norman. Perhaps there was never enough money here to do "restorations" in the Victorian age which defaced so many churches. As a result this small village church gives a wonderful feeling of continuous use.

In the long centuries after the fall of Rome the heathen Saxons and Danes completely lost the art of working stone. After the Cross returned to Britain it took many, many years to relearn the craft. There was no memory preserved by old men. For far too many generations there had been no building and no repairs. Men may have lived in the ruins of Roman villas but as they would have lived

42

in caves. They shored up a wall with a tree trunk, or stopped a hole with wattle and mud. Dry walling was just within their powers, but this seldom gave a wall higher than six feet and was done with naturally occurring stone slabs. Real building involved work in the quarries and the dressing of stone, not to mention the arch and the buttress. When the Saxons built Studland church they were working with very little to guide them. The Normans who followed were much more accomplished craftsmen, and yet it is unlikely that even they had any guide in the form of a plan. The instructions of the lord of the manor, or the abbot or bishop, were probably in fairly general terms as to size of nave and height of tower. The master mason, from his practical experience, pegged out his design on the ground and supervised every step of the work. He probably left many details of decoration to the craftsmen working under him. It is difficult to believe that some of the grotesque corbel heads at Studland church were ever commissioned by a cleric, or even by a noble lord. To me they may well represent the sort of creatures an unlettered workman might have associated with the heath. There were devils in this barren place where even the few bushes grew stunted and twisted. There were sudden bare hills, dry pits, quaking bogs, grey boulders and two mighty rocks, the Puckstone and the Agglestone which were undoubtedly intimately associated with evil, half-remembered, gods. Incidentally, these two rocks are fairly near the Studland road to the ferry at Sandbanks. They have been claimed as prehistoric relics of the nature of Stonehenge, but there is little evidence of anything other than a natural origin.

The main road from Studland to Wareham keeps as far as possible from the waters of Poole Harbour and runs under the cliff of the downs to Corfe. Between the road under the ridge and the sea is from three to five miles of ancient heath. There are isolated farms on pockets of good land and the Forestry Commission have done a great deal of draining and planting. There are few public roads, but it is possible to get a glimpse or two of the country in a car, on the highway from Stoborough to Arne, and on a road which wanders across Slepe heath nearly to Middlebere Farm, and then back towards the Wareham–Corfe road. During the 1939 War this heath was completely cleared of human beings and farm animals. It was used as a rehearsal ground for amphibious operations using live ammunition. From memory this battle training area was cleared in 1942. I was on the staff of the War Agricultural Executive

committee and we were given the job of getting all the corn crops out
of the area by a fixed date in autumn. Most of the sheaves were
stacked by the roadside near the Half Way Inn between Wareham
and Corfe. They were strangely shaped stacks, because the work
was done by service men with no farming knowledge. Much of the
grain was damp, because the land had to be cleared or the crop
abandoned, and the weather was showery. Potatoes were salvaged
from isolated cottage gardens, and some lovely black grapes from
the conservatory of the one big house to be abandoned. I suppose
the very indifferent grain was worth all the fuel oil expended on
saving it? The vegetables and fruit came from a very few settlements
and probably never reached the market.

My last evening in the battle zone was at Middlebere Farm. We
made tea in the farm house kitchen for a dozen or so sailors who
were helping and then discovered that the bath water was boiling.
There must have been a heater behind the grate. Two or three of
the ratings had baths—harvesting was a dirty job with that mildewed
oat crop. It was a strange sensation to have that mixed gang making
free of what had been so recently a home. A living farm had died,
which was something I had never experienced before, and there was
something horrible about leaving it in the evening, without bother-
ing to shut the gate between the cultivated land and the waste of
the heath. Certainly wars have produced just that sort of effect in
much of Europe, but not in England for a very long time. In a way
it seemed almost worse to be deserting this quiet house at the dictates
of our own army, and to be giving up the earth to our own tank
tracks and high explosive.

The story has had a happy ending. The heaths of Studland, Godlington, Newton, Rempstone, Wytch, Middlebere, Slepe and Arne
were not greatly altered. The wear by tracked vehicles at Bovington
had destroyed the heather in places, but tanks have been concentrated
there since 1916. This wild country on the shores of Poole Harbour
was only occupied for a very short time. The few cultivated fields
and pastures could soon be brought back to production. In fact
modern fertiliser knowledge, plus guaranteed food prices, have greatly
improved many fields. The Forestry Commission have drained and
planted some considerable amount of waste. A few roads which were
once very rough tracks, have been rendered passable for cars at all
seasons. Most farm houses, such as Middlebere and Slepe, were not
destroyed by live ammunition, and have been repaired and modernised.

Best of all the old church at Arne escaped serious damage and has been restored and rededicated. This group of heaths suffered little from the war and are in better trim than they have been in living memory, without having lost their character. However, some change arrived with the discovery of a new oil field at Wytch Heath, which has become the largest onshore field in the United Kingdom. At the moment most roads are narrow and well-surfaced, although many of them have the habit of ending at a locked gate or a "Private" notice. At Arne there is a car park opposite the church and visitors must walk the last three-quarters of a mile to the sea. This is probably a very good thing since although this lonely place is not crowded, quite a few cars turn up on summer evenings. Many many more would explore the creeks and beaches and heather knolls if they were easily accessible, and the quietness would go. The essence of this shore is peace.

Beyond Corfe Castle the heath road to Wareham crosses heathery open land to Stoborough at the end of the straight causeway over the alluvial Frome marshes. This village has its heath but the farming of the place was always in the river meadows.

The northern Purbeck ridge runs like a wall from the sea at Ballard Point near Studland to the sea at West Lulworth. There is one break at Corfe, and another on the shore at Arish Mell. Peaks on the ridge are few, the most notable overlooks Creech Grange and has a tumulus on top. Generally there is this distinct impression of a steep wall, of level height, and largely straight. Only very occasionally are there double walls or twisted country, in fact the only actual valley in the hills that I can remember is on a hairpin bend on the by-road from East Creech to Church Knowle. In spite of its remarkably uniform nature the ridge is like the heath in having no single name. Presumably it always had a sheep-grazing value and every section had a name associated with a village or farm. There is Ballard Down, Nine Barrow Down, Branscombe Hill, Ridgeway Hill and so on to Povington Hill, Rings Hill and Bindon Hill. Nine Barrows is self-explanatory and Rings Hill overshadowing Worbarrow Bay has a prehistoric fortified camp on the very edge of the cliff.

The clay workings in the corner west of Stoborough and centred on Furzebrook have already been described. It differs from the other low ground under the North Purbeck ridge in the tumbled chaos of old pits and spoil. Further west the heaths are flat with hardly a mark on the map except the occasional tumuli or barrow.

The farms and villages are all in the alluvial valleys of the Frome and Piddle. The view from Creech Barrow in summer is over level purple heather for ten miles to the chalk hills beyond Bere Regis. The two river valleys show as ribbons of green pasture with farm houses and churches hidden in the only old trees in this bare country-side. On the heath itself the aspen is almost the only natural tree. Rhododendrons have spread widely from plantings made a century ago along avenues to country houses, and the Forestry Commission have planted conifers on much of the drier land. The summer green of civilisation and cultivation is quite easily seen, however, and it is worth following the rivers to find the old settlements.

Going upstream on the Frome from Wareham, Stoborough has little to offer except two pubs on opposite sides of the main road. This is convenient in these days of heavy traffic, but hardly necessary, except in holiday time, for a tiny village one mile from a town. The importance of Stoborough is as the gateway to the heath, first near Arne, then to the very different heath of Furzebrook and the Blue Pool and to the shady lane leading to East and West Holme. I am not sure that the present condition of Holme Lane justifies a visit. Progress has been at work here. The lane is a good motor road; two water splashes have utterly vanished, and it is no longer what Sir Frederick Treves called "a delightful walk". It is still a pleasant shady bit of highway, but traffic now goes through at 60 m.p.h. In the 1930s I used to picnic there, and sleep for an hour after lunch, with no sound except the tinkle of peaty water over red gravel. There is sadness in the thought that even on Sunday afternoons a man can only find peace if he has a large farm of his own without roads. Dorset is the least damaged of all the southern counties of England, but quiet is hard to find near any good road surface. With a reasonably fast main road from Wool to Wareham it seemed a little unnecessary to touch this narrow lane on the other side of the river. It allows the cars of the staff from the Winfrith Heath Research Establishment to get to Swanage without going over Wool level crossing or going through Wareham. This may not be the reason for the road "improvement" but I suspect that such development will inevitably result from the establishment of the "light industry" so beloved of councillors. Is there no choice between becoming a museum, or growing into the sort of urban sprawl which has destroyed so much of the south-east of England?

At Holmebridge there is one modern improvement which has

not obliterated past beauty. The narrow bridge which carried the traffic on this very unimportant by-road is 600 years old. It saw a bloody skirmish in the Civil War when the king's men held it successfully against the Parliamentarians. Neither holiday traffic nor the industry of Winfrith were much impeded by this ancient bridge. The destructive factor here was the third major influence on the Heath—military occupation. Holme bridge leads to the firing area for tanks and anti-tank guns, shooting across Holme and Povington Heaths into the Purbeck Ridge, north of Tyneham. The Army needed a wider and probably a stronger bridge. To the delight of Dorset ratepayers the central Government paid most of the cost of the new bridge. What is even better the old one has not been removed.

The retention of Holme bridge is a blessing, but a small matter in the comparison with the loss of Holme Lane. Much worse things have happened upstream at Wool. This was a pleasant village in my youth with a wide main street and a thrilling connection with holidays. Wool was the station for Lulworth Cove and very busy with horse brakes and cabs in July and August. My elders complained that the railway had ruined the character of the village. Sir Frederick Treves wrote, "It was once a pretty village enough, but the railway has contaminated it." Today the railway is regarded as a dear old-fashioned relic. I find myself tending to defend the quaint level crossing which blocks the main Dorchester/Wareham road. At least I regard it with affection when travelling by train.

Wool bridge was very old. Built of grey stone, it was only wide enough for one car, and there were deep triangular recesses formed by the buttresses where pedestrians could shelter from passing carts. The old bridge lasted till the Great War when much of the parapet was smashed by army vehicles from Bovington. Today the river is no sort of barrier to fast cars, but the dear old railway crossing is still extremely effective.

The creation of Bovington Camp in the 1914–18 War led to the unplanned building of a bungalow town at Wool. Whatever may be said of Town and Country Planning since Hitler's war, nothing as bad as the Wool of 1920–39 has been perpetrated anywhere. The village has been "contaminated" much more efficiently since Treves wrote, and yet much remains. The Frome river is still an excellent trout stream. The super-modern industry of Winfrith differs from the factory development of a century ago in being careful to exclude effluent from streams. It is a paradox that farm and household cleanliness have done much more to foul rivers in the last ten years than local industry. Farmers have done much more washing of cows and cowstalls than was ever contemplated by our fathers. Housewives have used detergents and lavatory cleansers in a plague of hygiene. At last laws have been passed to control river pollution by countrymen, and there is hope that these laws will be enforced in time to preserve the sweet waters of Dorset.

The people of Wool have not lost their individuality. Some years ago the B.B.C. broadcast Christmas carols supplied by the village undertaker, who was said to have one of the best collections of these old songs in the English language.

South of the river is a wood by the side of the road to West Holme. A small notice board by an open gate carries the words "Bindon Abbey". The ruins of the abbey include the old fish pond, with a small island at one end which contains a hole in the ground, and this is claimed to mark the beginning of a tunnel which led under the river to Wool Manor. I hope this story is true. Secret passages are a fitting part of great abbeys, but it is a long way and a very damp one from the fishpond to the manor. Making such a passage would have been a great labour to keep secret.

There is a literary connection between the abbey and the manor. Thomas Hardy chose the old house for the unhappy honeymoon of Tess. When she wandered in her sleep she lay down in a stone coffin near the ruins of the abbey. The stone coffin is still there, and so is the picture on the walls of the stairs which distressed her when she went to bed. It is strange how the genius of Hardy made the fiction of Tess more real than history for most people. There was a Turberville family in Dorset and memorial brasses to them can be seen in Bere Regis church. The empty coffin at Bindon was that of Abbot Richard de Maners, but brasses and coffin are only of interest because of the fictional Tess.

The sadness of the few stones which are all that remain of Bindon Abbey is a recurring theme in Dorset and in most of England. We may be luckier than most counties in retaining the magnificent churches of Sherborne, Wimborne and Milton, with the great house of Forde, and the tithe barns of Cerne and Abbotsbury. Here at Bindon there is another flame of revival. The landowners, the Weld family of Lulworth, never deserted the old faith. At the earliest moment when Catholic Emancipation made it possible they opened a chapel in the abbey grounds. It was on the second floor of a dwelling

The River Frome by Wareham Bridge

house, very different from the glories of the ancient church, but unchanged in its witness to the Faith.

The next heath village up the River Frome is Moreton. Once again the meadows and ploughland are on alluvium brought down by the chalk stream, but the heath presses close, and deposits of river gravel have lead to much chaotic stirring of the surface. The great house is still the seat of the Frampton family who held the manor long before the house was built in 1778. It was a Squire Frampton who played a considerable part in the persecution of the Tolpuddle Martyrs. The church had been much restored before the war and required a great deal more rebuilding after being hit by a bomb. The cemetery is separate from the church, presumably because the old churchyard became overfull. Our forefathers must have used the same ground over and over again, but modern feeling on this point has closed all town churchyards and forced most villages to seek extensions. Here at Moreton the new cemetery is pleasant and well kept. It contains the grave of Lawrence of Arabia who died nearby in a motor-cycle crash on May 19th, 1935. A few miles away at Clouds Hill, Bovington, his cottage is open to visitors. He lived there when he had turned from fame to serve as an aircraftman in the R.A.F.

Further upstream on the Frome are Woodsford and West Stafford, both on alluvium and gravel. The river valley here is wide and the stream has been diverted in a dozen places to form water meadows. Most of these meadows are no longer irrigated but it is still possible to find the hatches, the feeders and the irrigation ditches of a system which was still flourishing in my youth. Water meadows differ profoundly from the flood meadows found in the Stour valley, crossing the heath near Wimborne, although superficially they are both just flat grassland. As the names imply, flood meadows are covered with wide stretches of shallow water when the river overflows. This brings down a certain amount of sediment which presumably has some fertilising value. In water meadows the water is diverted deliberately into side channels and then taken in shallow ditches along the tops of parallel ridges. A man called a drowner stops the ditches with a turf at certain places so that the water runs in an even sheet down the flanks of the ridges. Between the ridges is another ditch which collects the water and returns it to the main stream lower down. In flood meadows there is no control of the water which may come up in summer and cover good herbage with mud. The

Bere Regis church roof

water meadows are strictly controlled, and the water used is clear
and fast flowing. It is sent over the meadows in the depth of winter
and the main object is to keep the land from freezing. When the
danger of hard frost is over in March the water is cut off and the
grass grows a month earlier than on adjoining unwatered fields. It is
interesting how small is the margin between soil temperatures which
control growth. These meadows gain no advantage from the water
as moisture, because all fields are wet enough for growth in April.
There is no fertiliser of any consequence in the water and best results
are obtained from streams near their source where they bubble up
from deep springs. This water is purer than any town supply and
its only virtue for encouraging growth is that it is relatively warm.
Similar water, usually from artesian wells, is used in the Dorset watercress industry. It comes out at about 52 degrees Fahrenheit which is
well above the root temperature required for growth.

Most water meadows are no longer used as such because early
growth of herbage can be obtained by cultivating pedigree grasses,
and by using modern fertilisers. They are a feature of the Frome
where it crosses the heath, but equally so of the chalk valleys of the
Frome and Piddle. They made possible the large dairies which have
always been a feature of these valleys, just as flood meadows on
the Stour encouraged milk production along that river. The Frome
water meadows gave a living to villages which are basically on the
heath, such as Woodsford, Moreton and Wool. In the parallel Piddle
valley every village gives its name to a heath from Puddletown to
Bere Regis, but the villages and water meadows are almost entirely
on chalk soil. The heath has practically no influence on the villages
and never has in the past. Their story must come later in a chapter
on Chalk.

For the real heath villages we go back to the flood meadows on
the Stour near Wimborne. Corfe Mullen is one of the largest parishes
in Dorset, but fifty years ago the whole life of the place was along the
sides of the Stour where the village church stands just across the road
from the limit of the flood water. This water was often a mile wide
across the fields to the north. In recent years flooding has been less
frequent, partly through better care of watercourses, and partly
through less obstruction of the stream by ancient water mills. It may
be also that the general level of underground water has fallen owing
to the much greater use in industry, farming and domestically. The
river at Corfe Mullen made the meadows and this was along the

northern border of the village. Southward there was hardly a name on the map at the turn of the century. Today a small town has developed on the heathland very remote from the old church—so remote that the church has developed its own bus service to the crowded new houses on the Wareham road. This is partly a dormitory town for Poole and partly a place of retirement for the elderly. Since we must have more houses the heath soil must be the right place to put them. It has an unexpected advantage over good land. The cost of transforming this barren stuff to make it grow farm crops may well be too high. No one counts the cost of making a garden or a golf course. What is more a whole range of choice flowers grow best on sour land—rhododendrons, azaleas, heathers, lupins, brooms and hydrangeas. The indifferent turf which may be persuaded to grow gives no bulk of hay, but is slow growing and hard wearing, ideal for lawns. Houses on the heath can soon be hidden in pleasant shrubberies and be much less of a scar on the landscape than the new council houses jutting out of a chalk village like a sore thumb. In fact Ferndown, once no more than a valueless part of Heath Farm, Hampreston, has been "developed" to give "pleasant houses hidden in their own wooded grounds". I quote from an advertisement but without malice. Well tended gardens can give more beauty than barren heath, as long as somewhere we are left with enough heath to remember the eerie feeling of immense age, loneliness, and untamed stubborn resistance.

Very near Ferndown which is wholly new is the old village of Hampreston. It is on a blind lane off a by-road and by a Dorset miracle remains undeveloped in the modern sense. There is the small ancient church, a large farm house and a cluster of cottages. Agriculturally it is very much developed. The Stour made the flood meadows on the usual plan, but they have been greatly improved by modern science. The slightly higher alluvial land has long been cultivated very intensively as a market garden, and irrigated with artificial rain from the river. Even the heath has been nibbled into for the growing of horticultural crops. Market gardening, nurseries, and glasshouse culture are common in the Wimborne district in spite of the fact that the real heath soils are naturally barren. The reason was the very sudden growth of the Poole-Bournemouth centre of population. There is an enormous market for horticultural products which did not exist when the railways were first built. A century and a half ago one postman could deliver all Bournemouth's letters. It is significant that even a market for hundreds of thousands of people left most of the sterile sand uncropped by commercial growers.

Canford Magna, the manor of which once included Poole, has remained a village. Its river alluvium grows crops and keeps cows, whilst its heath is either covered by the houses of Poole or remains empty and poverty stricken. This was the seat of the Wimborne family and the village of Canford consists of what the lords of the last century regarded as model houses for the working classes. Similar cottages were scattered all over the estate, obviously built to the same plan at about the same time. They were at least weatherproof, and with decent windows, a vast improvement on the hovels they replaced. The survival of Canford as a village was probably due to the lords of the manor. Their great house is now a school, and this preserves the park as playing fields. It will be interesting to see if pressure of population in Poole swallows up the good land of Knighton Farm. Building here would be easy compared with the undrained bogs of some of the worthless acres. There is also the curious fact that people will often rush to preserve worthless soil if it is a common, and be content to see privately owned farm land vanish. Now within the county border, Bournemouth and Christchurch will almost certainly not be allowed to encroach on the New Forest. I have much less hope for the good land in the old Dorset village on the Stour at West Parley.

In the other heath villages of West Moors and Verwood the rivers have done little to alter the barren soil. Verwood is partly on London Clay which gives a reasonable agricultural soil, but otherwise this area has only been altered by buildings. Neither were parishes at one time. West Moors was a hamlet of West Parley, and Verwood a hamlet of Cranborne. Growth came to both before the 1914 War with the building of the railway. This cheap land was reasonably near Bournemouth and gave an ideal place for retirement. Houses increased after 1918 but the growth tended to fall off a little when motor transport replaced railways. Housing sites were more popular on main roads than on branch railways until the advent of Town and Country Planning. In 1931 Verwood had 1,605 inhabitants and West Moors 1,181; they have become small towns from isolated heath farms in less than a century.

Between the heather of the heath and the bare fields of the chalk is the long narrow strip of wooded country on London clay and gravel. This is now often planted with conifers but it was undoubtedly once natural woodland, and traces of the forests remain. From the Hampshire border near Fordingbridge the road through Alderholt, Edmonsham, Horton, Hinton Martell and Holt is beautifully shaded. Names like Woodlands, Pig Oak, Haythorn and God's Blessing Green bring memories of small green fields and a plenitude of timber. The villages on this narrow band of mainly heavy soil are close together, and their manor houses added to the woodlands in the last century by planting trees in their great parks. What with very old natural forest, replanting with commercial timber, and the amenity wood- lands, this narrow band of reasonably heavy soil is easy to follow from the outskirts of Cranborne through Kingston Lacy to Lytchett Matravers, and on to within a couple of miles of Dorchester at Stins- ford. The only break is where the alluvium of the Stour valley cuts across it between Corfe Mullen and Cowgrove. For the last ten miles between Bere Regis and Stinsford this natural woodland belt is narrow and does little more than give coverts for pheasants. All the villages in this area are on the chalk streams and have always looked to the chalk soils for their living. East of Bere Regis the villages are close together, and the older cottages are often oak-framed and of local brick. They are hidden in trees and are quite different from the near- by chalk villages. On the chalk the houses straggle along the streams, whereas on the clay they are scattered, with isolated farm houses. There is well water at shallow depth and in reasonable abundance through these parishes, but often no stream to govern the shape of the land and the site of the houses. Bloxworth is a good example since it is off a main road and has not been altered much by traffic. It is also far enough from any town to have escaped becoming a dormitory. From the small church of Bloxworth one rector moved to become cardinal archbishop of Canterbury. He was John Morton, and was one of the most hated men in England in the reign of Henry VII. That was the age when being a great churchman usually meant being a politician. John Morton became Lord Chancellor to the King, and was responsible for raising vast sums of money. Some of this money found its way back to Dorset, not to Bloxworth but to the neighbouring chalk village of Bere Regis, where Morton paid for the tower and roof of the village church.

The adjoining village of Morden is also remote from main roads. The church and most of the houses are in the trees of the clay but the great house, Charborough, and the park, are mainly northward on chalk. In the church is a memorial to Thomas Earle dated 1597.

This name ties up with that of the 1964 owner of the property, Admiral Sir Reginald Aylmer Ranfurdy Plunkett-Ernle-Erle-Drax. Morden church is said to have been "erected on the old site in 1868 by Miss Drax", and presumably the Earle memorial was from an earlier building. Charborough Park has samples of all the fantastic extravagance of its age. The park is of 650 acres and is surrounded by a high brick wall which must have cost an enormous sum even when labour was cheap. For two miles or so the main Dorchester/ Wimborne road runs along by the wall, and it is very obvious that the road goes round the park and does not follow the direct route across it. In my youth Charborough Park not only had its deer, but a zoo of other animals not unlike modern Whipsnade. In addition there is a tall tower in the grounds which gives a view for miles. This "folly" is one of the largest and most blatant in Dorset. Treves says, "It was built originally in 1796, was struck by lightning in 1839, and unfortunately re-erected."

Adjoining Morden on this woodland belt of soil is Lytchett Matravers. Here the main roads and the nearness to Poole have destroyed some of the natural character of the village. This is even more the case in Lytchett Minster. Matravers is worth a visit for its very old pub and for one of the best views of Poole Harbour. Lytchett Minster is best known for the unusual pub name of St. Peter's Finger. The inn sign shows St. Peter with finger raised in blessing. What is strange is the difficulty in finding the reason for the name. At first sight it would have seemed easy. A village called Lytchett Minster might be expected to have a great church like Wimborne Minster or York Minster, and such a church could be dedicated to St. Peter. Add to this that it was near the public house where the bell ringers went for relaxation, and you could imagine St. Peter's finger raised in blessing or admonition. It seems a pity that there is not a word of truth in all this plausible folk-lore, which I have just invented.

Lytchett is a Celtic name associated with woodland, and we should expect primeval woodland on the London Clay. Lytchett Matravers got its second name from a great landowning family, but Lytchett Minster never had a minster. It was once a hamlet of Sturminster Marshall and even Sturminster Marshall church is not dedicated to St. Peter. Lytchett Minster church has its original tower, but the small building was entirely rebuilt in Victorian times. There is nothing to show that the old church was any bigger. There is also very little evidence that the old church, which was destroyed by fire, was dedicated to "St. Peter ad Vincula". This is usually given as the origin of "Peter's Finger", but it seems strange that such a dedication was not transferred to the rebuilt church.

The next village on the wooded belt adjoining the heath is Corfe Mullen. Here the clay strip is very narrow although it gives some pleasant park-like land south of the old Somerset and Dorset railway. The main part of this very large village has already been mentioned as being on alluvial soil from the Stour river, or urban development on barren heath.

Across the river the woodland continues, with the great house of Kingston Lacy still inhabited by the Bankes family who have held the land for centuries. The first house was built by a Bankes in the seventeenth century. The name of the hamlet indicates that it was once a royal manor before passing to a John Lacy. In fact this region has much connection with kings. You will remember that Wimborne was a royal free chapel under the Normans and that after the Reformation Elizabeth I re-established the school. The connection goes back to Saxon kings with historical certainty. Kingston Lacy was part of Wimborne and shares the history and the legends. One reason for this is that the hamlet is between the very old town of Wimborne and a much older hill fort called Badbury Rings. This is on the chalk soil and in the neighbouring parish of Shapwick, but it influenced Kingston Lacy and the town of Wimborne. Here Saxon King Edward, the immediate successor of the great King Alfred, was encamped with a rebellious subject, Athelwald, in Wimborne. Athelwald thought discretion better than battle and withdrew without a fight. For tales of war we must go further back to the darkness which filled the centuries after the Roman army of occupation had withdrawn. Was there a King Arthur, and a Round Table, and knights? If so the fort of Badbury was old when he fought his great battle at the legendary Mount Badon. It is a likely enough spot for the Celts to have met the heathen Saxons. An invading army coming in from Poole would have found little on the barren heath to attract them and would have swept in over the most easily fordable point of the river. Alternatively if they entered the estuary of the Stour and Avon at Christchurch they might well have got their ships as far as Wimborne. Add to this that Badbury was on a Roman road, and a road which had not been neglected for very long. The conquerors drove their military roads on strategic routes. They had occupied and strengthened Badbury Rings. If Arthur and his Celts came back there they were returning to the home of their ancestors, who had been enslaved 700 years before. There was a road from Salisbury to Dorchester, and there were three mighty ramparts rising to a plateau with a lookout over three counties and the sea. If there was an Arthur he might have fought the heathen just where the Bankes family still continue to keep the heathen out of Dorset, by doing their best to keep the countryside alive.

It is desperately hard to preserve such a place as Badbury Rings from litter, noise and all that goes with a "beauty spot". Perhaps the old Rings do not mind. After all they once enclosed a very populated noisy town with a great deal of insanitary litter. The old families of Dorset saved it when our immediate forefathers might have put up tea shops and public lavatories. Today it is reasonably certain that Badbury Rings will not be destroyed. The old town at Badbury was inhabited by Celts, Romans, Angles and Saxons. It ceased to exist a thousand years ago. The fields my friends are farming along the River Allen have changed a dozen times in the method of their farming but remain producing food. The old landowners have saved them so far, and long may they do so.

Mention of the Allen brings me back from the calm sensible legends of Arthur and from the wild fantasies of modern reason. Unlike most streams the River Allen did not greatly influence the life of the people on its banks in the clay area. At one time it had a profound influence on the sewage disposal of Wimborne. The maintenance of an old mill on the outskirts of the town was intimately connected with Wimborne W.C.s. The same old mill held the water back along almost the whole course of the Allen so that all the farms along its banks had snipe marches which could not be drained. The farms and houses had their water supplies without the help of the boggy stream, and the stream has no villages on its banks after it leaves the chalk south of Witchampton. Only in recent years has it been possible to get sufficient fall to drain the old wet meadows on farms such as Hillbutts. Incidentally, this name is alleged to go back to the days of the long bow.

Having included Badbury Rings in this section on Kingston Lacy, although it is in Shapwick, I must mention the wonderful avenue of trees on the Tarrant Keynston/Wimborne road. This is said to have 365 trees on each side of the road and must be a bit of landscape gardening connected with Kingston Lacy Hall, and the Bankes family. I once tried to count the trees and made the number 367, but it is extremely difficult to count driving a car. The number of the days in the year would seem to be likely especially since our forefathers often used this sort of fancy in such things as the windows in a palace and the like.

North-east of Kingston Lacy the wooded belt widens to its maximum at Holt. Holt has its common on the heath but the farms are all on clay, or clay with gravel. The great house has an historic name—Gaunts. I am not sure of parish boundaries, and geographically Gaunts House may not be in Holt, but it is part of the same pattern of natural woodland. This is the England of old Gaunt's dying speech, "A dear, dear land" of great oaks, noble houses, green pastures and scattered farms. There are streams in Holt running either into the Allen or, via Uddens Water, to the Moors river. Once again, though, the streams, through this clay, drain water away instead of supplying it to a thirsty land. The farms are small and scattered. There are several open spaces which could be village greens, except that there is no central village in the usual sense of the word. None the less the farms of Holt are farms. They are quite different from the New Forest holdings just over the border in Hampshire. In the New Forest the pattern of agriculture for centuries has been a few enclosed fields used for hay, with grazing rights on the unfenced waste. At one time this led to a life of extreme poverty for the commoners. They lived off the Forest, never buying coal, but burning fallen timber, or peat. Instead of straw they cut the bracken in October as bedding for their animals. Their pigs lived on acorns and beech nuts for many months in the year. In comparison the small farms of Holt have always been much more prosperous during my lifetime. Recently the growth of Poole and Bournemouth has provided a ready market, but I think Holt has always been able to support a community which lived reasonably well from enclosed land.

The adjoining villages of Hinton Martell and Horton follow the same pattern of strong land and trees, but both villages are on the edge of the clay belt and are much influenced by the chalk. Indeed the strangely isolated Horton Inn, on a cross roads far from the village, is on typically bare chalk land. Horton has the remains of a great religious house which shows how far it is in fact from the adjacent Horton Heath. The old monks were very good judges of land, and their only settlements in the heath area were on soils very different from barren sand. Wimborne, Bindon and Horton could all yield fish, corn and flesh.

This area is sometimes visited for its connection with Monmouth. After the disaster at Sedgemoor the unlucky duke was found in a ditch near ·Horton disguised as a shepherd, but still carrying the Star of the Garter in his pocket. There was a price of £5,000 on his head and the hunt was keen. They took him to the nearest magistrate at Holt Lodge, and within seven days he was executed on Tower Hill in London. There was an ash in the hedge where they found him, and the place has been Monmouth's Ash ever since. I wonder how often the tree has been replaced? Certainly the original tree has not lasted since 1685.

Perhaps the best impression of this belt of clay between the heath and the chalk is from Chalbury. Here there is a hill which is only three hundred feet high but which manages to give a wonderful view over woodland, heath, fertile chalk and the distant Isle of Wight. This feeling of immense space seen from relatively small hills is a blessed peculiarity of Dorset.

If you find the view from Chalbury gives the best quick impression of the clay/tree country between the heath and chalk, it may be worth attempting an equally concentrated glimpse of the heath. Start from Wareham on the Dorchester road, branch off right at the sign-post marked Worgret Heath, one mile from the town, and go straight on to Stinsford. In this fifteen miles you can see some bits of original heath, the amazing chaos of gravel workings, the influence of Boving-ton camp, the effects of modern forestry and the way farming makes use of every better bit of soil in this sterile land.

IV

THE CHALK FRINGE

The northern edge of the chalk forms a bold escarpment which can be best seen from such open places as Batcombe Hill or Bulbarrow. This belt of chalk country averages about ten miles in width, and crosses the county from south-west to north-east. There is a general slope from the escarpment to the south-east where the chalk finally passes beneath the narrow band of wooded London Clay discussed in the previous chapter. The tilt in the landscape has led to three types of chalk villages. The top of the north-westerly escarpment has a few settlements at a height of 700–800 feet, with deep wells and no streams. Ashmore is a good example. The central plateau of 500–600 feet is crossed by parallel streams or winterbornes, and all the villages are in the narrow valleys about 200 feet below the level of the bulk of the farm land. Finally the third type of village occurs at about 250 feet where the chalk vanishes beneath the clay. Here village names may be given to neighbouring heath land, but the whole living of the place comes from the chalk.

To gain some impression of these different bits of Dorset it is desirable to take three journeys. For the edge of the heath and forest a start should be made at Cranborne, and the country explored through Witchampton to Shapwick, Winterborne Zelston, Bere Regis and Puddletown. A second trip would cross the river valleys from Winterborne Steepleton through Dorchester, Piddletrenthide, Milton Abbas, Blandford and Wimborne St. Giles. The final exploration of the uplands would deal with Handley, Tollard, Farnham and Ashmore.

For the start of the first journey Cranborne is ideal as an example of a well watered village on the edge of the chalk. It has almost everything. At one time it had a weekly market and was the "town" for a great deal of the surrounding countryside. Men have lived on this easily cleared dry soil long before the beginning of written history. There are burial mounds and ditches in plenty from early British times. The conquering Romans drove a great road straight across the country from Old Sarum to the occupied fort at Badbury Rings. This road misses Cranborne but can be seen plainly nearby where it follows the line of the much older Ackling Dyke, south-west of Pentridge and east of Handley. The later successful invasion by the Normans left a mark on Castle Hill just outside Cranborne. This was probably a meeting place for Britons and Saxons in turn but the Normans made it one of their fortresses. We are so used to seeing remains of immensely strong stone Norman castles, such as Corfe and Old Sarum, that we get the impression that the conquerors first swept through the country and then built these holding points at leisure. In fact the stone fortresses were merely a permanent form of the military strong points which were put up or altered in a great hurry as part of the original campaign. The first Norman castles consisted of a "motte and bailey". This is esssentially the same as the great mound surmounted by a stone keep which can be seen at Corfe, but they were put up very quickly as temporary buildings in the first flood of the invasion. Castle Hill, Cranborne, is a good example of such a fort which never became the permanent dwelling of a great lord. Instead the church already held the ownership of much of Cranborne land, and an abbey existed there when William the Conqueror gave the manor to his Queen Matilda. Nothing remains of the abbey except fragments, such as a pulpit bearing the initials of an abbot of Tewkesbury who died in 1421. Tewkesbury and Cranborne were closely associated until the Reformation.

Apart from the very large church the other great building in Cranborne is the Manor House. The two have a connection in so much that the more magnificent parts of the house were added to a Tudor manor by a Cecil in the reign of James I. Of all the great families who became immensely rich as a result of the Reformation the Cecils are outstanding. They were very powerful, and have had a profound influence on English history for a very long time. The inheritance of talent seems never to have run dry in this family, from Elizabeth I to Elizabeth II. Dorset is very rich in old families who have had great local influence, and who have preserved their heritage. It is unusual to find anything to equal the Cecils on the national and international stage. They were very much more than local powers, although here at Cranborne they followed the usual pattern of Dorset gentry in landscape gardening and paternal care for their tenants.

Cranborne's heath is so far away that most people would not

connect it with the village. It is known as Cranborne Common and is near Daggons Road Station. During the 1939 War part of it was ploughed by the Dorset War Agricultural Executive Committee, but without any outstanding success. The land round the heath is wooded and there is some development of small houses, which seems to have taken place mainly before 1930. It was probably influenced by the growth of Bournemouth, and the railway from Salisbury to Fordingbridge, Wimborne and Poole. This bit of semi-urban country had much the same history as neighbouring Verwood and West Moors. The railway has gone and there is no important road in the area, so recent growth has been relatively slow, but there must always be a danger from industrial Southampton, or residential Bournemouth.

Possibly Cranborne is best known for its "Chase". At one time this included all the heath down to the Avon and Stour rivers, and then rose to totally different soils on the highlands of the chalk at Ashmore. The heaths were probably always bare heather but the uplands grew primeval forest. I use the word "forest" in its present meaning of woodland. It has a much older and different meaning in place names such as New Forest or Epping Forest. These were royal hunting grounds and governed by an entirely different set of laws from those applying to the ordinary land of England. Generally forests were unfenced, and there were strict rules about the preservation of game. "Game" included almost every sizeable, edible creature, but of these deer were of prime importance. All the "vert"—timber and underwood—were the covert for the deer. There could be settlements in a forest with enclosed fields and villages. The inhabitants might have rights to cut peat, to collect fallen branches, to graze the open land with cattle, and to allow their pigs out at certain seasons to eat acorns. All these privileges were overshadowed by the over-riding fact that there must be no interference with the deer. For instance, almost always dogs were forbidden or restricted to a very small size.

Sometimes the ancient kings allowed their great nobles to have forest rights. In this case the area was usually known as a "chase". This was the position at Cranborne before the reign of King John. This monarch had a great love for hunting, as had all the Norman kings. John married an heiress who owned the Chase, but seems to have divorced the lady soon after he became king. He did not return her land, however, so that Cranborne became a forest. It remained royal until the time of King James I when it was granted to the Earl of Salisbury, of the mighty Cecil family.

Moving down the fringe of the chalk the villages have a tendency at times to fall into my second category of dry upland fields with cottages only by a stream, rather than well watered spreading settlements such as Cranborne. Perhaps the real test is if they are near enough to the heath to possess a common or near enough to the narrow clay belt to be well wooded. Wimborne St. Giles comes into the latter category although many of the plantations are less old natural woodland than the result of planting by the Ashleys, the earls of Shaftesbury. St. Giles is the home of this family which has had so much to do with bettering the conditions of labour after the Industrial Revolution. The village is still largely "model" in the Victorian sense, somewhat on the lines of the Guest family buildings at Canford Magna, but better preserved. The great house at St. Giles is very large but has been altered extensively since the original Tudor manor of the sixteenth century. It is much older than the pleasant little church, which is one of the few Dorset village churches to owe little on the outside at least to Roman Catholic origins. St. Giles church was rebuilt in 1772 when the Church of England was very much a Protestant foundation established by law. It is full of Ashley memorials and some monuments are much older than the actual building. To me its main interest is of a Protestant edifice on which a very great deal of money has been expended for many years.

The Protestant feeling of the present building is confined to the outside, which is very much of the period when churches were plain meeting houses, and the altar was a table. St. Giles' church was gutted by fire as recently as 1908, when the roof and most of the interior was destroyed. The restoration which followed was on what is commonly called High Church lines. The type of worship there is now certainly Anglo-Catholic as witness the notice in the church about services. This refers to "Sung Mass with Holy Communion", and to "Confession", and to "Requiem Mass". The decorations follow the richness and colour of Roman Catholic rather than Protestant churches. To low church taste it might conceivably be regarded as a shade too ornate, but it is quite outstanding in the loving care which is obviously and consistently spent on it. No church could be more spotlessly clean and with a feeling of being in more constant use.

One of the fascinations of Dorset is the way that not only great families like the Ashleys have persisted but so have lesser people. There are many farming families, many shepherds and farm labourers whose names are recorded in parish registers for centuries. The Hooper family have farmed in a big way in the county for a very long time and are still occupying thousands of acres of land. Some of them are now owner-occupiers but the tradition of the family was to rent land. It could hardly have been a tenant farmer who drank with Charles II in the cellars of St. Giles house. At any rate the king was so pleased with the wit and capacity of Mr. Hooper that he knighted him amongst the barrels. This original Sir Edward Hooper died before he was fifty. Possibly his capacity was stretched too often, and ever since the family have been noted for a temperate approach to life. To persist for centuries a farming family must be able to save money in good times if they want to maintain a decent standard in the bad years. They must not ape the gentry in extravagance, or they will join the poor in hand-to-mouth existence. Thrift and saving are not exciting virtues, but they have often preserved the fields of Dorset from falling into decay.

Travelling on down the edge of the chalk lowlands, Gussage All Saints certainly comes into my second category of purely chalk villages based on a stream. In some ways the same is true of Witchampton, although here the stream is the Allen with its very wide and marshy meadows. Just behind on the uplands Moor Crichel has been changed from typical chalk by very extensive planting of trees round large houses. Witchampton is mainly famous for its paper mill, a rather unexpected industry to find in a very rural setting. Treves calls it "one of the most beautiful villages in the entire county", so you can guess the mill is well hidden in trees. A century and a half ago Cobbett found another paper mill in the pleasant Hampshire village of Whitchurch. It made paper for bank notes and his wrath flowed over. Paper money was the curse of modern economy. Of this little river he said, "Oh mighty rivulet of Whitchurch! All our properties, all our laws, all our manners, all our minds you have changed." He would have undoubtedly hated the Witchampton paper mill just as much but I find the village still fitting Treves' description and singularly unchanged. Moor Crichel's claim to fame once rested on the sporting countryside where King Edward VII and the Kaiser once shot pheasants. It has recently achieved a status near to that of Runnymede, possibly with just as little justification.

When the barons forced the king to seal Magna Carta they were safeguarding the rights of the great nobles, with precious little thought for anyone else. When the owner of Crichel Down stopped the Civil Service in the 1950s from carrying out a good plan connected with farming, it is doubtful if the public weal was much in mind. Still, the Great Charter did result, after many centuries, in a foundation for justice which aims at being neither delayed, nor sold, nor denied. The Crichel Down Case may deter civil servants from taking un-constitutional action with the best of motives. Unfortunately it may encourage them not to take action at all. Dorset men are generally prepared to boast about anything connected with their county. I find myself wincing slightly when Crichel Down is mentioned in the same breath as, say, the Tolpuddle Martyrs.

All the villages on this part of the chalk fringe—Cranborne, Wim-borne St. Giles, Witchampton and Moor Crichel, have obviously been influenced by the nearness of the belt of London Clay. Like true clay villages such as Holt, the older small houses and cottages are of brick. In the centre of the chalk area cob walls and thatched roofs were universal in my youth for all buildings except the church, the vicarage and the manor. The sole exception was the school and the few brick cottages erected by squires in a brief prosperous period for agriculture, about 1860. Cob and thatch are expensive to main-tain and on the central chalk the red brick of the council houses has swamped the old character, except for the slightly better class small houses which were faced with flint. On the chalk fringe a few oak-framed brick cottages, with thatched roofs, still remain. So do small brick houses with tiled roofs from Georgian times because these were more durable than cobb and thatch. Thus the fringe villages have retained to a considerable extent a consistent use of materials, and modern dwellings blend rather more happily with the old.

Further south the nature of the soil has been greatly altered by the wide alluvial valley of the Stour. Shapwick on one side of the river and Sturminster Marshall on the other are on the 100–200 feet level and quite close to the clay belt, but the main influence on their life and agriculture has been the stream. The wide meadows have always supported large dairies and usually these have been com-bined with arable farming on the adjoining dry chalk fields. Most farms are large with big solid farm houses, and extensive buildings just on the edge between the flood meadows and the gentle slopes of the chalk. Barford Farm is a good example. In the bad times before the war it had two large dairies and also had much of the

Bulbarrow Hill

dry land growing grass to provide hay for the cows. When corn became profitable the old plough land could easily be brought back into cultivation. On this farm, and generally in this area, there was always a choice away from corn growing, and it was corn which lost money on the unwatered hills from 1870 to 1939. The great depression was survived by most of the farmers who could easily switch to cows in these fortunate villages on the Stour. As evidence of the extent of this switch the cheese factory at Sturminster Marshall in 1939 was the biggest in the world. Similarly a butter factory at the other side of Dorset at Chard Junction still holds the world record for hundredweights of butter made in one day.

Shapwick and Sturminster Marshall were so much influenced by the river which made cow-keeping possible that farm buildings were more commonly red brick cowstalls than cob barns. There was also a tendency for groups of cottages to spring up round dairies. Today the fashion is for concrete and asbestos to take the place of brick, but the villages remain spread out, just clear of the flood meadows, and there is no crowding into ribbons along narrow valleys.

West of Sturminster Marshall the fringe chalk villages are all governed by limited water supplies, and are mainly concentrated in valley bottoms. First there are three Winterbornes—Zelston, Thomson and Kingston. Beyond come villages in the Piddle Valley, or on a Piddle tributary such as at Bere Regis. In all cases patches of gravel tend to occur over the chalk and this may alter the flowers to be found in cottage gardens. The gravel is seldom workable as gravel but where it occurs the top soil may be short of lime. Agriculturally the lime shortage was often counteracted by digging into the subsoil for chalk, and spreading the lumps over the surface in autumn. Winter frosts were usually sufficient to break the chalk into powder. A similar procedure took place on flat-topped chalk hills where flinty clay is frequently found. I have heard my father describe this job which was common in his youth, one hundred years ago. It was a contract business done by two men who used donkeys with panniers. The use of tons of rough chalk has been replaced in modern days by ground chalk applied mechanically. This is also usually a contract job. It carries a government subsidy, and it is a valuable soil improvement, but by no means as picturesque as the donkeys must have been. Chalking has changed the acidity on the gravel patches in most fields, and it is no longer usual to see crop failures, or very definite

The Frome, Lower Bockhampton

areas covered in acid-loving weeds such as the yellow corn marigold. On the other hand it is not at all unusual to find lime-hating flowers, such as rhododendrons, azaleas, broom and lupins flourishing in gardens.

Of the Winterborne villages, Zelston has one pub with a very modern name, "The General Allenby". On the same winterborne just below at Almer is "The World's End", a solitary thatched house just off the main Bere Regis–Wimborne road. Whether it is the name, the solitude, or a cheerful host, I cannot tell, but the cars and motor-coaches flock to "The World's End" every summer evening.

Winterborne Tomson is not named on the Ordnance Survey 1:50,000 maps. Previous ones spelt it Thomson, and Victorian ones occasionally Thompson. The pronunciation is not affected by the spelling and is no more than a minor source of irritation to natives, unlike the changing of names in the Piddle valley to Puddle. The mention of natives is a reminder that Winterborne Tomson has remarkably few. The manor house went through a stage of becoming a farm house and this, with the farm buildings, was almost all that remained of the village. The old tiny church was a ruin, and its restoration in 1932 was due largely to Thomas Hardy and was a memorial to him. It is sometimes forgotten that Hardy started life as an architect which explains his interest in the building. The thought of a church as a memorial to one who was not a conventional churchman is not incongruous in his case. He would have gone to see the oxen kneel at midnight on Christmas Eve "hoping it might be so".

The last villages up this particular Winterborne are definitely not connected with the fringe of the clay. They stretch right across the chalk country to the escarpment in the north and all follow the pattern of long villages in a narrow valley with the farm land on a plateau right and left. The source of this unreliable stream is Winterborne Houghton, and it twists through Winterborne Stickland, Winterborne Clenstone, Winterborne Whitchurch and Winterborne Kingston before reaching Tomson and Zelston on its way to the Stour.

Bere Regis is the next village on the fringe of the chalk, and this has connections with the heath to which it gives a name, but is little influenced by the clay fringe. At Bere Regis the forested clay strip is only a few hundred yards wide, although it still gives a wooded skyline on the west, south and east of the village. The famous Wood-bury Hill Fair was held on the edge of the chalk and clay one mile east of the parish. This fair used to last for five days, but it was almost dead in my boyhood just before the 1914 War. Today the ancient earthworks of the early Britons are undisturbed by any annual wild revelry, yet a faint influence remained for at least twenty years after the death of the fair. As recently as the 1930s Bere Regis was regarded as the toughest police beat in Dorset. The reason can only be guessed as the settlement here of some of the extremely tough types from all over England who used to travel from fair to fair.

South of Bere Regis is another fortified hill called Hundred Barrow which like Woodbury Hill is just off the edge of the heath. The heath itself has a few burial mounds, but the fortified escarpments of our distant ancestors were almost all on the chalk, or very near it. Presumably chalk was normally free from trees, not heavily bushed, and easy to clear. It was not until the Saxons came that much was done with the heavy soils of the clay, whereas the heath could never have supported crops or animals.

Mention was made earlier of the benefactions to Bere Regis church by Cardinal Morton in Tudor times. He provided a wonderful painted and gilded roof in 1476. Large wooden figures project from the roof at strange angles, and there has been some argument as to what they represent. Their costumes are Tudor, and their countenances could be the weather-beaten faces of Bere Regis farm labourers. Undoubtedly the carver used local people as his models, but I have no doubt that they are the apostles. St. Peter has his keys and Judas his money bags.

Possibly more people go to Bere Regis church to see the Turberville tombs than for any other reason. They were a real family who held the manor for centuries from the time of Henry VIII and the church contains several well-preserved brasses and monuments. Yet, as at Bindon Abbey and Woolbridge Manor, it is not history people come to see but part of Hardy's amazing legend of *Tess of the D'Urbervilles*.

This church was old long before the Turbervilles held the manor or Cardinal Morton built the roof. Bere Regis was royal long before the Normans came. The Saxon Queen Elfrida came here after she had murdered her stepson at Corfe Castle. King John restored the pillars of the nave, and the word "restored" stresses the fact that the church was old even in his time. For the devout there is a feeling of continuous worship here which is very precious. For those who profess complete indifference this church should be visited because it stirs the imagination and tickles the sense of humour. It was tactful to carve the head of King John although he spent much of his life in very bad odour with the Church. Some of the other carvings have less obvious meanings. There is a huge dog hanging on to the ear of a creature which could be the devil. On the other hand King John was madly keen on hunting and the creature might be a wolf. Then there are vivid carvings of men in pain, from tooth-ache or from the results of gluttony. The vicar told me these were concerned with the results of the deadly sins. If so they are an awful warning and their carver was certainly a humorist.

Apart from the church, the village is dull, and my only interest lies in the watercress beds. For more than a mile an intricate system of gravel beds have been laid out and the water from the stream has been completely excluded. Instead water is obtained from deep artesian wells. Pipes are driven deep into the subsoil, often for 200 feet, and the water bubbles up under its own pressure to a height of two feet or so above the surface. This water from the depths is amazingly pure, infinitely better than any public supply, and never varies in temperature from about 52 degrees Fahrenheit. This feels cold in summer but is well above freezing point of course, and also well above the temperature at which plant growth is stopped. Bere Regis watercress gives fresh green food in mid-winter, and it is possibly significant that the far northern cities take more per head than the sunnier south.

The next four chalk fringe villages are all in the valley of the Piddle. The stream follows the wooded belt of clay which appears as a low ridge about half a mile from the valley bottom. All these villages upstream to Puddletown, extend beyond the wooded belt to the heath, and all give their names to heaths. From Bere Regis the road climbs the ridge and the obvious motor way drives straight on across the stream and over the heath to Wool. On the left a narrow road labelled "Hyde and Bere Heath Chapel" leads to quiet narrow lanes winding across the meadows of the valley. Eventually this lane reaches the heath and a wide road through gravel workings from Wareham to Waddock Cross. It is a delightful place to explore by car, but never forgetting the chance of meeting a milk lorry.

The road from Bere Regis to Turnerspuddle forks right off the Wool road just outside the village at Hundred Barrow. Within another mile it forks right again without any signpost. Turnerspuddle lies on both sides of the river. As usual in chalk villages there is a road along either bank but often with nothing but footbridges across the stream. Frequently only one road is tarred and this has tended to govern the placing of new houses. Turnerspuddle is peculiar in that the tarred road from Bere Regis goes to the church only. Beyond this point the stony lane goes on to Briantspuddle. There is no signpost but equally no notice claiming it as a private road. I found it passable in a car even in wet weather although some of the potholes were more than six inches deep. The rest of the village, on the other bank, is reached by a signposted road which goes from Throop Clump on the heath to Briantspuddle. The only way to reach the church from this side is by walking. The river was once used for irrigating water meadows at this point, and was diverted to form two channels. Both are crossed by foot-bridges, flanking fords which are too deep for cars. They were probably no barrier for horses and waggons except in flood time, but might well stop the smaller types of modern tractor. The walk over the foot-bridges is only a few hundred yards and it is certainly not worth taking a car into the uncharted lanes which give the only modern approach to the church. It is good to get to a lane and a ford which is remote from fret and strain. Yet even Turnerspuddle can hardly be called unchanged. The farm house at the end of the lane is old and mellow, but the sound of tractors is liable to drown the song of warblers in the willow thickets. The farm buildings have been patched, enlarged and repaired to fit prosperous modern agriculture. The sad, picturesque, mouldering thatch, and crumbling walls of pre-war years are gone. Treves talks of the church and farm house in "venerable companionship". It is a tiny church, and his phrase gives a charming picture of what it was like in my boyhood. I went back to see it in 1952. At that time there was a gaping hole in the roof of the nave; the arch between nave and chancel had been bricked up. The only part of the church in use was the tiny chancel which would have had difficulty in seating twelve people. In 1963 the hole in the roof had been mended and the church is watertight again. The brick wall still cuts off the chancel, but the fabric of the building is safe for the moment. It may be that twelve seats are enough. There is a church every two miles up this valley, which is still mainly agricultural in spite of the proximity of Bovington and Winfrith Heath. It is good that someone thought this small, rather plain little church worth saving.

Before leaving Turnerspuddle it might be as well to deal with the Puddles and Piddles. I do not think there is much doubt that

Piddle is the correct name of the river and that it means small stream. On Piddletrenthide church tower it is spelt Pydel and there was a Baron Pydel at Puddletown, but this goes back to the days before spelling was standardised. The baron is more likely to have taken his name from the village than to have named the river. In my youth it was usual to speak of Piddletrenthide, Piddlehinton, and Little Piddle, followed by Puddletown, Tolpuddle, Affpuddle, Briantspuddle, and Turnerspuddle. I am inclined to think this change to Puddle was Victorian "refinement", and I can remember elderly aunts referring to my native village as "Trenthide". The voters lists, when I last saw them in 1946, still referred to Briantspiddle, and Piddletown, but some six years ago a long County Council debate solemnly decided Piddletown should be Puddletown. The official position at present would seem to be that the names of my childhood, with the change after Little Piddle, are now established. If I sometimes vary the spelling in this book, may a native be forgiven for preferring the Anglo-Saxon piddle? From the beginning of time Mr. Punch has used "Puddleton" for his most remote and dim-witted community.

Briantspuddle was described by Treves as "a very rudimentary, very pretty hamlet". He would certainly not have used this description today. Briantspuddle was the centre of an enormous agricultural experiment between the wars. Sir Ernest Debenham, head of a great London drapery business, decided to apply big business methods and modern science to agriculture. The idea is quite familiar today when huge companies are making large profits from farming big stretches of the countryside. In the 1920s most of the money coming to the land was from rich men who kept their estates in good order through pride of ownership or to preserve sporting amenities. Very few bought land and farmed it with the idea of making a profit. At that time prices were low for farm produce and many farms were going derelict. Similar land in Wiltshire was being let for £1 for three acres. By 1963 such land was fetching £7 for one acre, so it is plain that conditions for Sir Ernest Debenham's experiment were very different from those enjoyed by industrial farmers to-day.

At the bottom of the depression in the early 1930s the estate being farmed must have covered more than ten square miles. Old cottages had been restored and some very good new ones erected. Some of the new ones had seven bedrooms, with the object of providing accommodation for the single workers in the intensified departments of farming. Poultry and pigs, for instance, were kept in huge units. In addition there was a milk factory selling milk in cardboard cartons made on the premises, plus equipment for large-scale cheesemaking. The main egg farm had a packing station for eggs which was ten years in advance of its time. In Briantspuddle a whole new "estate" of cottages was built up a little coombe in the hills. These were set back from the road with green lawns in front and a plentiful planting of trees. It is now a charming addition to Treves' "very pretty hamlet". At Briantspuddle there was also a pumping station which supplied water to most of the cottages, fields and farm buildings on the estate. There was also an electric generating plant more than sufficient for the needs of a small town, and an efficient estate office. "Pretty" it still was, but by no means "rudimentary".

Unfortunately the experiment failed in so far that a great deal of money must have been lost, and most of the land was re-sold before times changed for the better agriculturally in 1939. The reason was partly the very low prices which meant that most of the farmers who survived did so by spending nothing and taking what the land would give. It was a time when hedges became overgrown, ditches were uncleared, old buildings were patched with second-hand materials, and implements obtained at the bankrupt sales of "gentleman farmers". This was no time for new buildings, new fencing schemes, new cottages and new implements. In addition, the notion of keeping pigs and poultry on extremely intensive lines was before its time. There was little knowledge of how to control disease, or how to live on the edge of a disastrous outbreak without going over. Possibly the latter is the basis of successful modern intensification. There was also no guaranteed prices, no grants for fertilisers, liming, drainage and new buildings.

Out of it all has come a large number of extremely good cottages and farm buildings. In Affpuddle, Briantspuddle and Milborne St. Andrew the mark of Sir Ernest Debenham can be seen on the whole countryside, and not only in utility but in beauty.

Treves found Briantspuddle rudimentary and of Affpuddle he says that its "sleep has been unbroken by the last hundred years or so". This was largely true when he wrote it in 1906, and to some extent it is still superficially the case. This village is still small and wholly agricultural. To the townsman it must seem sleepy and unchanged. Town industry has a habit of being noisy, restless and assertive. These small settlements round old stone churches, separated by only a mile or two along the stream, grew up when England was feeding herself from her own fields. When cheap American grain flooded the market in the last century they seemed to fall upon sleep. If industry does the same thing it dies and the land it occupies is probably blasted for ever. Affpuddle could sleep without dying. The weeds increased, but weeds can be beautiful. The old cottages started to deteriorate, but were no less picturesque for being insanitary. Once English land was needed again the life came back to the soil in a flood. For decades old men had repeated stories they had heard from their fathers about wheat growing on land which looked sterile. Once the need returned those fields on the chalk soil awoke, and today more and better crops are being grown than ever before in history.

Tolpuddle just across the river is equally small but its peace has been destroyed for the moment by the extremely busy main road which is the sole street of the village. Only on the back road from Affpuddle can you get the peace of the water meadows, and the sight of the gracious old house by its pond, within a hundred yards of the perpetual fumes and rush. Of course all the world knows that the peace of Tolpuddle was disturbed in 1833. As usual a fair section of the world have got the story of the Tolpuddle Martyrs slightly wrong. It is very common to hear it said that the Trade Union Movement started in this Dorset village and this is certainly not true. What is true is that what happened in this village had an enormous influence on the future of Trades Unions.

George Loveless was a farm worker and a chapel man. In my own memory being a Nonconformist local preacher branded a man as being a ranting radical. The nearest modern equivalent of "radical" is the American McCarthy image of Communism. Such a man would not be popular with the squires, the Established Church, or the farmers, although no one questioned his industry and honesty. The local farmers had agreed to pay wages of ten shillings per week at a meeting presided over by the vicar of Tolpuddle. They broke their word and paid only nine shillings which was later cut to eight. The vicar flatly denied having given any pledge on the matter, and the local justices said wages were no longer fixed by them—which was true—and that farmers could offer what they liked. This was the signal for a reduction to seven shillings with a threat of six shillings in future. At this stage George Loveless called his fellow workers together since it was "impossible to live honestly on such scanty means".

They formed a Friendly Society which was quite legal and asked for advice from a Trade Society in London. Obviously Trades Unions already existed or this could not have happened. It seems certain that nothing could have been done from the legal angle if the men had merely agreed not to work for less than a reasonable wage. The chance to get at them arose from the understandable requirement suggested by the London men that an oath of secrecy should be taken. This was seized upon as breaking a law governing secret societies which had been passed in 1797 during the Napoleonic Wars which ended in 1815 to deal with a naval mutiny. More than forty labourers had joined the society in October 1833 but only six were arrested, of whom five were known Wesleyan Methodists. They were charged with conspiracy and, after a hurried trial, before a grossly prejudiced judge and jury, they were sentenced to transportation for seven years and shipped off in chains in 1834.

There is a happier end to the story. By March, 1836, a free pardon and passage back to England had been secured, although it was not until June, 1837, that Loveless reached England, and four of the remaining five did not get back before 1838. It must be remembered that at that time all members of Parliament belonged to the aristocratic or rich middle classes. Thus the men who insisted on this gross injustice being remedied were of the same class and with the same interests as those who committed it. There is a feeling for truth and fairness in England which goes very deep.

Memorials to the Martyrs abound in Tolpuddle. The little chapel where they worshipped has been preserved and is entered through a rather heavy memorial arch which is out of proportion to the tiny meeting house. There is a pleasant wooden seat under the trees with a view over the meadows and a row of good modern houses provided by the T.U.C. for elderly farm workers. These are visited annually by a T.U.C. procession with banners. Unfortunately the harmony was disturbed a few years ago by a dispute with a Communist section. George Loveless has not been completely successful in promoting unity.

Puddletown is only two miles upstream from Tolpuddle but on the 1902 Ordnance map the two villages were separated by two parishes—Burleston and Athelhampton. I find it difficult to account for Burleston which shows no sign of ever having been more than

a couple of farms with a handful of cottages. Athelhampton has a
church, one mile from Puddletown church, but only a hundred yards
from the great house of Athelhampton Hall. This was the seat of
the ancient manor of Piddletown, held by the Londons and then
by the Pideles, or Pydels. I have mentioned this spelling before.
The Pideles I suggest took their name from the village. Is it possible
that the Londons were responsible for a curiously named lane in
the adjoining village of Piddlehinton? This short lane, which now
ends in a farm track, is called London Row. It seems much more
likely to be connected with the Londons, lords in the next village,
than the very distant city.

In the early thirteenth century Athelhampton passed to the Martins
who lived there for more than four hundred years. Tombs of the
Martins are in a side chapel of Puddletown church and date from
1250 to 1595. The church at Athelhampton is modern and may
have been built to replace the private chapel in Athelhampton Hall
which was allowed to go in 1862, when the gatehouse was pulled
down. The Hall remains as one of the glories of Dorset, and is still
lived in and open to the public from Easter to September.

In the garden there is an ancient pigeon cote in perfect repair.
In general these circular towers had windowless walls and the pigeons
got in through the top, where an arrangement called a lantern allowed
them to enter but kept out the rain. The whole of the inner walls
consisted of nesting holes which often went in for two feet. The
general impression was of a brick wall with every other brick removed
from top to bottom to leave a hole. In fact the holes were nearer the
size of two bricks and there were a thousand such nest holes in some
cotes. Thus with two pigeons in each hole and two young there were
up to 4,000 birds feeding on the tenant's crops. The ownership of a
cote was a very unpopular right enjoyed by the lord of the manor,
or by some church dignatary. It provided pigeon eggs and also
squabs—young pigeons at the point of flying. To collect the eggs
and squabs it was necessary to use a ladder to reach the higher nest
holes. It must have been a nuisance to climb down every time to
move the ladder, and our forefathers invented an effective device to
save time. This was called a potence. It consisted of a large beam
in the centre of the tower which was pivoted top and bottom so
that it rotated freely. A cross beam jutted out from the top of the
central column and from this a ladder was hanging close to the wall.
The operator collecting eggs on the ladder merely had to give a

slight pull on a nest hole to move the ladder round the wall to fresh holes. The potence at Athelhampton still moves as freely and easily as if it was on the most modern ball-bearings, yet there is not even a way of oiling it. It was this invention of a revolving ladder which settled the circular shape of the dovecote towers. Some of the older ones were rectangular, but Athelhampton goes back to the thirteenth century, so the potence was discovered fairly early in our civilisation.

In the nineteenth century most of Puddletown, as opposed to Athelhampton, passed to the Brymer family, who erected a new manor house near the church. They were responsible for much of the church restoration, the building of new cottages and a reading room, and for the preservation of the character of the village. Between the wars a few houses not needed for estate management were sold, and since the end of the last war several large farms have been sold to tenants. This sort of sale invariably changes a village but not necessarily for the worse. It may be that Town and Country Planning will save the countryside as effectively as the old squires preserved it although on different lines.

In Puddletown the death of the late squire has meant that the Home Farm is let, and there is no job of keeping the house in butter, cream and fresh eggs. The keeper was too elderly to seek employment with the syndicate who now run the shooting. The Victorian gardens and greenhouses are run by a skeleton staff who sell the produce on commercial lines. This is a contraction of old splendours. On the other hand the owner-occupier farmers have put up many more new buildings than have been erected since farming was last prosperous before 1870. Then because skilled farm workers are not easily replaced there has been a tendency to improve cottages. Farmers need fewer workers but each man is responsible for very large amounts of capital in the form of livestock and machinery. To attract a skilled worker it is essential to have electricity, bathrooms and waterclosets. I think it is probably true that farmers as owner-occupiers have improved the few cottages they need quicker than landlords would have done. Of course the landlord often had many more cottages to deal with, often let at rents of a few shillings to old retainers or their widows. The tendency in most villages is for vacant cottages to go to outsiders, to retired people and to town workers. Almost always this means very considerable improvement to the fabric. Puddletown is typical of many villages in which existing houses have been vastly improved by new owners. It is also typical of villages which have recently had public sewage schemes, and have become desirable as building sites. The council houses already form a separate community, and this is now being supplemented by a new privately owned building estate. So far the village remains a village, although most of the inhabitants earn their living in town.

Houses are in good repair, gardens contain more flowers and less potatoes, people are well fed and well dressed. Only the elderly have any roots in the place, but this is not necessarily a bad thing. There is certainly no one left who can undertake the planned planting of miles of countryside on the lines of the old landscape gardeners. Puddletown has more than one example of this sort of activity. The most spectacular is an unfenced straight lane, a mile long, which runs through pine woods. On either side of the narrow tarred road there is a wide edging of grass and heather, and then an impenetrable bank of rhododendrons twenty feet high. When these are in flower it makes a royal avenue of purple against the darkness of the evergreens. On a June evening this mile of road through the heath is lovelier than any garden path I have ever seen. It starts about one mile from Puddletown and used to be a favourite Sunday evening walk. Today there may well be fifty cars there on any evening of the week and the boot of every car is stuffed with broken twigs and large branches. Even so two banks of blossoms each a mile long stand up reasonably well to the pillage, although after the first week the thick wonder of the flowers does not start much below seven feet. Possibly the picking does not injure the bushes, the pruning of flowers may well make them stronger. Yet there is something senseless in taking away enormous numbers of blooms which will drop soon. The massed effect of so much colour should not be lessened by stripping everything within reach. A few more hundred cars might force the owners of the land to put up a barbed wire fence. Already the Forestry Commission must be desperately worried by the fire danger in the very valuable forest behind the rhododendron avenue.

Puddletown church has a restored chancel but this is not used by the choir. They still occupy the old wooden gallery, dated 1635, at the back of the church, stamping up the stair just before the service starts, and leading the congregational singing from behind. All the rest of the church is equally free from innovations. The roof is of

Spanish chestnut, and was saved from death-watch beetle thirty years ago. The pews are of the old-fashioned sort, each with a door, narrow seats and high sides. Children are completely invisible in them, and even adults have difficulty in seeing the parson except when he is in the tall pulpit. It is still possible to meet members of the Antell family in this church. Old Mrs. Antell told me how cousin Thomas used to come out to see her husband and to ask his criticism on the latest chapters of a new novel. She could remember her husband working with four employed shoemakers in a little room, with a rammed earth floor, lit by a hanging oil lamp. Thomas Hardy stood in the middle and read his latest inventions about Weatherbury, Casterbridge and Mellstock. This is very much the Hardy country.

Further upstream from Puddletown the Piddle river no longer skirts the fringe of the tree belt, and Piddlehinton and Piddletrenthide are well in the main chalk country of deep valleys and bare uplands. The last fringe village is over the ridge between the Piddle and Frome just outside Dorchester. Stinsford is Mellstock of the Hardy novels. It consists of three distinct hamlets. One clusters round the church where the poet's heart is buried. Here there are four sizeable houses, three in the village and another a mile away at Higher Kingston. The largest, a huge Georgian mansion, and another which used to be the dower house, now accommodate the Dorset County College of Agriculture. Farm institutes are designed to give a twelve months' course to young people who have already had at least one year's practical experience on farms. They do not aim to turn out agricultural scientists who are catered for at colleges and universities. The main aim is to give a working knowledge of science and modern techniques to young people who will become farmers, managers or responsible heads of such farm departments as the dairy. In some cases a further year of education is provided in advanced studies on, say, machinery or management. Most counties now possess colleges although before the war there could not have been more than ten in England. Two were in the south-west in Somerset and Hampshire.

The second hamlet of Stinsford is Lower Bockhampton, on a quiet by-road, which crosses the Frome water-meadows on a series of narrow bridges. The old grey bridge, over the main stream at the end of Lower Bockhampton's one street, is a marvellous place to lean on the parapet in evening peace.

The third hamlet is Higher or Upper Bockhampton—Dorset normally uses the word "Higher" in preference to "Upper". This settlement consists of a lane which runs up a narrow coombe and stops at a gate. It goes through a farmyard, past a prosperous farm house and group of cottages, to a solitary small house at the top. This is where Thomas Hardy was born, and by the final gate there is a memorial stone erected by American admirers. Picture postcards describe this house as "Hardy's Cottage". Any countryman who knows the squalor of real cottages in the past realises that the child born here was outside the labouring class. In fact he came from a lower middle class family who had enough food to eat and clothes to wear.

What interests me about the house is its situation. From the top of the coombe all its windows look out on the fertile valley and the kindly green hills beyond. It is on the absolute edge of the good soil and behind it is the sterile heath. To an imaginative young boy that barren waste could be cause for dread. Later he wrote of it as "retarding the dawn". The pagan gods and the grim fates were always there, just over his shoulder. It is well worth making the journey to Hardy's birthplace to sense the influences which must have shaped his early years. For preference go early on an April evening, when all the cultivated land is full of life and hope. Go when the swallows have come back and the bluebells are in flower beneath the first dainty leaves of tall beeches. Open the gate to the heath after you have seen the friendly front of the house, and look at the blank back. See the dead heather and the litter of broken bracken from last year. Wander a little to strange unnatural pits in the ground, to sad patches of bogs, and to meaningless tracks which lead nowhere. It will be a great help in understanding Tess.

V

THE CHALK—TYPICAL UPLANDS

THE chalk villages associated with streams or winterbornes form the largest single section of the Dorset countryside. Generally the valleys are very narrow, with room for little more than a road, the stream, and a row of houses. The sole exceptions, on the genuine solid chalk foundation, are the Frome for a few miles above Dorchester where the meadows may be a mile wide, and the Stour below Blandford. Both rivers, and the Piddle, have much wider valleys when they skirt or cross other formations, but even the sizeable Stour river has a very narrow valley when it first cuts through the chalk between Hod Hill and Shillingstone Hill.

It is difficult to suggest a tour along anything approaching a straight line which will give a true impression of the chalk uplands. The valleys run roughly parallel to each other about three miles apart, and there is always a road through the long villages in the valley bottom. These villages are an old form of ribbon development and there is a church in each valley every three miles or so. By following the valley roads the traveller gets an impression of a thickly populated sheltered countryside, blessed with tall trees and abundant water. On the other hand by following one of the roads which cut across the valleys, such as the Dorchester–Blandford–Salisbury, the sole impression is of bare hills with few villages, and little in the way of soft delights. Almost invariably on this crowded highway the charms of the villages are completely hidden from the road. In exploring my native chalk uplands I propose to wander up the valley by-ways whilst at the same time always returning to a route which runs north across the ridges. This will not be by the Dorchester–Blandford–Salisbury highway, but by quiet lanes roughly parallel to it.

The first chalk valley is the Winterborne south of Dorchester which has Winterborne Abbas at its head. Only the first three villages, Winterborne Abbas, Winterborne Steepleton and Winterborne St. Martin follow my standard description of ribbon development, with only a stream, the houses and the road in a narrow valley. After Winterborne St. Martin—sometimes called Martinstown—there is only a very small road, and the stream cuts by Ashton Farm, under the great fortress of Maiden Castle to Winterborne Monkton, Winterborne Herringston and Winterborne Came, before joining the Frome river at West Stafford. Dorset is infinitely varied, and there is no such things as a typical chalk stream. There is not even a standard scheme for exploration by motoring down the valleys on obvious roads.

Winterborne Abbas is at least like scores of other villages in having the stream running by the walls of many of the houses, on one side of the single street, with little foot-bridges between the front doors and the main road. The name Winterborne stresses the fact that the running of the brook is uncertain. The springs break in the autumn. The first major bubbling up of clear, sparkling water is just west of the village, near the spot where the Devil's Nine Stones can be seen by the roadside. This is a circle of stones, only a few yards across, but giving the impression of a very miniature Stonehenge. The look of this circle, near the capricious spring in the wood, was quite enough to connect it in Victorian times with Druids and religion. Here was a well and a grove for the delight of the mystic. It was sometimes claimed to be a sort of chapel of Stonehenge, and at others an altar half-way between the fortified towns of Maiden Castle and Eggardon Hill. The line across country is reasonably accurate for the latter explanation, but there is little evidence of any religious connection. Modern thought regards these small stone circles as the remains of round houses, and this could well be a site for a hut near the Winterborne main spring. In a wet winter other springs rise for nearly a mile further up the valley along the side of the main road to Bridport.

The underground water in the chalk moves up and down for considerable distances. At my home in the floor of a valley most of the wells were about thirty foot deep. In a very dry summer they went dry and after a wet autumn they overflowed. This movement of at least thirty feet is quite enough to account for the Winterborne streams drying up in summer. What is more difficult to understand is how some deep springs coming out at the foot of steep hills can be never failing and scarcely changing. Yet at the same level, by the side of the stream fed by these springs, a well can show a seasonal rise and fall of thirty feet. Water is mysterious stuff.

Ramparts of Maiden Castle

Like most Winterbornes there are springs occurring at various points along the valley bottom. After the main spring has failed at Winterborne Abbas, and the bed of the stream has dried for several miles, there may still be water lower down at Winterborne St. Martin, which will again fail before Winterborne Monkton. This breaking of springs along, or just off a stream, is quite common on rivers as opposed to winterbornes in the chalk country. The Piddle has been known to fail below Piddlehinton but has always revived again before Puddletown.

Winterborne Steepleton as the name implies has a steeple instead of a church tower. This is very unusual in Dorset on old churches, and this church is very old. As so often happens in small farming parishes the churches of Winterborne Abbas and Winterborne Steepleton have to be served by one parson, but at least the buildings are maintained. This is important not only because beautiful buildings should be preserved, but because there can be no certainty that villages will die. Without the slightest doubt there has been an enormous reduction in the number of people getting their living from the land, or from connected trades such as smiths, saddlers, hurdle-makers and thatchers. On the other hand even in remote places unexpected sources of employment arise. Not far from Steepleton was an establishment on the bare hill which arose in connection with cables and wireless. Quite a few people worked there and similarly unpredictable industries can repopulate any sleepy hamlet with a renewed need for a church.

Winterborne St. Martin is mainly famous as the site of an old fair. The houses do not line the roadside at one end of the village but there is quite a substantial unfenced green. At one time the gypsies gathered here for horse trading, whilst on the other side in a small field the sheep were penned. This was the last fair of the year in the Dorchester district and was dying in my youth. The nearest railway station was four miles away and motor transport did not arrive in time to save it. It is interesting to notice how the old fairs withered when sited away from the railways, and how quite important markets grew up near isolated railway junctions. Today markets and fairs have tended to move out of town centres, as witness Exeter, Salisbury and Shaftesbury. The remote railway junctions have mainly lost all meaning.

Half a mile below Martinstown the main road goes right over the ridge before dropping into the coastal strip near Upwey Wishing

Well. The stream turns left to go through empty fields to Winterborne Monkton and the road by its side is very narrow, unsignposted but quite passable. Just to the north the ramparts of Maiden
Castle tower over the little valley. Few people have seen the gigantic
earthwork from this side because the road between Ashton Farm
and Winterborne Monkton is so hidden and anonymous. A more
usual view is from the Dorchester–Weymouth road or from the
Dorchester–Martinstown road. From either it is very impressive, and
it is well worth taking Maiden Castle Road on the very outskirts of
Dorchester towards Weymouth, opposite the cemetery. This road
passes through a modern housing estate and beyond the built-up area it
continues as a metalled, though narrow road to a large car park almost
at the foot of the green ramparts of the ancient earthwork. Originally
open fields, cars used to get stuck here in wet weather and the farmer
has a graduated tariff for pulling them out by Land-Rover or tractor.
I have heard him say that the highest charge is made after lunch
on Sundays, when he has to be awakened from a nap to do the job
himself.

Maiden Castle is the largest earthwork in England and has a very
long history. The first enclosure was only ten acres in extent and
it may have been walled in some 2,000 years before the Romans
came. Apparently it was a place where people slept at nights round
fires in pit dwellings. They got their food and water from outside
and this suggests that they did not fear a siege. Enemies were passers-
by along the ridgeways on either side, or came from other local
camps. They were not invaders who would camp out and invest
the fortress with an organised army.

After the passage of many centuries the original ten acres of town
seems to have been deserted. No one can be sure if there was a sudden
great plague, an exhaustion of local soils by over-cropping, or a
period of peace which made the fort unnecessary. The latter seems
very unlikely. Whatever the cause it was abandoned to the extent
of being used as a very important burial ground. A long mound
1,790 feet in length was used as the burial place for one man. Eric
Benfield in his fascinating book about Maiden Castle points out
that this man's skull had been pierced and his arms and legs broken.
Benfield suggested this may have been part of some magical rite to
use the brain, possibly by eating it. The legs may have been broken
to stop him walking away. It all happened long before the dawn
of written history, and all that is certain is that here was a very

important man, so important that his fellows could undertake the colossal labour of building this enormous mound with flint tools, in the middle of what had been a town.

Why people left Maiden Castle no one knows, why they came back no one knows, but come back they did in the early part of the Iron Age. Benfield points out that this does not mean that iron tools were used in the construction of the new fortifications. They may have been erected before iron had come into general use. The walls of the old town consisted of one earth mound with a ditch both outside and inside. The new bank was held up by timber and Benfield thinks this confirms that iron was available. They present a wall to the enemy and not merely a steep earthen slope. The new wall enclosed sixteen acres and it had an eastern and western entrance. These entrances were a weakness and were later guarded by new walls faced with stone—a big advance in ideas of fortification.

This second town on the old site seems to have endured for a few centuries, and then to have been suddenly expanded to such an extent that we are left wondering why it had to be made bigger. The new enclosure covered not sixteen acres but forty-six which is an enormous increase. It seems to imply some sudden jump in population, but there is nothing to suggest conquest by a larger tribe. This could well have taken place, however, as long as the invaders were of the same culture. Without writing there can be no record except tools, weapons, pottery and the like to identify the inhabitants. The history of the next stage in the tale of Maiden Castle is written in just this way.

Suddenly Roman swords and arrows appear. The gates are broken, the platforms of the slingers on the wall are destroyed. In a town where only a very occasional burial had taken place in thousands of years there is now one great common grave. In the grave the skeletons are hacked by Roman swords or carry Roman arrow-heads in their bones. The great fort of Maiden Castle met a professional army and was overwhelmed.

The army moved on and did not repair or occupy the ramparts as they did in so many other places. A minor fort, by the ford over the Frome at nearby Poundbury, may have been occupied, but Maiden Castle was abandoned. The pacification of the countryside was later centred on the new town of Dorchester, which was wholly Roman, except for the nearness of Poundbury just outside the wall.

Centuries later when Rome was declining, there was a small Roman temple of sorts, little more than a hermit's cell, at Maiden Castle. The Celtic inhabitants had drifted away long before this. The remnant which survived the massacre of the conquest may have lived there until Dorchester became established. They were Roman subjects, taxed slaves, but fairly comfortable. The only point of living on that bare waterless hill was safety. Now they were under the heel of Rome, but that meant they were also under the shield of Rome. It was a softer life by the sweet Frome waters. Only a religious fanatic would move back to hardship, and the Roman who did so was also old-fashioned. Perhaps the reason he went to the cold winters and fiery summer heat of the grassy mounds was because Christianity had become the official religion of the Empire, and he wanted to escape.

The solitude of Maiden Castle has never been disturbed since the Romans left. There are forty-six acres of easily ploughable land inside the ramparts, but it was not ploughed even in the desperate food shortage of the last war. There was a Government directive forbidding local Agricultural Executive Committees from ploughing barrows and ancient dykes, but there was only one long barrow which would have seemed obvious to a committee member. I was on the staff of the committee and cannot remember any serious suggestion of ploughing. It may seem a little strange to outsiders but there is a long tradition against disturbing this very ancient place. At least one of the Saxon invaders is buried there with his arms, so the Saxons certainly had a look at it, but there is no record of a settlement. There would be no luck in ploughing Maiden Castle. After dark it is not pleasant to be alone there, at least it was not pleasant during the war when there were no friendly lights from Dorchester.

On the other hand there may be no mystery at all about the lack of ploughing, before or after the war for profit, and during the war for national need. Maiden Castle is part of the estate of the Royal Duchy of Cornwall. They would certainly not have allowed ploughing in peace time, and their land was exempt from committee ploughing control during the war. Ploughing on Duchy land was by agreement—never withheld in my experience—but not by Order. It may well explain why corn was not grown, but I stick to my statement that no one wanted to plough this haunted land.

The ramparts on the Winterborne side are very close to the road and river, which wind through a very narrow valley between the castle and the ridge from Abbotsbury to east of Weymouth. Winterborne Monkton is usually regarded as being in a cul-de-sac just off the Dorchester–Weymouth road. The by-lane is closed by a gate at the Monkton end, has no signpost, and looks like the beginning of a private drive. Winterborne Monkton village is small and centres largely on one farm. The stream is dry for quite a bit of the year. There is nothing to attract the holiday traffic which thunders along the coast road three hundred yards away. In fact it is difficult to get in or out of the narrow entrance to the village when the traffic is at its peak. The result is an oasis of peace almost within gunshot of fret, frustration and danger. Perhaps within "a sling throw" is better than "a gunshot" if we remember the distance weapon of the old castle just above this little natural cup in the hills.

After Winterborne Monkton the stream crosses the main road and a by-road winds along nearby. There are two parishes between here and the Frome river but no typical chalk village. There is no narrow, steep-sided valley, and Winterborne Herringston consists of a large farm isolated up a lane, and Herringston House which is a mile away and nearer Dorchester than anywhere else. Winterborne Came is similar in having no village, but is more famous for possessing an excellent golf course. There is one large farm quite near the golf course but a long way from Came House. The church is adjacent to the house, but, most unexpectedly, the rectory is three-quarters of a mile away, just across the Dorchester–Wareham main road. It is a thatched building easily visible from the road, and famous as the place where William Barnes died.

My father told me that he could well remember Barnes, dressed exactly as in his statue outside St. Peter's Church, Dorchester. He wore black knee breeches with stockings, not gaiters, a long black coat and buckled shoes. In his old age he still liked to walk the mile into Dorchester on Wednesdays and Saturdays—market days. Barnes died in 1886 and my father was born in 1860, so there is no reason to doubt that father remembered this very striking old man whose poetry was very well known in his native Dorset. His parish of Came was combined with Whitcombe, a hamlet just over the low hill, which consisted of the church, one charming farm house and a few cottages. Barnes rectory was about equally distant from Came and Whitcombe churches, which possibly accounts for its unusual isolation.

Neither Whitcombe nor Winterborne Came has any village and they do not fit any of my classifications. Whitcombe Farm climbs slowly up the chalk hillside with very large fields, largely unfenced, and with few trees. It is a road worth taking for at the top of the ridge are many barrows and a wonderful view of Weymouth and Portland, but this is for a later chapter. Winterborne Came and Winterborne Herringston are much more wooded but mainly because they contain a lot of park land. The existence of the very old town of Dorchester undoubtedly led to the building of many stately homes in a two-mile radius.

Having reached the Frome at Stafford, in those water meadows where Tess met Angel Clare, this particular Winterborne has made a complete semi-circle round Dorchester from the Devil's Nine Stones at Winterborne Abbas. Before exploring the upper part of the Frome valley it is as well to look at the capital town.

Today the word "capital" certainly applies, and this has always been the case to a considerable extent. It is true that Sherborne is the seat of the Suffragan Bishop, and was once the home of the County Council, but it lost the council to Dorchester in my young days. Dorchester now has an enormous group of County Council offices whose foundation stone was laid on the day of Munich in 1938. Already an additional floor has been added on the original flat roof and two large separate buildings erected. I have not the slightest doubt that the accommodation is already cramped. Other Government offices include the Rural District Council and the Town Council, plus the Ministry of Agriculture and the Inland Revenue. Every town in this country now has its half hour in the morning and evening when the streets are crowded. The London rush hour has had its publicity and its horrors are well known. Few people realise how recently the same type of congestion has spread. Melksham in Wiltshire has a population of only 9,000 people but it took me twenty minutes to drive through it when I arrived at the moment when the factories closed one evening in May. The Dorchester rush is about 5.15 p.m. when the Government and Local Government offices disgorge their staff. Incidentally a ghastly new word has been coined for this dispersal. It is known as "the out-muster". Quite a few from the Dorchester out-muster make for the Weymouth road which is definitely unpleasant for a short time every morning and evening. It is a little unusual to find people leaving small towns where they work for a much larger one where they sleep. Generally dormitory towns are smaller. In the case of Dorchester and Weymouth the draw is of course the sea, and the move was made easy by the very cheap and frequent rail service. This service is now less cheap, but all offices are a way from the stations and Dorchester is well supplied with car parks, especially the County Council.

It is a relief to write "Dorchester is well supplied with car parks", because I seem to be half criticising a place which has been "town" for me from my earliest boyhood. Let there be no mistake, Dorchester is a town with every reason to be proud. My very last criticism is of urban sprawl and this has been confined to two sides. The green meadows were a shade too difficult to drain for the early speculative builders and the Duchy of Cornwall were reluctant sellers. In my boyhood quite a bit of Dorchester was inside its ancient walls. The line of these is still marked by beautiful avenues of trees called Walks. The river was the barrier on the north but the Walks give a square outline on the other sides, which shows exactly how the Romans first laid out their new town. As I remember it there were only a few modern things outside the walls—the railway stations, the brewery, the public gardens and a few rows of houses near the gardens and brewery. The village of Fordington certainly touched the Walks but no one then confused Fordington with Dorchester. Fordington was a tough place. The police never went down Mill Street except in pairs, at least so my parents told me. I never went to Mill Street myself until a few months ago, although there was always a fearsome urge to do it. Today it is a pleasant place with charming views over the meadows. Even now it is just possible to guess what Mill Street was like, especially if you read *The Mayor of Casterbridge* before starting. It was from Mill Street that the famous skimmity ride started, and some of Hardy's ghastly old hags were common in Dorchester less than sixty years ago. Then, too, Fordington was part of the Duchy of Cornwall Estate. They were prince's men, whereas Dorchester people regarded themselves as king's men. There is a long history of differences between our monarchs and their heirs.

Even to local people it is surprising how far the parish of Fordington extends. Most of us think of a rather grey village clustered round a green by the large old church on the eastern fringe of

Dorchester. Here there are obvious remains of a mill, and town dairies with every old appurtenance of a village outside the walls of a town. What is not so fully realised is that when Dorchester spread, in the opposite direction from this old village, it was doing so in the parish of Fordington. The old church of St. George's is just off the Wareham road leading east, but when they first built a new church for Fordington it was within two hundred yards of the centre of the borough of Dorchester, but outside the wall and on the Bridport road leading west. Actually this new church was later moved to a site just off the Weymouth road leading south, but the fact remains that Fordington goes half-way round Dorchester, always hugging the old wall and almost all of the modern housing estates are in Fordington.

To my mind Fordington needs a cheer leader, or a public relations officer, or something of the sort. It turns its worst face to the world with a kind of fierce, inverted Dorset pride. The faces of the houses on the street side are as grey as a northern mining village. Only when someone opens their back and front doors at the same time do you see the hidden gardens at the back. Perhaps Fordington men are very wise. If they could fool me for fifty years—born eight miles away—they may well conceal their pleasant urban village from the rapacious developer.

To some extent the borough of Dorchester hides itself in the same way as Fordington. There are gardens behind some dull streets although I fear they are tending to vanish. There are strange changes in architecture in the main streets which have not been obliterated by the standardised shop fronts of the more universal of stores. In the back lanes there are queer bits of surviving wall where red brick restored the ruins of the town fires of two thousand years. No two houses are alike; there has never been a master plan, thank God. The Old Theatre on the corner of Trinity Street survives as I write, although it may be gone when this is read. The actor Keene once played here. Long before my time it was a quality shop for glass and china. It is empty at this moment and its future is obscure, but I hope it is not merely a valuable site. I hope that whatever it becomes it will retain what I meant by a "quality shop". It has a distinction now even in desolation. By 1977 it had become a memory.

Like most old towns Dorchester has had more than its share of fires and old buildings are few. St. Peter's church is mainly fifteenth-century with a twelfth-century south doorway. Outside the walls in Fordington, St. George's is partly Norman. Holy Trinity is a very ancient parish but the present church is wholly nineteenth-century. There were Tudor almshouses at Napper's Mite in South Street, now shops, and there remains part of the old Grammar School adjoining, which is now an auctioneer's office—a long established firm of auctioneers. For the rest there is a café in the house where Lord Justice Jeffreys lodged for his Bloody Assize, another café in an old house at the Top-o-Town, but no imposing block of ancient buildings. There is not even any block of Georgian buildings but rather a happy blending of styles and materials. A fragment of Roman wall in West Walks is remarkably like the lower courses of houses in Colliton Street which are probably Tudor. This was a new town only two thousand years ago and it is still up-to-date. Underneath is the chalk, but to reach it you have to dig ten to twenty feet through the black earth created by human habitation. Before you reach the clean, undisturbed whiteness you are more than likely to strike an inlaid Roman pavement at any point within the walls or Walks. Even outside the walls are reminders of Rome. In my grandfather's youth the railways came to Dorchester and it was some sort of miracle which stopped the destruction of the Roman Amphitheatre —Maumbury Rings. I have heard it argued that such a destruction would have been justified since the Romans destroyed a neolithic temple to form their theatre. At least it would have been in the lavish tradition of towns which possess so many treasures as Dorchester.

Leaving Dorchester on the Blandford road it would be possible to skirt the heath for five miles, and then to strike through the heart of the upland chalk towards Salisbury but this is a very busy and dull route. It is far better to turn in the opposite direction for three miles towards Bridport, almost back to Winterborne Abbas. For the first three miles the road is almost straight. Then, at the bottom of a hill, the main road goes left but a minor road goes straight on. Without touching a village this road sticks to the top of the ridge for a further six miles when it ends in a five crossway just outside the great earthworks of the fortress of Eggardon Hill. This is the edge of the chalk and gives a marvellous view of the mixed soils and tumbled land of the west, and the glories of the coast. After being inaccessible for some years the Iron Age ramparts of Eggardon Hill are now open to the public, and its wide views are shared by many roads and rights-of-way. My own favourite is the one marked "Unsuitable

for motors" which is a little stony but completely passable. At
this moment, though, we are concerned with chalk uplands, and
any road back or northward will reveal beautiful hills and valleys
with very few farms. The general aim is to reach the village of
Maiden Newton but it would be a pity to miss the almost complete basins which hide respectively Compton Valence, Shatcombe
Farm, or Wynford Eagle. Unfortunately no single road can include
all the beauties of the chalk plateau, and it is hard to have to make
a choice. Both Wynford Eagle and Compton Valence are examples
of whole villages centred on one large farm and cut off from railways and bus services. Wynford Eagle can also claim a very beautiful house surmounted by an eagle in golden stone. Kipling lovers
will be interested to know that this was one of the manors of De
Aquila, the Eagle, who held Pevensey Castle in Sussex after
Senlac. Wynford was owned by the Sydenhams from 1551, and
Thomas Sydenham was regarded by many as the father of English
medicine.

Maiden Newton is on a main road and has no obvious beauties
for the passing tourist. To stop and pause is quite another matter.
The church is fascinating, and there are a dozen corners where
pleasant houses sit in green lawns. Two main streams meet here,
the Frome and its tributary the Hooke, both almost equal in size,
and henceforth making the sizeable Frome river. In this district the
Frome has cut so deeply into the chalk that the main village is on
the Upper Greensand. The same thing happened at Wynford Eagle
and even in that completely isolated hollow of Compton Valence.
Maiden Newton is not only a centre for roads but of springs, quite
apart from the two main streams.

We have seen that the brook from Wynford has cut into the greensand and the same is true of the Hooke which comes to Maiden
Newton from Toller Fratrum and Toller Porcorum.

There is a great deal to be said for exploring Dorset on foot along
its rivers, and the Maiden Newton district illustrates what I mean.
There is a motor road to Toller Fratrum, but it is a cul-de-sac. Only
by footpaths is it possible to follow the stream to Toller Porcorum.
Equally there is a back road down the Frome to Frome Vauchurch,
to Frampton, and Bradford Peverell but for much of the distance
it is not a motorway. Minor roads follow the Frome upstream to
Cattistock, Wraxall, Rampisham, and Corscombe, but it is much
eaiser to get an idea of the shape of the land from the streams. Only

in cutting across the chalk hills to Sydling is it rewarding to take the obvious tarred road.

Of all the possible by-ways from Maiden Newton, my favourite is the back path to Dorchester on the other side of the stream from the main road. The way is tarred for a mile or so to Cruxton Farm. Thereafter it is a farm track which I once covered by car in dry summer weather, but this does not mean that there is any right for vehicles. Possibly the reason for the decay of the back road at this point is that the next farm on this bank of the Frome—Notton —has a road bridge over the river and can therefore reach the main highway on the other side. Again between Frampton and Muckleford there is a public bridleway through the parkland of Frampton Court and beyond Muckleford you can now drive all the way to Dorchester. Between Bradford Peverell and Dorchester there is an impediment which must always have forced the back road away from the riverside. The stream cuts along the side of a hill which is almost a cliff and on this hill is the old fort of Poundbury. Almost certainly the old road has always skirted Poundbury and dropped into Dorchester where the Victorian barrack gateway still stands and serves as the Military Museum.

So much for the road which can only be explored in part by car, but, for the elderly, much can be seen by a series of excursions from cars, with the aid of the one-inch Ordnance map, or better still the 1:50,000 map. No lesser map is of any real use since none of them show anything but crowded roads. On this wrong side of the river is the best of the valley. First Frome vau Church (usually written Frome Vauchurch) is almost part of Maiden Newton. It has a tiny ancient church which is beautifully kept and which gives an impression of eternal, living peace. This is no sleepy relic. Peace is not a negation, but a very positive, real thing, which our Saviour left with us.

The roads carry no signposts and very soon after the church this one finishes in a farmyard. It is a curious farmyard which probably would not have survived by the side of a main road. No one has cleaned it up and I do not mean moved out the dung. There are modern efficient asbestos buildings here, plus the ruins of old chalk-stone cottages and sheds. In a sense it illustrates how the old Roman villas survived, under the ashes of the centuries, up to a level of a foot or two. No one cleared them away, and in the end their ground plan was buried. In two thousand years' time excavators will find the site of late English cottages—*circa* 1850—just outside Frome Vauchurch. But unless this book survives they will probably be labelled "Humanist hermitage, late Elizabeth II".

On an adjoining cul-de-sac of tarred road Cruxton Farm has the same mixture. Here there is a beautiful old house, lovingly tended. It could have been a small manor, which had become the home of a prosperous yeoman, then sunk with the 1860–1939 depression, and revived in the last decade. To me there is a pleasure in guessing the story of a house. If you share this experience you can check your guess by going to a reference library and consulting the enormous tomes of Hutchins' *History of Dorset*.

Having written this I had to check Cruxton, and Crookston or Croxton was certainly a manor. William Crox gave thirty marks to have seizin of the vill in 1205.

For the rest, Cruxton has a highly efficient range of modern buildings, some good dwellings, and a few derelict cottages. Everyone of these isolated farm settlements away from villages has become smaller. I imagine Cruxton once had a cowman with four or five people to help him, a shepherd, four carters or so, and perhaps three or four general labourers. I am guessing at the size of this farm, but it applies to any 600-acre farm on the chalk with, say, sixty acres of valley pasture for cows. It meant at least nine cottages, grouped round the buildings and farm house. Today there would be either a shepherd or cowman but probably not both. Specialisation is preached by all economists. There might be three tractor drivers, but no general labourers so that four cottages would suffice. In many villages some of the old cottages have been purchased and vastly improved by town workers or retired people. In the isolated settlements they had gone before site values reached the proportions of a racket.

From Cruxton downstream there is no motor way. If you walk you pass Notton Farm, and then soon find a road again on the outskirts of Frampton. Most of the village and the church is on the other side of the stream, on one of those ghastly main roads which have transformed quiet village streets into death traps. To really see Frampton the best thing to do is to cross to the quiet side of the river and take a road up the hill. There is no signpost. You just go at right-angles to the river uphill and very soon you can look down on the lovely wooded valley. It is wooded mainly because the Sheridans once lived in the very great house of Frampton Court.

It was here that the Game Laws were drafted in the last century, which still govern English field sports.

The great house at Frampton was demolished between the wars, leaving several extremely pleasant, large, country houses in the vicinity. The park, and the roads of the park, have fallen on hard times. There are lodge gates, with high-sounding names like Peacock Lodge, but inside the roads are pot-holed, and only the classic stone bridges give any hint of past glories. It is possible to get along the river to Muckleford, but probably hardly worth the effort, except as an escape from crowds.

The name Muckleford sounds foreign to Dorset ears and so does the adjoining country house—Quartre Bras—more usually Quarter Brass when I was young. Across the river the main road now by-passes Stratton, thus eliminating one of the county's worst death traps. The narrow village street has houses lining both sides with their doors opening directly on to the road outside, without the vestige of a pavement. Safety and a degree of peace have returned to Stratton.

Sticking to the back road, the lane is very narrow and winding, but traffic is not heavy. Unfortunately what there is can be defined as "local" which means that the habitual users know the road so well that they go far too fast.

The little village of Bradford Peverell is the last on this side of the stream before Dorchester. Its church has a spire, which is unusual in Dorset, but not an ancient one. The houses in the older part of the village are hidden in trees and most of them look over the rich Frome meadows. The car headlights give a continuous illuminated display on the main road across the valley, but even on a still night the noise is distant and slight. For three-quarters of the people of England this sort of quiet must be almost unimaginable.

Going up the Hooke river from Maiden Newton again involves some walking, but only between Toller Fratrum and Toller Porcorum. This valley gets its living from the chalk hills on either side, but the river has cut through to the greensand which tends to give many springy and boggy patches which are not typical of chalk valleys. Toller Fratrum gets its name from the Brethren of the Order of St. John of Jerusalem. They levelled a site on the hillside overlooking the stream for their monastery. The lovely stone house with mullioned windows dates mainly from the Reformation, but probably the old religious establishment was used as a stone quarry.

Here the fields have always been well tended throughout my life-time, and looking down on the village from White Sheet Hill gives an impression of secluded prosperity. The rest of the Hooke valley is much wilder. The tendency to springs and bogs by the stream and up the slopes is not the only reason. The hills are more wooded than in most of the chalk country with a fairly large proportion of "rough grazing". It may be that the woods and coppices round Great Toller gave it the name Porcorum. In the old days pigs were woodland animals and lived for much of the autumn on beech-mast and acorns. The boggy, shaded, rough grazing was ideal for wandering pigs, but not by any means as good for sheep or cattle, and obviously unsuitable for cultivations. Sheep on boggy land are liable to a parasite of the liver called fluke, and cattle on rough grazing may suffer from a disease carried by ticks called red water. Modern drainage, clearing and chemical knowledge have improved the valley but the land above Toller, through Kingcombe to Hooke is still more wild and lonely than the open country of plain chalk streams. At Hooke itself the largest spring I have ever seen used to gush out of the steep hillside, and was immediately used for water-cress. Today this is one of the principal sources of supply for the local Water Board, who have erected a rather expensive but attractive building on the site.

Perhaps the best impression of this rather wild and lonely country-side can be enjoyed from the hill top south of the village. Here five roads meet and all of them are worth exploring as long as you are in no hurry to get anywhere in particular. You can reach Hooke Park by one lane and this is a stretch of primitive woodland where there are deer in abundance. Or you can drop to North Poorton and Loscombe—which should surely be Lost Coombe. Another lane goes to Higher Kingcombe, and yet another to Wytherstone Farm and Powerstock. Most of these delectable places are outside the chalk belt and are only mentioned here because of the strange road junc-tion just outside Hooke on the edge of the chalk. The Ordnance map calls this spot Mount Pleasant, which is very suitable, but I have always known it as Drag North.

Back at Maiden Newton the road up the Frome valley is still influenced by greensand although here again most of the farm land rises in typically bare chalk hills. At Cattistock the greensand strip is quite wide enough to give flat pasture fields, and a valley bottom which is much more than a ribbon of road, stream and houses. To

me the village has the personal interest of being the place where
Wightmans first settled when they came down from the Scottish
Lowlands. One corner of the churchyard contains a number of
headstones mainly of farmers, and registers show innkeepers and
butchers. This is hardly a likely source of pilgrimage for many
visitors, but in my youth Cattistock had another unique attraction.
The church only dates from 1857 but it had a carillon of thirty-
five bells. The sound of these on a summer evening, heard from
the encircling hills, drew hundreds of visitors even before the days
of motor cars. Unfortunately there was a serious fire in the tower
in 1940, not caused by enemy action in spite of the date. The tower
has been rebuilt, but with a modern peal of eight bells. Other
claims to fame for this pleasant village are that it is the home of
the Cattistock Fox Hounds—properly pronounced Catstock—and
that the nearby Tudor mansion of Chantmarle is now a centre for
police training.

Further up the valley Holway Farm and Lower Wraxall show
the typical influence of the greensand in the occasional boggy field
but the hills lack the wildness of the parallel Hooke valley. Higher
Wraxall is in an offshoot valley from the river, and is almost surrounded by chalk hills. It is not a cul-de-sac as far as roads are concerned, and one road continues beyond it over the hill. In other
respects it is like a half dozen other chalk settlements which are
complete dead ends. There is a house, in this case a manor, a dozen
cottages and some farm buildings. For centuries such places must
have been completely isolated and self-sufficient.

At Rampisham the greensand has almost vanished and the chalk
hills close in to form a typical narrow chalk valley, with large open
fields on either side. There is a trace of wildness on the hill to the
south where poor woodland goes up to acid soil, on the summit,
near the new wireless station. This is a windswept place, very
different from Rampisham village and the Tigers Head Inn. This
is a cosy pub by the clear river, and it is almost hidden in fine
trees.

Just beyond Rampisham is Benville Lane and this is virtually
the end of the Frome valley. The chalk goes on as a high ridge on
the left carrying the Maiden Newton–Crewkerne road through
lonely country. Benville Lane meets this road at Toller Down Gate,
which was a toll house, and nearby was the site of an old sheep
fair. Today it is merely a cross roads. On the Beaminster side the

hamlet of Toller Whelme is tucked away a few hundred yards from the highway, and is the most south-westerly settlement on the chalk. Once it belonged to Forde Abbey and there are remnants of an old grange which speaks of a flourishing community. Much later a church was erected in a brief spell of prosperity in the last century. Before 1939 the farming depression had brought poverty to remote farms and Toller Whelme was more remote than most. Only good farmers and very strict economy kept it from going derelict. Today it is alive again, or at least the land is alive. Wholly agricultural communities, completely cut off, all need less workers and less houses than they did when they were built.

A mile on the north side of the main road on the ridge is the village of Corscombe. The church is half-way down the hillside and looks over the wide vale of changing clays and limestones. Below the church is the village, on the chalk, but not in any usual steep-sided valley. Corscombe's valley has only a steep chalk ridge on the one side. In fact it sits a little way up that pleasant dry hillside, keeping its feet out of the mire towards Halstock.

Finally the chalk ends spectacularly where the Maiden Newton–Crewkerne road plunges off the ridge at Winyard's Gap. Heights can be impressive without amounting to much in the way of measurements. At the point of the ridge above the public house in Chedington parish the height is only just over 800 feet but it gives the impression of a mountain. Dorset, Somerset and Devon are spread out below. It is a fitting site for a memorial to the men of Wessex. The inscription reads, "To the memory of all ranks of the 43rd Wessex Division, who laid down their lives for the cause of freedom 1939–1945. This memorial is a replica of that erected on Hill 112 near Caen, the site of the first major battle in which the Division took part. July 10th to July 24th, 1944."

Once more back in Maiden Newton we forsake the valleys for the eastward journey over the ridges of the chalk. In all the chalk valleys there are roads which go over the hills and down the other side. Many are still no more than farm lanes, only practicable for farm motors, but every now and then one has become a tarred road. This is the case with the road from Maiden Newton to Sydling, except that here the road does not bother about Sydling village, but leaves it on the right as it drives straight over the next ridge on the way to Cerne Abbas.

The Cerne Giant
Piddletrenthide
Wynford Eagle church

Sydling has its own stream which rises in a hollow of the hills called Up Sydling. This is very like Higher Wraxall, previously described as being almost surrounded by hills, but Up Sydling is a complete dead end. Although the road ends in a farmyard, lanes and bridleways continue upwards to the ridge of Batcombe Hill to the north, to Ayles Hill westward, or to Elston Hill on the east. In this quiet spot a rifle range was established during the 1939 War and remained in use for some years afterwards, closing an old ridge way for most daylight hours for much of the year. This ancient road, which was possibly an alternative pack-horse route from Dorchester to Sherborne, can be traced from Charminster to Hilfield in Blackmore Vale. It was at one time just possible for a car but would now need military or farm transport.

The main village of Sydling St. Nicholas is wide enough to have roads on both sides of the stream, but only just. The hills on either side reach 650–700 feet, and the pattern of farming is the usual chalk arrangement of a few acres of valley pasture with large plough fields on the uplands. There are still many picturesque thatched cottages in the village, but possibly the state of repair is slightly lower than in some neighbouring parishes such as Cerne Abbas. Much of Sydling is owned by Winchester College, an undying landlord with no need to sell portions to pay death duties. This was an advantage through the very bad times for agriculture between the wars. It does not help when there is plenty of money about and far less cottages are needed for farming. In such circumstances the new non-agricultural owner of a cottage is likely to retain old beauties such as thatch, and at the same time to spend money on paint and drains. The appearance of a village can be improved by the landlord cashing in on present site values. This a private owner is more likely to do than a college or any corporate body. In fact when a college or any private owner does sell derelict cottages they are almost always blamed locally. There is a sentimental affection for mouldering, insanitary cottages, probably connected with the fact that until recently they were let at 3s. per week or less. It is forgotten how often landowners could only save such accommodation by replacing the roof with corrugated iron. New owner-occupiers, guided by planning authorities, keep their cottages looking as if "someone lives there" as we say in Dorset. Sydling can show its corrugated iron but it remains one of the most charming villages in the district. The narrow road up the valley only goes on to Up

Milton Abbas village
Gold Hill, Shaftesbury

Sydling. The road over the hill misses it by half a mile, so that Sydling feels withdrawn from much of the fret of traffic.

From the Syd valley over the hill to Cerne is the usual three miles of almost straight up and straight down. A cyclist is always walking, working extremely hard, or free-wheeling. The top of the hill is flat enough to cultivate, and I have described this Dorset chalk hill land as "plateau". This is fair enough as long as you do not think of plateau as flat. It would be difficult to find enough flat land for a football pitch. During the war when a new airfield was needed only one site could be found in all the chalk belt of twenty miles by ten. The valleys are not only steep-sided but all the uplands are rolling.

This is especially the case round Cerne Abbas, and it is from the Sydling road that we look over Cerne to a steep rounded hill beyond, which carries the famous Cerne Giant. This is the crude outlined figure of a man, carved through the turf to the white chalk. The narrow trenches forming the outline need cleaning periodically. The work has been done very thoroughly once to my knowledge in the last thirty years. I think the giant might well have vanished if left untouched for much more than a century, although rain might have kept the steeper, downhill outlines scoured. If this guess is accurate the giant must have been cleaned several times during the centuries when a Christian Abbey flourished in the valley at his feet. Without the slightest doubt the old abbots had tremendous power and might have hastened the hiding of the giant, rather than his preservation, if they had so desired. Probably G. K. Chesterton was stating a fact when he said:

> "*It is only Christian men*
> *Guard even heathen things.*"

Generally the church took over and christianised old pagan festivals such as the winter feast of the shortest days. Or they blessed with a saint's name an old pagan magic spring—there is a wishing well in the churchyard of Cerne Abbas, of pure, cool, clear, unfailing water. I have never traced any effort at civilising or christianising the giant. The figure of a naked man, with a club in his hand, and every indication of virility, must have been difficult to fit into any moral story. As a child I remember being told a tale, with obvious connections with Goliath and David, which was the nearest possible approach to respectability. It said that a giant threatened Cerne and went to sleep on the hillside. A shepherd boy went up in the night and slew him, whereupon the people of Cerne carved round the outline of the body, which is 186 feet from head to toe. Presumably they filled in other details such as the eyes and ribs later. At least it is true that several friends of mine have provided supporting evidence for the legend that sleeping within sight of the giant is a powerful fertility spell for women.

The true story of the giant still causes long arguments amongst archaeologists. In my youth he was invariably described as being contemporary with Stonehenge or Maiden Castle—neither very exact periods—with 5,000 B.C. thrown in for good measure. Actually there is an enclosure with pit dwellings on the top of the ridge above his head, but with no necessary connection. A more recent theory may have owed something to the Wiltshire chalk downs above Fovant. Here the soldiers in the First World War carved their regimental crests in the chalk much on the lines of white horses or giants. It is suggested that the Roman soldiers of occupation carved the god Hercules on this Dorset hillside. There are stated to be similar figures on Roman coins of the period. This makes him two thousand rather than seven thousand years old. Some writers find mystery in the absence of early reference to the giant in abbey records, and are inclined to think of him as a relatively recent agnostic, or a devil-worshipping joke. Here I refuse to follow. The abbots may have tolerated the giant, but certainly did not approve, so why mention him. I refuse to knock one month off two thousand years. I also refuse to join the local school who, several years ago, wrote passionate letters to the press demanding that the giant's aggressive masculinity should be veiled.

Cerne Abbas is like Maiden Newton in having a stream which has cut through the chalk to the upper greensand. This, as usual, gives a wide valley, with many springs, and plenty of room for streets, side streets and back streets, instead of the narrow length of true chalk villages. For that matter Cerne is rather more than a village. In my grandfather's time it had a tannery, a malt house and was very much the "town" of the surrounding district. In my own youth it had a police station, a Rural District Council, a Magistrates Court, and the only doctor in a five-mile radius. There is still a doctor, but neighbouring villages now have their own practitioners. There is no longer the need for the sick or their relatives to walk three miles and back over the wind-swept hills for a bottle of medicine—not that they would need to walk nowadays, even if doctors were thinner on the ground instead of thicker.

Cerne Abbas has fewer inhabitants than it used to have and it is no longer any sort of market. One corner is still labelled Pitch Market where farmers pitched sacks of corn as samples for sale. Probably the dissolution of the abbey started the decay, although it is usual to blame everything on the fact that the railways did not come within eight miles. Actually my grandfather described Cerne as a "run down" place, even when the stage coaches were still prosperous elsewhere. I think it must have declined before railways, because some coaches did not bother about it. My great-great aunt kept an isolated pub at Giant's Head, one and a half miles away, on the ridgeway parallel to the valley road from Dorchester to Sherborne. Here the coaches changed horses and my relative saved £3,000 in thirty years, mainly from bread and cheese for coach passengers.

All the writers of my youth found Cerne a dying settlement. "Here are empty barns, gates falling off their hinges, and doorways grown up with weed." It was a fair enough description fifty years ago but is certainly not true today. There were a number of old houses in Cerne originally built by fairly prosperous tradesmen, and going back to Tudor days before the Reformation. These had often been plastered over and were in a state of decay not superficially different from the appearance of Victorian mud-walled hovels. Yet underneath they were very different. New modern owner-occupiers have found treasures, and not only in the beautiful street of old houses opposite the church, which was always obviously built for prosperous people. The many good old Tudor and Queen Anne houses in small Dorset towns are in basically the same tradition as the wool manors of the Mendips and Cotswolds, except that they did not belong to extremely rich men. These houses were put up by a new middle class which had not broken into the gentry, but were well-fed citizens of Cerne, Beaminster, Bridport and the like.

Apart from the abbey, Cerne was a commercial town with no resident rich landowner. It has no great manor built from the ruins of the abbey.

Of the abbey one magnificent gateway remains of all the splendours, and a tithe barn which has been turned into a dwelling.

The gateway was in a farmyard in my youth, but the old farm-house was purchased by the late Lord Digby and restored as a small country house. Portions of this house and garden were undoubtedly originally part of the abbey. It was called the Abbey Farmhouse, and some of its later walls may well have been made of old stone in the sad period when the mighty building was used as a quarry. Of the abbey church only foundations remain. Cerne had its own parish church which was distinct from that of the monks. For the rest one remnant persists which is little more than a series of earth banks and a name on a map. We have seen how the kings had hunting forests and the very great nobles owned chases. The slightly less powerful nobility owned parks in which deer were confined. The abbot of Cerne had his park, fit for a prince of the Church. It is still shown on the Ordnance map, west of the village in a pleasant coombe, and it must extend to well over 100 acres.

A mile northward is Upcerne, happily off the main road, with a beautiful manor house. From here a rough but passable road leads to the top of the great chalk escarpment above Batcombe. There are gates across this road, and the surface on a very steep hill is of sharp flints. It is not for those who have tender feelings for cars or tyres, but it leads to downs which will remain utterly peaceful until someone officiously surfaces the track. It will then become a beauty spot.

Still further upstream but on the main road is Minterne Magna. I think the original settlement was Minterne Parva which is a farm nearer Cerne on the stream but just east of the main road. The present Minterne is right on the main road and has been completely based on the great house, which was erected not long before the First War. There is a memorial to a Winston Churchill in the church, and a more recent connection between Digbys and Churchills is young Mr. Winston Churchill, who is grandson of the most famous owner of the name, and of the late Lord Digby. This Lord Digby once took me through the gardens which are the glory of Min-terne. The chalk hills close in very abruptly round the house, but the stream has cut through into slightly acid Upper Greensand. This gives ideal soil conditions for azaleas and rhododendrons. A belt of woodland fills the valley for about a mile below the house, and this is planted in a hundred seemingly natural clearings with flowering shrubs of all kinds, rhododendrons being a speciality. For many years it has been possible to visit these gardens, at their best in spring, on payment of a small fee. During much of this time the late Lord Digby lived in the Abbey Farmhouse at Cerne, with Minterne House empty. Today the new Lord Digby may make different arrangements but as I write it is still possible to see these wonderful grounds.

Below Cerne, down the valley, is Nether Cerne, which is only one hundred yards off the busy road and yet lies in deep peace. There is an old church, and a manor house, with mellow stone windows, and a very few other buildings. In my young manhood the well-to-do farmer who lived in the house was not a member of the Church of England. In other similarly small isolated parishes the squire, who held the gift of the living, was not always on speaking terms with the parson. There is not invariably complete sweetness and light "where every prospect pleases", although I would stress that there was no rancour at Nether Cerne.

Within half a mile downstream is another church at Godmanstone. Here nearly all the houses are on the main road which is the sole village street. Farm roads cut up the hillside and one passes the lonely Bushes Barn into the Sydling valley. Like many other tracks over the Dorset hills this is a public path and bridleway. Much of my cross-country motoring has been done as the guest of friendly farmers.

I have described these chalk valleys as parallel, but generally they converge on either the Frome, Piddle or Stour. Nevertheless the basic plan is parallel, in that there is upland plateau between them for most of their length.

Here I am tempted to leave Godmanstone for no other reason than the fact that the landlord of the pub is a friend of mine. It is a pleasant pub but I would have liked to perform a record. No one previously has ever written any book or leaflet about Dorset, Wessex, or even the pubs of all England without mentioning "The Smiths Arms", Godmanstone. You see it is alleged to be the smallest licenced house in the country, but I swear I have seen almost a hundred people in it.

These are the facts. It is an old smithy, single storied, with a thatch roof which comes right down over the small windows. With an effort I can believe the legend that a king stopped there with a horse which had cast a shoe. The king wanted a drink, but the smith was unlicenced, so naturally a licence was immediately conferred. From memory this story is attached to Charles II whom, you remember, did really knight a drinking companion in the cellars of Wimborne St. Giles. The explanation about the smallest public house attached to this reasonably large room is simple. Only the old smithy is licenced; the landlord's living quarters are in a separate building, and are a private dwelling. The story brings the public in and sells a lot of postcards, but there is actually plenty of room. The landlord has a natural friendliness and hardly needs any help from beautiful surroundings, or a charming old building, or the legends, to be busy.

The Cerne river joins the Frome just below Charminster. This gives a wide flat stretch of water-meadows, and a bewildering maze of natural and artificial streams. In the past the river was diverted and split to feed a mill at Lower Burton on the old road to Charminster, another mill at the bottom of the Grove in Dorchester, and at least one more in Fordington. The whole lay-out of mills, streams and water meadows was immensely complicated by the making of the New Sherborne Road to Charminster which cuts right across the meadows. This new road was built in the turnpike days of the nineteenth century and a turnpike cottage is the only dwelling on this 1½ miles of low embankment.

It is now extremely difficult to be sure just where the Cerne originally met the Frome. Today most of the Cerne water would seem to go well north of Dorchester to Grays Bridge, whereas the Frome follows an artificial cut under the old town walls, past the prison to Fordington Mill.

In most of the parish of Charminster the Cerne river gives the familiar farming pattern of a few meadows in a narrow valley with plough land on dry hillsides rising steeply from both river banks. It is only where the valley joins with the Frome that a really wide stretch of meadows alters the layout.

Round the old church Charminster is charming, although the name is merely a corruption of Cerne Minster. Downstream there is one wonderful old house from early Tudor days when men first started to build great houses as dwellings rather than castles. Wolfeton House was built by the Trenchards from 1505 onwards and retains its towered gate house. It is still a dwelling, but is no longer occupied by one family.

For the rest Charminster has been influenced by Dorchester for a long time. An old County School for Boys educated many prosperous farmers' sons in the very early days of this century. It is now two houses with several fairly large dwellings in the grounds. Similarly there must have been another dozen Victorian "good" houses in the village before the last war. Of smaller houses there is a between-wars row of bungalows lining the Sherborne road, a couple of separate post-war council housing estates, and a very new private development area. In many respects the village has become suburban, but the fields are still very close. Dorchester is not big enough to obliterate the countryside, and Charminster meadows are too wet to make building sites.

Back at Cerne the route over the ridges goes up a very steep hill, and straight down into Piddletrenthide. This means leaving the Frome valley for the Piddle, and these two parallel streams do not meet, although they enter the sea very close together in Poole Harbour. Most of the Piddle villages so far have been mentioned as being on the fringe of the heath. Piddlehinton, Piddletrenthide and Alton Pancras are typical of the chalk mainland. They are all in the very narrow valley, all have ancient grey churches with square towers. The farms in each village stretch from the valley up one hillside only. If a farmer has both sides of the valley you can be quite certain two farms have been amalgamated in modern times.

Driving down the narrow road there is nothing to make the tourist pause, and no obvious change between the three villages. I was born in Piddletrenthide and naturally "I know different". There is no pub in Alton Pancras and no chapel. In Piddlehinton there is also no chapel but one pub, whereas in central Piddletrenthide in my father's time, there were five pubs, two chapels and a Salvation Army meeting place—hardly a barracks because it was only used occasionally. Not that Piddletrenthide is all that much larger than Alton or Piddlehinton. I think its superiority was entirely due to land ownership, although even this is not immediately understandable. Alton Pancras can be dismissed in a word. It had, and still has, a resident squire who could easily forbid licenced premises and Nonconformists. Hence no pubs and no chapels. At the turn of the century the then squire accepted a Nonconformist farmer for his best farm; the family are still in the farm but they have to go two miles downstream to Piddletrenthide for chapel.

Piddlehinton is superficially similar in ownership to Piddletrenthide. Until recently they were both owned by colleges. The "hind town" is still owned by Eton College, and the "thirty hides on the small stream" was held by Winchester College from the Reformation till well after the last war. The different character of the villages must have been caused by the attitude of the colleges. I think Eton were the more conservative, and were quite prepared to allow Piddlehinton a pub, but not a chapel. Certainly, like Alton Pancras, one of their large farms in my childhood was let to Nonconformists who had to walk two miles each way to Piddletrenthide to chapel, twice every Sunday. Incidentally I have only recently realised that Church of England people often drove a horse and carriage to church, but that these well-to-do chapel people always walked. I now believe this is based on the rigid interpretation of the Old Testament rules about the Sabbath, and was also observed by Orthodox Jews. My father always walked on any Sunday outing, but previously I imagined it had a purely commercial basis in giving his horses a needed rest. After all they were worked very hard during the week.

Returning to the subject of the differing villages, I believe that although Eton was an absentee landlord it must have taken a much more paternal interest in Piddlehinton than Winchester took in Piddletrenthide. Winchester favoured a system of long leases, often for the lives of three named individuals. My grandfather bought the house in which I was born, plus three half-acre plots of pasture one mile away in 1880. My father's life was one of those involved, and he lived to the age of ninety, so that we had the property until after the last war. This form of half-gambling tenancy meant that once a man had obtained a lease he was quite safe for life. He could be a drunkard, a radical, a poacher, a Nonconformist, or anything considered undesirable by conventional squires, but he could not be evicted.

I have found that the energetic, skilled countryman starting with no money is usually a rebel. He tends to use his extra earnings as a pieceworker either on an occasional drinking orgy, or to support parties or churches opposed to the Establishment. It explains our five pubs and two chapels. It also explained why Piddletrenthide had a very high percentage of skilled men such as carpenters, wheelwrights, blacksmiths, hurdlemakers, well-diggers and thatchers. This was one of the very few villages where a man could be free as long as he could pay his rent. It was the one red blot on an extremely true blue parliamentary constituency. Probably it was not a coincidence that Piddletrenthide church was always "high" and Piddlehinton "low". In a very low village the church had to be high in self defence.

All three village churches in this stretch of the Piddle valley are beautiful. Piddletrenthide is by far the most impressive in size and height of tower. We natives claim it as the finest village church in Dorset, but this depends a little on whether Beaminster and Cranborne are classed as villages or towns. For the rest there are the marks of prehistoric men on the hills, the houses crowded by the stream, the odd new house in sites made possible by piped water, but all not wildly changed.

Conducting a stranger round Alton Pancras, I think I would take him up an unsignposted road, turning west off the main road on the north side of the village. It ends in the farmyard of Holcombe in a perfect basin of hills. There is nothing more to see and no possibility of riding further, but it is very much in the centre of Dorset.

In Piddletrenthide I would go to the church and then through the churchyard to a small lane to Morning Well. Here springs bubble out of the base of a steep wooded hill into a shady pool. Let us settle on the mystic number of seven springs, although some dry in the summer. It is an enchanted place, raising memories of holy wells and pagan groves. It is easy to imagine that the church was built on its knoll between the springs and the village to cut off the power of the old gods. If it is true they were not evil gods, for this is a place of comfort in a thirsty land, a place of bird song, and of sunshine on a gently rippled pool.

For Piddlehinton my viewpoint would be just out of the village on the crest of the hill towards Charminster, where it is possible to avoid seeing the raw 1938 Army Camp just out of the village.

Continuing across the ridges from Piddletrenthide, there are two side roads out of the valley close together near the manor house. One runs 1½ miles to Plush, which is another hamlet at the end of a coombe in the tradition of Higher Wraxall and Up-Sydling. In the case of Plush the narrow road goes on to a pass in the hills between Ball Hill and Nettlecombe Tout. It then descends to Mappowder and Blackmore Vale on utterly different soils. The ridge of the pass beyond Plush is very far from "the madding crowd". It is called Folly, and there must have been an element of folly in siting a public house at this spot. Plush is a mile away, the road is no more than a lane. In living memory there were never more than

a dozen houses scattered over a radius of a mile, and the shape of
the land makes the ridge a wind funnel, yet in my youth Folly
had a farm house, three cottages and the Fox Inn. This had been
the case in my father's youth, which means for at least a century.
The explanation for the farm is simple because springs of never
failing water are plentiful. The pub may owe its position to the
fact that Plush had no pub, probably as the result of a ban from
some past squire. When a new squire got a licence in Plush just
after the last war, the "Fox" at Folly was forced to close. The old
innkeepers usually regarded the running of an isolated pub as a
part-time job, which their wife could look after until regular cus-
tomers turned up in the evening, or it might be as a roof for retired
service men or policemen who wanted an addition to their pen-
sions. Certainly there could never have been a living in the "Fox"
at Folly.

The old inn is now a pleasant private house, the cottages have
gone and there are only two dwellings left on the ridge. Eastward
there is a lane and track which leads to the top of Nettlecombe Tout,
one of the major peaks along the wall of the chalk escarpment which
cuts across the county from Shaftesbury to Winyard's Gap. A little
further east is Dorsetshire Gap. This is a break in the hills which is
very noticeable from the other side of Blackmore Vale, looking
towards the main escarpment. There is no road anywhere near it,
but a maze of ancient trackways, and marks of dyke, ditch, camp
and burial grounds. I once walked there when my brother-in-law
had Folly Farm and we wanted to go to a farm sale at Hartfoot
Lane. Apart from hunting men and rabbit trappers I have never
found more than a dozen people who have discovered Dorsetshire
Gap, which shows how lonely it is.

This journey to Plush and Folly is to the edge of the chalk hills.
My route across the rolling central plateau is up the other eastward road from Piddletrenthide Manor towards Chesilborne. This
road is now fenced and tarred but I remember it when it crossed
the open down turf with hardly a trace of rut or hoof mark in the
grass.

About one mile from Piddletrenthide there is a hollow in the
hills to the south of the road which shelters the isolated farm of
Doles Ash. It is typical in being in a hollow within reach of well
water. A mile further on, and north of the road is a deeper hollow
called Lyscombe. This is yet one more cul-de-sac, similar to Up

Sydling, in an almost closed basin of the hills. A tiny stream flows southward out of the valley, and there are fragments of a religious house dating from Norman times. Doles Ash and Lyscombe are exactly what always occurs on the chalk. Wherever there is a combe with water there will be a farm, and if it is a sizeable hollow the Church were fairly sure to have an interest in the best of the land. This three miles between Piddletrenthide and Chesilborne displays one startling departure from tradition which is quite new. On the very top of the hill a farm has been created with a modern house and buildings. Everywhere the farming of the chalk has been completely altered by piped water, and the springs and wells no longer dictate where a man can live. Will it change the character of the bare chalk hills? I think probably not very seriously. Farms run big on this soil and one group of buildings on 500 acres can be hidden in trees. Our forefathers had isolated cottages with rain-water tanks on the hill tops, and these were usually sheltered by trees or high hedges.

Chesilborne village has its narrow street, a pub and an old church. It now has to share a parson, and the old vicarage has become a charming country house. In my early memories it was far too big for the vicar and must have been a millstone round his neck. It could have been lost, whereas it is now safe for more centuries of beauty. Near it is an old farm house, part of which is Tudor. The village has not been in the hands of one owner for several generations, and has been farmed largely by owner-occupiers. This type of ownership often tends towards frequent changes. Families may have to split farms if there are several children, and although brothers may agree as partners the next generation probably will not. There is seldom a tradition of inheritance by the eldest son in middle class families as there is with the nobility. Possibly for one or other of these reasons there have been a large number of farm boundary changes in this area.

Down the valley is Chebbard Farm, home of a noted herd of Friesian cattle, and from here my road goes over the hill to Dewlish. Here there is a large manor house still in private use as a dwelling, but it is no longer the home of the squire of the village. Dewlish farms are mainly owner-occupied, which is not at all a bad thing in times of agricultural prosperity even for preserving old buildings. Equally in bad times farmers are not bad preservers. They may not be guided by any love of beauty. Frequently in the past they have

put corrugated iron on old thatched roofs, but the walls have remained
and enough has been left to make restoring ancient glories a possibility. Farmers as a class like things to remain much as they remember
them from their youth. The real destroyers have always been the
very rich. Many old manors were deserted in Georgian times because the rich squire or his lady wanted the glories of new houses
with high rooms and enormous windows. Often the manor became
a farm house and in Dorset this frequently meant that it survived,
sometimes to return to the status of a Country Residence, but equally
to retain its connection with the earth on which it stands. The largest
farm house in Dewlish gives me the impression that it was never
built for a farmer, although farmers have preserved it for many
years.

The road over the ridges goes on north-eastward roughly parallel to the main Dorchester–Blandford road. The turning off the
valley road is north of Dewlish towards Milton Abbas, but the
valley should be explored a little more before returning to the
hills.

There is nothing quite like Melcombe Bingham and Melcombe
Horsey. The manor house at Melcombe Bingham, first built in
Plantaganet times, is a perfect example of a Tudor manor, which
was never replaced by a Georgian palace. It is all in warm Ham
Hill stone, with mullioned windows, and an air of solid security far
removed from pride or grandeur. For more than six centuries it
belonged to the Binghams, who later set their mark on the New
World. An American ambassador named Bingham came back a few
years ago to see the home of his ancestors.

The old stone church is immediately adjoining the manor, and
visitors often hesitate to seek the church because the approach appears
to be the entrance to a private house. In fact in summer the church
is completely hidden in trees. Rather naturally the owners of the
manor have not put up any direction sign to the church—local wor-
shippers know precisely where it is. Thus tourists may miss this completely untouched gem of a house, which was already mellow in the
days of the first Elizabeth.

A couple of miles away a lane leads to the dead end of Melcombe
Horsey, which is probably the best of all the basins in the hills,
sheltering under the great chalk escarpment. Like Up Sydling there
is no through road, and motorists have to turn back near the big
house.

As with so many of the deep hollows just behind the main chalk ridge, the springs have cut right down to the greensand, and the whole circular valley around the manor is on good, deep soil, free from flints. This is land which could always be switched from good plough to good pasture, and it is not surprising that the house speaks of a long prosperous past. The basin in the hills is very much a settlement on its own and it is slightly surprising to find another village straggling along through a very narrow gap between the ridges and yet not a parish. Dorset has got over this difficulty by referring to this settlement as Hartfoot Lane. Actually part of it is in Melcombe Bingham and part in the even more distant parish of Hilton. To make things even more complicated the names Higher and Lower Ansty come into it.

This must be near the geographical centre of Dorset. Hartfoot may be the correct name but "Arfurd" is nearer the local pronunciation—Dorset men *do* drop their aitches whatever the scholars may claim. In my youth I remember it as full of incredibly old people. The dialect was the richest in the county and the least contaminated by Devon or the New Forest. Every "yokel" story is fathered on Arfurd Lane. It was here that a cottager rushed to get the pig out of the sty to stand with front hooves on the wall, and to share the march past of the band on the Friendly Society Feast Day.

Here there is the only pub for many miles and here I played my first game of shove-halfpenny. Straight across the road is a massive building which is now part farm, part barn and part an extremely good village hall. I remember it as a brewery, or at least as a malt house, possibly both. Great waggons pulled by superb shire horses used to lumber through these lanes, usually with the driver fast asleep. I have driven a horse myself from Ansty to Piddletrenthide without one wakeful moment. This is old Dorset still, but the roads hold more dangers.

Having arrived at Ansty it is hardly worth going back to Dewlish to cross the hills to Milton Abbas. It is easier to slip down into Hilton, which has the parish church for the district although it probably has less inhabitants than its old brewery hamlet. This is yet another basin in the hills with the springs coming out of greensand in the valley bottom, but with the farming on the chalk slopes. It was part of the Milton Abbey estate when it was owned by the very rich Hambro family. The Hambros took great pride in their pheasants and King Edward VII was a frequent visitor. As a result there was a great deal of planting on the hill slopes and in more scattered clumps of woodland. Probably, too, there had been a good deal of planting in the older days of landscape gardening. At any rate Hilton and its hills are much more heavily wooded than most chalk villages.

Probably the best way to approach Milton Abbas is from Hilton. From the roadside there is first an amazing view of the great church and the enormous mansion attached to it. The mansion is not old, except for the monks' dining hall, and is impressive mainly for its size. It is now a school, having gone through all the usual history of being sold away from the church at the Reformation.

Later its history was by no means usual. Seeing it from the Hilton road one is conscious that the church and the mansion are quite alone against the background of the wooded hills. It is perfectly normal for a large Georgian house to be alone in its park, but not for a church, and certainly not for an abbey. Always an abbey attracted cottages, a market and probably a small town. This was the case at Milton Abbey before 1786.

When Joseph Damer acquired the estates he found a large and rowdy village near the great church, just where he proposed to build his new Gothic mansion. He therefore had it removed. It was as simple as that. Goodness knows what he destroyed of beauty, but at least he put something back elsewhere. A mile away in a steep narrow coombe he built a new village. This could be called the first bit of town planning for small houses. Damer provided a wide street, straight up the hill from an artificial lake. On each side of the road was a grass verge in the latest 1965 style. The houses were semi-detached cottages, although no one had yet thought of that ghastly word. They were thatched and were completely square. Between each pair was a chestnut tree. There were twenty dwellings on each side of the street, all absolutely and mathematically alike.

Today the chestnut trees have been removed because they were old and unsafe, but in most cases young trees have been planted. The houses are privately owned, and in many cases the two semi-detached in each block have been turned into one. The general, rather weird look of Milton New-town has been preserved very faithfully. "Newtown" is my name for it. The real post-war new development is on the top of the hill, out of sight of the street. For that matter the higher part of the street departed from the 1786 tradition before my time with a church, a school, a pub and some Victorian houses.

The tiny stream from the lake at Milton Abbas looks hardly big enough for minnows, yet when the lake was cleaned out some twenty years ago a salmon was found in it. How this fish got up the brook and over an embanked road to the lake is a mystery. It is very unlikely that any breeding took place, and if this did happen the young salmon would have had to face several large and hungry pike. Between the lake and the village of Milborne St. Andrew the brook used to work a mill, with another mill just below Milborne. This was only made possible by storing water in fairly large mill ponds.

Milborne is on the main Blandford–Dorchester road, and hides most of its charms from the traffic. There is a model of a large white stag by the roadside. This used to be an inn sign from the old coaching days, but the modern village inn is on the opposite side of the street. Off the main road Milborne straggles along by the stream which winds its way to Bere Regis. Much of this part of the village is very old and charming. The influence of the short Debenham ownership, mentioned in the last chapter, can be seen in a huge milk factory on the main road to Blandford, plus a large number of concrete poultry houses on the other side of the village.

Back in Milton the road over the hills switchbacks to another Winterborne valley, mentioned previously because it finishes on the heath beyond Winterborne Zelston. Winterborne Houghton, Winterborne Stickland, Winterborne Clenstone and Winterborne Whitchurch are all typical chalk upland villages in narrow valleys, but with the additional complication of an uncertain winterborne instead of a steady stream. I think this has led to rather larger farms because the space available for well watered small dairy holdings is even more limited than is usual on the chalk. The watercress industry had improved the water supply at some points by boring deeply with artesian wells. This was even before piped supplies became commonplace but the old influence of the unreliable stream is still apparent. As usual, in a land of very large farms, there is a big gulf between the prosperous manors and big farm houses, and the bare old cottages. In other districts smaller, mixed farms give a number of grades of houses and more tradesmen, more inns and more chapels. This was an austere land in all the decades of depressed

The Northern edge of Cranborne Chase

arable farming, and it has still not caught up with the friendly cosi-
ness of West Dorset villages. This Winterborne valley is typical of
the upper chalk in providing villages in deep valleys but north-
eastwards the plateaux between the valleys tend to spread out into
wider chalk uplands. This could have been part of my classification
of dry chalk heights if the Stour river had not happened to cut
through.

The Stour is not a chalk stream in the same sense as the Frome
and Piddle. It is fully grown before it reaches the line of the chalk
hills. It does not rise in them but cuts across them. It breaks the
rampart of the escarpment, south of the British camp on Hod Hill,
in a narrow pass, but thereafter it is much more than a normal chalk
valley. No longer do we get a village consisting of a ribbon of
houses, with a road or track on both sides of the stream. The Stour
often has villages or a town on both banks: starting with Durweston opposite Stourpaine, Bryanston opposite Blandford Forum,
and Blandford St. Mary opposite Langton Long. The valley still
remains fairly wide at Charlton Marshall and Spetisbury before
returning to a village on both banks with Shapwick and Sturminster
Marshall.

It is still true that the bulk of the farm land is up the chalk slopes
and that most of the farms are large, but the river has had more
influence on the soil of the villages. Meadows are wide and there
are far more old dairy buildings as opposed to corn barns.

The town of Blandford Forum is the centre of this chalkland
stretch of the Stour. The ancient borough has a very long history
as a market town, and until well after the 1914–18 War there were
important sheep fairs. In modern times it is usual to think of a farm
market solely as a place where animals are sold. This was not the
case in the old days, and not even well into the present century.
Market day saw the sale of butter, cheese, cream, fruit and garden
vegetables, not by auction but individually by the producers or
their wives. Even fat cattle were not sold by auctioneers when my
father was a young man, but by personal bargaining with the owner.
The Town Council took a toll on all sales. Blandford still appears
in guides with "E.C. Wed and M.D. Thur", but the cattle, sheep
and pig markets are no more. The fair ground for sheep sales has
been covered in houses. Why the weekly animal market vanished
is difficult to explain. Motor transport has made it possible to hold
much larger markets at fewer centres, but there seems no obvious

Sherborne Abbey

reason why Blandford market should have died and Sturminster Newton greatly increased. The death of the summer and autumn sheep fairs is more understandable. The types of sheep which used to be brought here in thousands were Hampshire Downs and Dorset Downs. These sheep were all kept on the folding system and this method of husbandry died out when machines replaced men on the farm. In England as a whole there are at least as many sheep as in 1939 but almost all of them graze freely on grass. The daily moving of pens on turnips, swedes, vetches, clover, sainfoin and such specially grown fodder crops can only pay for a few flocks making a high price for ram lambs. The Down breeds are still needed for crossing to give quality lamb, but only ram sellers can afford the cost of the folding which is necessary to feed lambs born at Christmas. The grass counties maintain sheep numbers, the arable chalk hills have scores instead of thousands. Numbers of ewes at the great Salisbury Fair fell from 20,000 to 800 between my boyhood and middle age. Blandford Fair vanished completely.

Superficially it seems that Blandford has lost its contact with the surrounding countryside which used to be its lifeblood. This is by no means the case. It remains a shopping centre and a service centre for much of modern agriculture. In every old market town a great many crafts supplying farming have obviously been greatly reduced in importance. Saddlers, smiths, and wheelwrights are few, but mechanics have increased. My personal view is that few market towns ever owed their prosperity to farming, in spite of all the speeches at the Fat Stock Show Dinner. Blandford certainly had a number of industries in the eighteenth century, such as lace, wigs and nets. In 1914–18 some shops must have benefited greatly from the nearby camp, and today light industry is increasing.

Like most old towns Blandford Forum has suffered from fire. The last and worst was in 1731 when the town was almost completely destroyed. There are a few old almshouses, from 1682, but practically nothing to suggest that this was a town in Norman times. One advantage has accrued. Just as Wren planned a new London after their Fire, so did John Bastard play a large part in rebuilding Blandford. In the Market Place the Georgian Town Hall, the principal buildings and the Georgian Parish Church blend together very happily. Red brick was largely used, but Georgian brick can give a feeling of permanence and prosperity.

Downstream on the Blandford Forum bank the tiny village of

Langton Long is on the quiet "back" road. The valley is very heavily wooded, almost certainly as a result of planting around the great house. This is not the natural woodland of old chases and forests but arose in the days of landscape gardening, and when coverts were being planted for game and foxes.

The wooded slopes on the opposite bank, just across Blandford bridge, may have had a utility reason, especially where the slope was too steep for agriculture, but here again most of the Bryanston woods were planted for sport. The enormous mansion was the seat of the Portman family. It is now a public school but the local pack of foxhounds are still known as the Portman Hunt. With the present value of land it is difficult to imagine the wealth which could keep the great expanse of Bryanston Park as a playground. It is equally difficult to imagine how the huge house could have been designed for one family. This fantastic wealth existed side by side with Tolpuddle Labourers getting six shillings per week. The next sizeable buildings to be erected in the countryside were the Workhouses.

The adjoining parish, also just over Blandford bridge, but on the left hand, is Blandford St. Mary. This is pleasantly wooded but by no means as thickly as Langton Long or Bryanston. Again the woodlands obviously date to the days of Planning for vistas or for sport. At Blandford St. Mary there was never a family with fantastic riches derived from the Reformation or from the Industrial Revolution. The manor house was part of the Priory manor, which means that it was a solid Tudor dwelling which was "restored" about 1776. Since then some of the lovely Tudor work has been rediscovered, which is a fairly common history for Dorset manors, as opposed to Georgian or Victorian palaces.

Upstream Durweston and Stourpaine on opposite sides of the river are fairly typical of chalk villages except that they are on one bank only. The pattern of a steep rise from the valley to flattish arable on the uplands is familiar, and yet noticeably different. These uplands are wider and wilder. Bonsley Common between the Stour valley and Turnworth is strangely alien after the tame plateaux between the streams near Chesilborne, and Piddlehinton and Charminster. Much of Bonsley was successfully ploughed during the last war but its outskirts and the surrounding woodlands give the impression of great age. This feels as if it was primitive forest into which agriculture has encroached, instead of planned woodland.

The top of the hill above Stourpaine gives the same impression. Ash Oake Coppice and Free Down form part of that dry upland which made my third division of the chalk. Without any doubt Durweston and Stourpaine are still peaceful, civilised villages, in the tradition of sheltered valleys and wide cultivated fields. But there is just a hint of a starker land on the hills, which the old squires never quite controlled and the old parsons never quite managed to sign with the cross. A land where the farmers' wages were not the sole source of income for a few secret men, especially after sunset.

This is the point to change to a chalk country which was neither entirely fashioned nor governed by the little streams and winter-bornes.

VI

THE DRY UPLANDS

It is difficult to fit the chalk countryside into a rigid classification. There is no very firm line between the rolling chalk hills and the dry uplands, but there is something to be said for giving the northwest of the chalk a chapter to itself. Most of the journey follows the main Blandford–Salisbury road, and seems at first sight to be a repetition of the country in the parallel valleys of the last chapter.

It is probably true that Pimperne and the lower Tarrant and Gussage villages do belong to the rolling land of cultivated hills and narrow valleys, but they do not fit exactly into the pattern of the central chalk. Pimperne, for instance, is not in a deep valley and has a very small stream. The higher part of the village merges into woodland which is essentially part of Cranborne Chase.

There is Norman work in the church, but no famous house and few picturesque cottages. If Pimperne has a claim to fame it is that one of the most up-to-date pig keepers in England farms there. What is more he was "brought up respectable". For generations his family have been corn and sheep farmers, which is the natural agricultural occupation on the chalk. Pigs in modern days have little connection with the soil any more than hens. Men "take to" pigs, or poultry, or horses, and it can happen to any village. Not that modern pigs offend the senses of sight or smell. There are thousands of pigs at Pimperne, plus a contracting system for the supply of skim milk and pig feed to other farmers, but it is inconspicuous. The only unusual result is that men come to Pimperne to work every morning, whereas men sleep in other agricultural villages and leave to work in town.

The Tarrant villages in the next dip underline my classification difficulty. Tarrant Gunville, at the head of the valley, is definitely in the dry upland section although it has some springs. It is the home of the Farquharson family who once hunted the whole of Dorset. Their great house is Eastbury and the fantastic thing about the present large mansion is that what remains is only one wing of the original building. Everything else was taken down and sold piecemeal in 1795, although it was only finished in 1738. Eastbury was not built by the Farquharsons but by a curious character, George Bubb Dodington, who inherited a fortune from his uncle. The architect was Sir John Vanbrugh, and the building must have rivalled Blenheim Palace, which was also designed by Sir John. It cost £140,000 in the eighteenth century, and it would be difficult to imagine what this means in terms of modern money. When I last saw it two medium-sized fir trees were growing straight up from the pillars of the gate house, and I could not discover if they were deliberately planted in the masonry or were self-sown. The Park of Eastbury has its clumps of trees, and all the usual planting associated with landscape gardening, but the woodlands to the north and west are another story. Patches were cleared and cropped by Ronald Farquharson in the 1950s of what was primeval woodland. Other patches were cleared thousands of years ago for ancient camps. Bloody Shard Gate and Bussey Stool Woods give the impression of being outside the quiet land of Dorset, which was civilised so many years ago. It is easy to understand that this was beyond the reach of the law for countless centuries. You know what "outlaw" means in this country, where the only road is the remnant for one the Romans made. Actually it was a place for outlaws, and poachers, and smugglers as late as Georgian times.

Tarrant Hinton, further downstream, and on the main Blandford–Salisbury road, is almost wholly without woodland. There are big dairies in the valley, and large arable fields on the hill. The Tarrant stream is very nearly a winterborne here, at least in very dry seasons, and it has not cut a deep valley. There is practically nothing which is unploughable from the point of view of slope, and nothing which is too wet. The village inn has been greatly influenced by the enormous amount of traffic on the highway and by the fact that the army camp is only about a mile away. The stage coach produced some pleasant pubs, but the casual trade from cars on an arterial road has not inspired any brewer to build or rebuild with much character.

The Tarrant brook has a village every mile, or at least a settlement with Tarrant as a prefix. Tarrant Launceston might well be passed unnoticed, as it is only a large farm by the roadside, within a half mile of Tarrant Monkton. This village is most unnaturally wide for a chalk settlement on a very tiny stream. It has the usual road on each bank, but these two roads are both tarred and 200 yards apart. As usual in this valley the farm houses are large and well built. They date from the time when farming was prosperous. The world price for wheat in 1817 was 96s. 11d. per quarter, in 1854 it had fallen to 72s. 5d., but this was still highly profitable. Compare it with 46s. 11d. in 1870, 31s. in 1911, and 87s. in 1964. The farmer in 1964 received a subsidy which raised the price to about 102s. but this was, of course, in a very depreciated currency. Compared with 96s. 11d. in 1817 it explains why farm houses of that date had wine cellars, and stables for half a dozen riding horses. Remember there was no income tax and wages were very low. It is difficult to give a fair figure for wages because there were other considerations such as free cottages, but they were so low that an iniquitous system had been invented for adding to them from the parish rates. Possibly when wheat was at its highest the wage may have been 12s. a week. It certainly fell below 8s., and was still as low as 12s. in my boyhood before 1914.

These figures explain the excellent farm houses built by rich squires in good corn-growing districts such as Tarrant Hinton and Tarrant Monkton. They also explain how farming families who did not try to ape the gentry managed to live when their income was cut by as much as two-thirds. Such families had reserves, and were ready to stride forward when prosperity came back. The workers had nothing and many of their hovels were no more improvable than old pigsties. Generally these cottages have vanished in the Tarrant valley, as they have in the rest of the chalk country. Mud walls and thatch are best removed, and a fresh start made on sites which are now worth ten times more than the original dwellings. Possibly the quiet valleys will see a considerable amount of building on old foundations in the near future. The universal private car has removed the need for trains and bus services. Already the army camp on Monkton Down, and the 1941 aerodrome at Tarrant Rushton had stopped the slow decay of Tarrant Monkton, which seemed absolutely inevitable as soon as a tractor replaced a horse.

Tarrant Rawston and Tarrant Rushton, before 1939, had almost vanished, and the war seemed likely to complete the process because a large farm on the hill at Tarrant Rushton was taken for a flying field and the house, cottages and buildings obliterated. These villages are unlike other chalk villages in many ways. First that farm on the hill was unusual, several hundreds of feet above the stream. Then the valley itself is different from the rest of the Tarrant vale in being extremely deep and narrow. At one point the road runs under a very steep chalk hill called "The Cliff", and the name is only a slight exaggeration. The villages are not unusual in being close together, although half a mile is near even by chalk standards. Both churches are worth visiting. Tarrant Rushton for its age and Tarrant Rawston for its situation. There are other Dorset churches touching, or very near, manor houses, but this is in the garden of a pleasant farm house. Church and farm house belong together, and the description "garden" is literally true. This is not a graveyard which has been tidied, but the mellow pleasance of a comfortable home.

At Tarrant Keynston the valley widens again to the same type of wide curves as at Tarrant Hinton. The hills are extremely rich in barrows, earthworks and ancient trackways. It is very near the great fort of Badbury Rings, and there is a Celtic earthwork called Buzbury Rings half-way between Keynston and Blandford, just across the road from the golf course.

Both Tarrant Keynston and the last Tarrant village, Tarrant Crawford, are much influenced by the Stour river. Keynston dairy house is actually on the main river, and the old abbey at Crawford was certainly placed here because of the well watered fertile countryside.

The diversion down the Tarrant valley started on the dry hills at Tarrant Gunville and finished in the rich meadows of the Stour. The main route over the ridges drives straight on from Tarrant Hinton over hills which have few hedges. This is Salisbury Plain country where the upland fences are of modern barbed wire. Here there is none of the sudden steepness of the typical chalk valleys. There is a dip where a by-road runs off to Long Crichel, but only any sign of a stream in extremely wet weather. The Ordnance map shows an extremely thin blue line running from the other side of the main road at Chettle but does not dignify it with a name.

Chettle village is in a dead end but not the usual chalk type such as Up-Sydling or Lyscombe. There is no basin of land almost surrounded by extremely steep hills. This is more in the nature of a shallow dish and the barriers to the west and north are of woodlands or bare, waterless hills. There are roads through and around

Chettle, but nothing beyond the village seems to lead anywhere inhabited. The village itself is completely dominated by the lovely Queen Anne manor house. In my youth and into the 1939 War this was owned by Major Castleman, who farmed his own land in the best traditions of fifty years ago. This is not intended as a sneer. He kept a flock of Down sheep and folded them in the traditional manner. His arable land was extremely well cultivated. He kept pedigree Channel Island cattle and made butter from their milk. He drove round his land daily in a smart four-wheeled carriage, accompanied by four pedigree sporting dogs, and with a groom to open gates. It did not pay, of course, but it was an interesting survival of a way of life. This was how squires lived on their own land as opposed to the extremely rich nobility with hundreds of villages. The squire had no superior save the monarch, but he was not remote from his people. He knew all his employees and was not separated from them by anything more than a foreman who was of their class. Today I believe Chettle is still farmed by the family, in the female line. The house is still occupied, but the methods are modern and profitable.

The next dip on the Blandford–Salisbury road has a small stream which finishes up in the Crane. Here there are three villages, Gussage St. Andrew, Gussage St. Michael and Gussage All Saints. St. Andrew is nearest the ancient woodlands of Cranborne Chase, but most of the farm land is in very big, open, arable fields. The turning off the main road is just past the Cashmore Inn, a lonely public house which must always have owed most of its trade to the highway. Gussage St. Andrew could never have been a large village and today it is scarcely a hamlet in the usual sense of that word. It is a large farm and such farms do not need many cottages. At the back of the farmyard is a small, ancient church. It has no tower or steeple but there is a small, wooden construction on one end which probably housed a bell. Sir Frederick Treves described it as "a derelict church in an open field". He goes on to say that it might be mistaken for a barn. Very happily it is now far from derelict. I found it locked, but with the key hanging by the side of the door. The obvious intention seemed to be to welcome visitors, but to remind them to keep the door shut. Birds, or even pigs and poultry from the adjoining farmyard might easily be a nuisance. There was no porch, and from the outside the walls were rather like an old barn, with very few windows and those not of the conventional Gothic of most old churches, or Victorian restoration. Inside it was perfectly plain with no arches, or aisles, lit by candles with one modern oil lamp. It was beautifully kept, including the narrow, mown, grass path which was the only approach.

At Gussage St. Michael and Gussage All Saints the valley closes in slightly into something more nearly resembling typical long narrow chalk villages. This is still a country of large farms and few inhabitants. Only the prehistoric circles and barrows speak of a time when it was thickly peopled. There is something significant about the ruined church at Knowlton beyond Gussage All Saints, near the Cranborne–Wimborne road. This is completely derelict, with no houses near it, and it is built in the middle of an ancient earthen circle. A Celtic civilisation has passed, the Christian church bells are silent, but small larks still sing in the empty sky.

For the rest of the chalk land of Dorset there will be no more need to suggest that it remotely resembles the tame uplands and narrow villages of the central area. Beyond Cashmore Inn the great road climbs into a waterless country. On the right of the road is Pentridge which has no present connection with any other place, but was once part of a Celtic system of defence and communication of very obvious importance. Near here is the great Bokerly Dyke which barred the easy way into Dorset between Pentridge hills and Cranborne Chase. Later the Romans drove their Old Sarum–Badbury Rings road over the Dyke, and the modern highway makes one of its few bends to cross it in comfort. The Dyke has the ditch on the northern side, which seems to suggest that it was built by Dorset men. Not only is it on a pass between the hills, but the chances are that there were dense woods of the New Forest to the east, of which Martin Wood in Hampshire is a remnant, and the thick wilderness of Cranborne Chase to the west. The Celtic men of 1,500 years ago had no liking for tangled woodland and the Dyke guarded the way through from one stretch of bare chalk downs to another.

On the west of the main road are Handley village and Woodyates. Woodyates manor house dominates its surroundings, in the manner of Chettle, by which I mean that the owner farms the land. The rest of the village is separate on the main road, right on the county border. It has other farms and a building which was once a very important coaching inn. The road to the manor was private when I first went there, and the squire had devised a method of enforcing a speed limit. He had made slight dips across the road at an angle which would do no harm to a car at 12 m.p.h. but would wreck any chassis at much over 20 m.p.h. These have now been levelled out, but there are a few diagonal slight ridges as a reminder of the old system of dips. The speed limit is still 12 m.p.h. and no driver with any regard for his car would do much more than 30 m.p.h.

A couple of miles short of Woodyates and Bokerly Dyke and the county border, is a cross-road on a bare hill top which gives the impression of being very windswept and high. Windswept it certainly is, but the height above sea level is only 303 feet, which illustrates how some of the little hills of Dorset can give a strange impression of space and size, quite apart from figures on a map. The signpost on the cross-road carries the name "6d Handley", and the "sixpenny" always interests strangers. I am quite sure that the Road Surveyor who commissioned the signpost had a sense of humour. He knew perfectly well that the sixpenny was nothing whatever to do with money. It goes back to the Hundreds of Saxon times when Handley was partly in the Hundred of Sexpena. Indeed he need not have put sixpence on the signpost at all, because almost all locals refer to the village merely as Handley.

This village seems to lack a reason for being precisely where it is. There is no stream, no sheltering hill, no great house, and no important ancient or modern highway. There had to be a village to deal with a reasonably fertile stretch of upland farmland, but this is a big village, and within only a few miles of the old market town of Cranborne. As some indication of its size there is a report that in a great fire in 1892 one hundred people were left homeless.

Immediately surrounding Handley the fields are large and mainly ploughed, but the ancient woodland of Cranborne Chase is on the north and west. Between the fields and the woods there used to be 300 acres of scrub-covered down known as Handley Common. It was requisitioned, cleared and ploughed during the war by the Dorset War Agricultural Executive Committee, and it was a wonderful sight to see 300 acres of wheat. Presumably when the war ended this land was due to be returned to the commoners of Handley. Local farmers, and in particular Mr. Dibben, a committee member, were dead against allowing this workable land to return to waste.

To prevent this happening the consent of those with common rights had to be obtained for such rights to be extinguished. This took quite a lot of discussion, but eventually agreement was reached, and the land passed to the ownership of the Dorset County Council. Like most County Councils they already had a landed estate let to small-holders, in fact they probably have more farming tenants than any other estate in Dorset. The County Council then proceeded to divide Handley Common into six holdings of about 60 acres. Houses, cow-sheds and farm buildings were provided and piped water was laid on. The first three holdings were let in 1960 and the last three in March, 1964. To me it makes a very happy story. Good land lying waste is a sad sight, and there is no large population anywhere near Handley who are starving for access to land for recreation.

The old woodland immediately north and west of Handley is very largely in Wiltshire. How Tollard Royal could possibly fail to be part of Dorset is a mystery, but such is the truth about this old hunt-ing lodge favoured by King John. In fact the main road from Cran-borne to Shaftesbury is in Wiltshire, beyond Woodcutts, until it plunges over the edge of the chalk escarpment to Melbury. The descent is so steep that the road has been engineered in a zig-zag, with frightening hairpin bends.

The village of Ashmore is just off this road high up in the hills. Handley cross-roads gave an impression of being high at 303 feet; Ashmore at over 700 feet scarcely feels as if it is on a hill top. The village is set in trees and in the centre is a very large pond. It is only occasionally that a glimpse of the land to the south-east is caught by the casual visitor. Here the country falls away into the blue dis-tance, with a view over the chalk, the clay and the heath for a score of miles. The extent of the view is enough to indicate that Ash-more is on a hill, but the approach from the Tollard-Shaftesbury road is on the level. Only the approach road from the west is at all steep and there is certainly not the same feeling of living on a cliff which applies to Shaftesbury.

The trees in Ashmore village have been planted in clumps and avenues; the old forest of Cranborne Chase is harder to find. Through the centuries some of the woodland has been replaced with conifers, or turned into park land as in the Larmer Grounds on the county border. There is no longer a great expanse of primeval forest such as still exists in remote parts of Britain. The age of the Chase is sug-gested and not always obvious. Some of the surviving clumps of

trees were obviously never planted, for there is nothing planned
and orderly about them. The oaks are not giants but tough survivors
on this curious soil of red clay overlying the chalk. The villages,
the manor houses, and the modern Forestry Commission have beaten
the old Chase, yet it is still easy to realise that most of these villages
started as clearings in the hunting grounds. None of them have
streams or any obvious reason for their situation. There was a break
in the trees and a squatter built a hut. His descendants assumed grazing
rights and fenced in a bit of land for hay. Probably they were there
before the nobles claimed the chases, or the kings reserved the forests
for hunting. It was accepted that such men could graze acorns with
pigs in autumn, but the deer always came first. Men were not tempted
to try to farm where ploughing was banned, and even grazing was
restricted. The settlements at Ashmore, Woodcutts and Farnham
remained small until the hunting of the deer went out of fashion.
There are still wild deer in the district, fallow and roe are fairly
common, but unless a search is made for them they are seldom
seen. They do a certain amount of damage to root crops by pulling
up far more than they eat, but turnips are not widely grown in
modern farming, and the grazing of pasture at night is seldom
noticed. The foresters who cultivate trees in plantations find them
a bigger nuisance than any other countrymen. Once the woods
were regarded as covert for the deer and now deer have to be reduced
in numbers because they damage the trees. It is another example
of the strange changes in country life. Another is that ploughable
land is now more valuable than good pasture. The old parks attached
to country houses were dotted with trees, and when the squires
gave up treating such pasture as a deer park or a zoo, they could
let it for grazing at much the same price as treeless grass fields. There
may have been some virtue in the trees as shade for animals. At
any rate they were tolerated by tenants much as hedgerow timber
was tolerated round grazing land. The return of the importance
of the plough has made a big change. Much of this area of flinty
clay over chalk was park land, or held by landlords with a delight
in trees. Farmers had cider orchards near their farms and these have
nearly all vanished in the last twenty years. Even the owners who
did nothing to maintain their woodlands spent no money on clearing
them.

Today bulldozers have made clearing relatively easy and ploughable land is worth ten times what it was in 1939, so orchards, parks

and even woods tend to disappear. Yet enough remains in this district to preserve the memory of forest, and park and coppice. The Pitt-Rivers family set their mark on the district in the spacious days before 1914 and their influence remains. I cannot remember the great days of Larmer Tree when General Pitt-Rivers succeeded in shocking most of the countryside. The tree was on the county border, and may well have been the meeting place for the Chase Courts, much as the Speech House was the meeting place in the Forest of Dean, and the King's House in Lyndhurst for the New Forest. The general opened the park to the public, which was wholly admirable. The trouble was that he opened it on Sundays. I can remember elderly Nonconformist relatives describing it all with obvious disapproval. Apparently there were brass bands, and horse brakes from as far away as Poole, rather on the lines of the modern coach party. There was even dancing round the tree, with a suggestion of pagan rites, all made much worse by happening on a Sunday. It sounds very harmless now, but the Victorians had strong views on the Sabbath, and this went even further than Popery and the Continental Sunday. The hint of Nature worship was certainly not as bad as a return to Rome, but dancing on weekdays never led to any good.

It was probably all part of the intense interest which the general took in every form of ancient civilisation. He devoted immense quantities of labour and money on excavating the many circles, ditches and mounds which abound on this part of his estate. Perhaps the most important was a British village at Woodcutts which was later occupied by Roman settlers. This seems to have been a rather different occupation than the use of the old earth ramparts as a military post. The Romans at Woodcutts may have been men retired from the legions, or civilian administrators. There is at least some evidence of family life.

As a result of his excavations the general accumulated a wealth of specimens. To house these he built a museum, in a field about one mile from the village of Farnham. The inn at Farnham is named the Museum Hotel. It is a large inn and a magnificent museum, but in an unexpected place. The main road is a mile away, and the nearest sizeable city is Salisbury, which is a dozen miles distant. It must mean that no one drops in to waste an hour as they would in a great town. All visitors must be genuinely interested, since no one could arrive accidentally unless they were lost. The museum used to attract many visitors, so that the general's site for it may not be as odd as it appears at first sight. On my last visit a party of Devon farmers were keenly interested in a collection of old agricultural implements. This was very much at home on the chalk hills, but the museum has been closed for several years and most of the exhibits are now in Salisbury Museum.

The excavations at Woodcutts have been carefully filled in and there is little to be seen on the site. Quite near it is another common which was cleared and ploughed successfully during the war. This was still ploughed in 1964, but there were no houses nor buildings on it, so presumably it has not been let as a separate holding or holdings. Woodcutts Common is not as big as Handley which is only half a mile away, but it must have been well over 50 acres.

A few miles farther away, in Tarrant Gunville parish, another sizeable patch—Holmes Common—was also ploughed during the war. It is very unusual for large areas of potential arable land to have been left as commons, and it is peculiar to this part of Dorset. Possibly it goes back to the old customs of Cranborne Chase. In other parts of the county most of the land still surviving as common is worthless heath, or very wet pasture. Anything ploughable was enclosed about 100 to 170 years ago, and so was most of the better grazing pasture. In a chase there was much less temptation to enclose, because the tradition persisted that ploughing was banned. The price of wheat was dropping, and the greed for land was falling in Victoria's reign. I do not know when Cranborne Chase was officially cleared of deer, but the Act to slaughter in the New Forest was not passed before 1858, when a register was compiled which is still the authority for forest rights. There was a somewhat similar date in Dean, so it is reasonably safe to assume that ploughing in the Chase was difficult until after the main rush of enclosures on land under ordinary law.

The war saw the ploughing of three big commons in this area, none of which have returned to their old state. The war also saw a change in farming thought away from the idea that pasture was not only the most valuable form of land but that it was difficult to restore land to grass after ploughing. In all the old leases there were heavy penalties for ploughing pasture. These were first suspended by war regulations and have now lost most of their meaning. Good husbandry has gone to the opposite extreme, and suggests that in many cases the best way to improve a pasture is to plough it and to re-sow with cultivated grasses.

The plough has altered and is still altering these old wooded chalk uplands, but this is still a lonely land. There are deep, shady valleys far from roads and great bare downs towering above the comfortable little farms of Blackmore Vale. In all Dorset there are few places more remote from any form of industry. This is a fitting place to leave the chalk, on the top of Spread Eagle hill, with the empty land behind and the crowded small fields below.

The church tower, Beaminster

VII

THE BLACKMORE VALE

I KNOW at least half a dozen places from which I like to show strangers Blackmore Vale, but almost any spot on the chalk escarpment from Shaftesbury to Winyard's Gap will serve. The attraction is the sudden arrival on something approaching the edge of a cliff, with the wide, green, wooded plain far below.

Coming to it from the highest and driest of the chalk uplands at Spread Eagle Hill the village of Melbury Abbas is typical of the long line of greensand villages at the foot of the chalk ridge. There are springs in abundance, tall trees, shelter from every wind and a feeling of having reached a harbour. The larger farms stretch up the slopes of the downs unto the chalk but they owe much of their value to the good valley soil.

In the first chapter a list of greensand villages was given numbering twenty-nine. These are not all in Blackmore Vale, some are on the other side of the chalk ridge and their farms live almost wholly on chalk soils. The springs from these pockets of greensand form the headwaters of the chalk streams—Frome, Hooke, Cerne, Piddle and so on. These have already been discussed. On the Vale side of the ridge the greensand is much more a narrow continuous belt with a line of springs forming brooks draining into the Stour. In fact much of the flatter part of the Vale could be called the Stour valley, although this might give a false impression of that changeable river. We have seen it transforming the Heath with silt at Hampreston, and flowing through chalk hills at Blandford. In the Vale it is placid, meandering through meadows, and usually remote from villages. This is because much of the time the river winds through flat clay lands whereas the villages are on adjacent drier subsoils. This is true even of villages which take their names from the stream such as the Stours and Sturminster Newton. They are not on the river in the sense that the Piddle villages are on the banks of that stream.

West Bay, near Bridport

Melbury Abbas may be typical of greensand villages, but the one greensand town which adjoins it is utterly different. The actual sand of this formation gives flat land as a general rule, but there can be greensand rock, and where this occurs it can act as a sheltering cap to the softer subsoil. At the edge of the rock cap the sand has washed away in the millions of years of geological time leaving an abrupt hill. On such a hill the town of Shaftesbury stands. It juts out into the Vale at the end of a ridge coming in from Wiltshire. On three sides the descent into the Vale is so steep that the roads can only reach it by means of hairpin bends. All around the town the valley greensand is rich in springs, especially at Cann where a water mill is still working, but on the hill top water has always been short and the burgesses have long had to pay good money for it, mainly from Enmore Green. The church of St. James is just under the town, so close that you look straight down on the top of the tower from the ramparts and get the impression you could pitch a stone on it. St. James always had water, but for centuries it was said that beer was more common in Shaftesbury than any other fluid.

The situation of Shaftesbury would suggest that it would be easy to defend. Only on one side are large ramparts necessary and there is much less need for walls and ditches than at most of the Stone-Age hill forts of Dorset. Yet there is very little evidence of Celtic occupation, nor of any Roman fortress. Shaftesbury is certainly ancient, but its period of importance started in Saxon times. Its wealth rested on the Church and it had no military importance.

At one time there were eleven churches in addition to the great abbey church. St. Peter's is the only ancient building remaining, although St. James church under the hill is on the old site. Of the abbey practically nothing remains except the foundations, which were excavated and left exposed. Between these half-hidden, pathetic bits of masonry there is green turf. The utter destruction seems to have taken place very quickly after the Dissolution, and was terribly thorough. For the last few centuries Shaftesbury has been no more than a small market town with a view. The railways passed it by, but the motor age has brought an enormous increase in traffic. The town is on the A30 road, which is probably the most important of the three highways from London to Exeter. It is unlikely that trunk roads do much to increase the trade of a town. In Shaftesbury the A30 assisted in moving the old cattle market from the very centre of the town to a much more convenient site outside.

This enabled the market to increase and probably increased the number of real shoppers from the surrounding countryside. This is commendable, but it is probably the sole benefit from the road. In every town parking problems cause the tourist to seek refreshment outside in wayside cafés and inns.

Shaftesbury may have been written off as dead or dying in the early days of this century, just as Cerne Abbas was condemned. Both are very much alive but without the shining glories of the past. It is hard for us to realise how wonderful buildings could have been erected in an age when most of the population lived on a very primitive plane. It seems miraculous that the old civilisations and arts of Greece and Rome could have survived, or have been revived.

Our first firm knowledge of a town at Shaftesbury was of King Alfred in the year A.D. 880. He is said to have "built this city", but probably this means that he repaired and fortified an existing settlement. Alfred endowed a nunnery of the Benedictine Order which was consecrated in A.D. 888. Later Saxon kings enriched it with manors, but its era of greatness started when the body of King Edward was brought here from Wareham. The murder of King Edward by his stepmother at Corfe Castle is one of the bits of history which stick in most people's memories from school days. The young king weary and thirsty from hunting called on his stepmother at the gate of the Lodge. She handed him a goblet of wine and gave the signal for one of her servants to stab him in the back. The king's last reaction was to try to escape, but he was mortally wounded. His horse galloped away but Edward slipped from the saddle. His foot caught in the stirrup and he was dragged in a bloody trail along the Wareham road. That at least is the history most of us remember. The dead king was succeeded by his stepbrother Ethelred, who gave the monastery and town of Bradford-on-Avon to Shaftesbury Abbey. The murderess also gave rich endowments. This sort of retribution for sin was common in early days, but it was not the main source of the riches of the nunnery. King Edward's body was buried in the great church and very soon started to gain a reputation for miracles. Edward was made a saint and martyr. By A.D. 1001 he was given a shrine in the church, and his relics were venerated by pilgrims for centuries, until the Reformation wiped everything away in 1539.

For the visitor in a hurry the best impression of Shaftesbury can be gained near the ancient church of St. Peter. Very close to it a massively buttressed wall holds up the Abbey Gardens and the only straight road comes from the Vale to the town. Gold Hill is so steep that it is in steps like the famous main street at Clovelly and the cobbled lane is utterly untouched by any wheeled vehicle. Visitors in a hurry, however, should not try to "do" Shaftesbury in half an hour. This is a place to explore slowly, with time to absorb the feeling of a thousand years of history. My own favourite illustration of the wealth of these old religious houses is contained in a saying from the Middle Ages. In essence it claims that if the abbot of Glastonbury married the abbess of Shaftesbury their son would be richer than the king of England.

Down in the Vale the greensand strip is actually a bit more complicated than my description has implied. The villages are almost all on the upper greensand where the springs arise. Next to this there is a narrow band of extremely impervious clay called gault, and another thin strip of lower greensand. The lower greensand in Dorset is short of lime, and gives a brown rather poor soil, although in some counties it is used for market gardening. The gault is never more than a field or so wide, and only influences the landscape in that it is often below the upper greensand which is the reason why springs are so common. Rain soaks into the chalk and upper greensand but cannot penetrate the gault clay, so that when the tilt of the strata is suitable the water gushes from the sand as springs.

When I use the word greensand in North Dorset I am lumping together the upper greensand with the occasional outcrops of gault and lower greensand. The essence of the whole area is the abundance of springs combined with well-drained building land. The villages do not line a stream as they do on the chalk and the roads are not confined to valleys. From Melbury Abbas the Shaftesbury–Blandford road does follow the line of the greensand through Compton Abbas, Fontmell Magna, Sutton Waldron, Iwerne Minster and Shroton, sometimes called Iwerne Courtney. The road, however, is not shut in by serious slopes and occasionally climbs to the foot of the chalk hills to avoid boggy places or to cut a corner. This is very noticeable between Compton and Fontmell where the road is high enough up the side of the chalk hill to give a charming glimpse of the Vale.

Possibly this is the only stretch of the road which is outstandingly beautiful. Elsewhere the villages are slightly withdrawn. At Compton the bit of the village on the highway is tidy and clean but there is a combe in the hills on the east, called East Compton which is really beautiful. At Fontmell Magna there is a charming house on the east of the road which was once a mill. The springs at the foot of the chalk fill the mill pond and flow as a wonderful clear stream to the village. It is not much wonder that this stream, within a few hundred yards of its source, once supplied a brewery. There is no water in the world like the untainted, sparkling springs which have filtered through three hundred feet of clean chalk.

West of the road the remainder of the village of Fontmell is spread round twisting lanes out of the noise of the traffic. Sutton Waldron forsakes the main highway completely, apart from a very good modern farm house with its set of buildings. Here at least half the farm land used to run up the chalk hills and spread out on the flat top of the downs. The rest of the village is wholly in the vale and without much in the way of a centre. With an abundance of springs there is a tendency for each farm to be a separate little unit. At Sutton Waldron they are fairly large and very good so that each is almost a hamlet in itself.

Iwerne Minster is possibly the most interesting of this belt of greensand villages. Within living memory it has twice suffered a complete change which has no connection with soil or natural causes. Early in the century it was owned by an extremely rich man who turned it into a "model" village. The little shops were fitted out with signs. The houses were made weatherproof. The owner had some strong liking for diamond-pane windows and half-timbering, but it was very well done. Already the village was unusual in possessing a church with a steeple, so there was nothing glaringly incongruous in using red brick for new cottages, especially since it was a pleasant red brick. Iwerne Minster was set in trees and gardens. Its houses were varied and definitely pleasant, although there may have been a suspicion of straining after the Edwardian idea of the picturesque. Then between the wars the whole place was sold. The mansion became a public school under the name of Clayesmore. Most farms were sold to farmers and there was an abrupt check in the flow of industrial money. This did not lead to deterioration in the condition of the houses which had been excellent. A new prosperity came to the whole countryside after the war and a rich squire was unnecessary. Modern building of council houses has been of red brick, of course, but this blends well with those put up sixty years ago. Iwerne Minster is still a model village, and the brick is only noticeable if you go straight to it from its neighbouring parishes.

Iwerne Courtney has nothing to do with the main road at all. It lies on a loop which turns off the highway and comes back to it half a mile lower down. Here the greensand is very near the chalk which rises in a cliff to the south of the village. In fact just beyond Shroton the Shaftesbury–Blandford road cuts through one of the narrowest and deepest chalk valleys. It is only surpassed by a minor road joining it from the west. This passes between Hod Hill and Hambledon Hill, both of which are crowned with huge earthworks. Hambledon's ramparts are immense and they last saw war in fairly recent times. During the Civil War the locals became thoroughly fed up with both king and Parliament. They banded together and occupied Shaftesbury Hill with the object of enforcing peace. It is said that there were 5,000 of them, badly armed and completely untrained. Cromwell quickly dispersed them but some 2,000 regrouped on Hambledon. To deal with these he sent fifty dragoons who were quite sufficient. There was no great slaughter. Cromwell reported it as "some small execution . . . I believed killed not twelve of them, but cut very many".

Hambledon had one other connection with war. Wolfe trained some of his troops here who were later to capture the Heights of Abraham at Quebec.

Hod and Hambledon are wholly of the chalk, but Hambledon overlooks the extremely good greensand of the Vale at Shroton. Here some of the fields are very large and have always been fertile. For many years time was dated in this part of Dorset by Shroton Fair. Old men recalled events by the number of months they had happened before or after this event. It rivalled Woodbury Hill and like Woodbury Hill it has vanished without a trace.

Beyond Shroton the greensand turns away eastward from the Blandford road and follows the chalk ridge through Childe Okeford, Shillingstone, Okeford Fitzpaine, Belchalwell, Ibberton and Woolland. A reasonably well-used road connects these as far as Okeford Fitzpaine, but the last three are as little known as any villages in Dorset.

Possibly Childe Okeford is one of the best places for looking up at the chalk hills. I was born on the chalk and my natural reaction is to take visitors to such places as Hambledon Hill where they can see the grassland of Blackmore Vale, stretching into the blue distance, far below them. In more ways than one the man from the arable farms of the chalk looks down on the Vale. What I had only realised recently is that one of the chief claims of the Vale is that you can look up to the nobility of the great chalk escarpment. This is especially true at Childe Okeford, and although it seems strange to me to look up for my view, there is biblical justification—"I will lift up mine eyes unto the hills."

Childe Okeford is a prosperous village, with one small rise called Gold Hill. The land is adaptable for grass or arable and there are abundant springs. The water from these finds its way into the Stour, which is as usual remote from the houses and flows in the neighbouring clay land. There is no village touching the river from Hammoon to Durweston; Shillingstone comes fairly near but is on the other side of the railway.

Shillingstone is on the main Vale road in Dorset from Sherborne to Blandford. It has the same view of the chalk hills, but is less immediately under the downs. Being much nearer the Stour river the springs of the greensand have had less influence on the farming. In fact there are wide meadows here of alluvium which can give fattening pastures, as opposed to the rather rushy dairy land which is usual where greensand meets chalk in a narrow strip. On the hillside, all along the chalk wall of the downs, there have always been the scars of old chalk pits. Sometimes the chalk was merely spread on the acid soils of the Vale and left for the frost to powder it. Sometimes it was burnt to make lime and used for local building. Since the last war there has been a great deal more building and also a subsidy for applying lump or powdered chalk to the soil. As a result the old white scars on the green downs have increased greatly in size. For the first forty years of my life they seemed quite unchanging. After all, taking a few dozen tons of chalk from a hill consisting of nothing else left only a fresher surface on an ancient hole. In the last ten years the taking of thousands of tons have enlarged the scars, but still with no very serious effect. The chalk cliff is 300 feet high and it goes on for many miles. Some by-lanes are rendered slippery in wet weather by the chalk lorries, but the Dorset landscape suffers very little.

Shillingstone village is much more charming than most places directly on a main road. It has a delicate village cross which has been restored in recent years. The word "restoration" raises fears, especially since Shillingstone cross has been completely rebuilt, but here restoration is successful. The plinth of the cross seems to be very ancient whereas a similar cross at Childe Okeford looks entirely new.

Okeford Fitzpaine, the next greensand village, is directly under the ridge, and two of the few good roads across the escarpment start here. One climbs across the slope for more than four miles up a fairly gentle incline to reach the top of Bulbarrow Hill. The actual Bul Barrow is 902 feet high which makes it the second highest hill in Dorset. From here it is alleged to be possible to see the Bristol Channel and the Isle of Wight. I can vouch for the Isle of Wight, but the mountains of Wales might have been cloud in the evening sky. The other hill road from Okeford Fitzpaine goes steeply over the ridge and down to Turnworth on the chalk. On several occasions on this road I have seen bags of moss by the wayside. This was a usual sight during the war, and I believe the moss from this very old turf had a high medicinal value.

To me Childe Okeford, Shillingstone and Okeford Fitzpaine are very similar. They have always given me a feeling of prosperity. The soil is good and the buildings substantial. Since the villages are on the border between the relatively tree-less chalk and the oaks on the clay, the building materials are very varied. For instance, in one old house at Okeford Fitzpaine there is one part of timber-frame and brick, touching a wing of flint facing and with stone mullion windows. There is also some extremely good house thatch-ing. This thatch faces a difficulty from bird damage which is very much worse than it was in my youth and can only be controlled by protecting the thatch with wire netting. The birds bore holes into the thatch into which a man could put his arm. I believe this is a relatively new habit and is not due to the modern shortage of thatched ricks in farmyards, or thatched cottages. There is another new bad habit of pulling straw from the ridge of a thatched roof and drop-ping it on the ground. This happens at any time of the year and seems to have no connection with nesting. Most of the thatch in the three villages is protected by wire but this does not show from any dis-tance, and does not detract from the charm.

The industries of the villages seem to fit into the countryside. There are the lime works, a centre for ready-mixed concrete, a milk factory and private schools for girls which naturally provide lessons in riding. Why is it that girls love riding horses whereas most boys are uninterested?

The last three real greensand villages, Belchalwell, Ibberton and Woolland are smaller and poorer relations of the Okefords and Shillingstone. I get the impression that after a man had worked all his life in an isolated farm down a lane at, say, Belchalwell, his ambition would be to retire to the higher civilisation of Shilling-stone. Certainly these last three villages have something in common. At Woolland there is a notice in the church porch which refers to "The Hillside Churches". I have the impression that all are now under one vicar and certainly his description of "hillside" is apt. At Ibberton in particular the church is not merely on high ground but half-way up the great chalk escarpment. The road to it stops at a farm and thereafter is labelled "Bridle road to church". Remains of steps still survive on the way from the village to the church, and Treves said there were fifty of them.

The view over the Vale from Ibberton church is superb, but the way up must be a real test of devotion for the elderly. At the turn of the century the building had almost fallen down. Inside there is a photograph which shows a broken roof and bulging walls, but these have now been restored and made safe for many years to come. Outside is a plaque in memory of Lionel Seymour Plowman—incumbent 1899–1927. "During his incumbency the church was rebuilt." This is an excellent job and must have seemed utterly hopeless for a tiny village.

Ibberton church contained two interesting relics. One was a Book of Homilies, dated 1673, which has, after three centuries, been stolen. The other is an enormous earthenware pitcher, said to be 150 years old. I should guess it as holding three gallons, or certainly more than two gallons. In it the bell ringers used to collect cider at Christmas to drink in the belfry. Any ringers who climbed the hill to the church carrying that jar certainly needed a drink.

At the foot of the hill, in a farmyard, is a small building which was a Wesleyan Chapel, dated 1884. This must have been built at a time when the village church was beginning to get into a sad state. There is no steep climb to the chapel, but it is no longer used for worship. When I last saw it, it was full of hens in cages—the battery system. This somewhat spoiled my pleasure in the saving of the old church. Perhaps a more proper feeling should be an amazement that a handful of poor people could ever have built a chapel in this remote spot, and within a few years rallied round to save the village church. I would bet the chapel-goers gave something

towards helping the church. In a village there can be a great deal
of lack of harmony between the Established Church and Nonconformists, but pride in the old church building is largely shared.
This was where our fathers were christened, married and buried.
Indeed for marriage and burial staunch Nonconformists used to turn
to the church quite naturally in my young days, except the more
highly educated.

Woolland church is again part way up the side of the ridge, and
is unusual in having a spire. This spire, however, is not ancient,
and the whole church looks as if it had been built within the last
eighty years. If this is true it was almost certainly re-erected on
an old site. Next to it is a house which could be Tudor and looks
like a rectory. On the other side is a mansion overlooking a large
park. Woolland House seemed to be empty in 1964 when I last
saw it, and the very extensive outbuildings were in poor repair,
since carried out. This was an old manor and the building varied
greatly in age. It had one point in common with most good houses
sheltering under the ridge—tall chimneys are essential. The wind can
produce some queer eddies here and tall chimneys are less likely to
smoke. In support of the vicar's use of "hillside" for his churches,
I would point out that this one stands at 440 feet, the valley below
is 250 feet, and the hill behind is 900 feet.

After Woolland the greensand north of the ridge is very narrow
and only influences the farming in producing springs of abundant
water. This is especially the case at Buckland Newton which supplies
half the Vale. Before reaching Buckland Newton there is Stoke
Wake, tucked right under Bulbarrow and the ancient fortified
earthwork of Rawlsbury Camp. The view is magnificent and this
is a favourite spot for Sunday picnics with all the disadvantages
of litter, but so far without any permanent buildings. Stoke Wake
has a new church adjoining the manor house but there is little in
the way of a village. Almost all the land is Kimmeridge clay which
tends to produce isolated dairy farms with one or two attendant
cottages.

Buckland Newton has a village centre plus a number of outly-
ing hamlets or farm settlements. The reason is that Buckland has
no less than five widely different foundations—chalk, greensand,
limestone, Kimmeridge Clay, and Oxford Clay. Wherever there is
a true village centre in Blackmore Vale it is on something other
than clay, although clay makes up the greater part of the area.

Mappowder and Hazelbury Bryan are compact villages on limestone. On either side they have clay, Kimmeridge to the south and
Oxford to the north. The clay fields are flat, permanent pasture, and
the hedgerow trees are rather stunted oaks. Perhaps the best sign
to look for of a change from clay is the way tall elms replaced the
poor oak—until Dutch elm disease struck.

Where a civil parish has been established on the Kimmeridge Clay
it is seldom a village. Manston is a good example. The pub is on
the roadside but most of the farms are at the ends of short lanes.
West Orchard and Margaret Marsh are equally scattered. In this
"Vale of little dairies" there is often no obvious plan or purpose
for a collection of houses, such as the chalk streams provide, or the
springs of the greensand. Of the Vale clays the Kimmeridge is the
best since it is usually well supplied with lime, and in places the
Stour river has dropped rich alluvium. This is especially the case
at Hammoon, where there is a compact village on a lane connecting
two main roads. Here is a church, two farms, a few cottages and a
lovely old manor house which is still thatched.

The other main clay belt of Oxford Clay is flatter than the Kimmeridge. It was a royal hunting forest, and the same soil goes through
to the Gillingham forest in the north. Little remains as a reminder
that this was a playground for kings. There are a few names, such
as King's Stag and Buckhorn Weston, but no great expanse of woodland. There is a "Green Man" inn, very near King's Stag bridge,
but no one seems to be quite certain whether the green man was
a keeper, a poacher or a Morris dancer. The legend of the King's Stag
is equally hazy. A king—Henry III—is alleged to have spared a white
stag because of its beauty, and to have put it under royal protection.
Later the king's orders were disobeyed by a nobleman and the king's
stag was killed. A fine called white hart silver was then laid on
the whole forest. The silver was certainly collected, but it might
have been an acknowledgement for grazing rights, with White
Hart Bridge as the meeting point, rather like the Larmer Tree in
Cranborne Chase.

Because clay land is flat and clay villages scattered there is little
spectacular scenery on the Oxford Clay. The charm of the place
is of small green fields, of deep pasture, of peace and of quiet. There
are interesting churches at Pulham, Hermitage, Wootton Glanvilles
and Holnest. The old manor house of Round Chimneys near Wootton
Glanvilles became a farm house after having fallen into decay. This

was the home of John Churchill who became the first earl of Marlborough, and gives Dorset a strong link with that remarkable family. Holwell, miles from the county border, was once part of Somerset. This "Somerset detached" arrangement was once fairly common. Apparently if a great nobleman had one manor, remote from his main estate in another county, he might elect to pay his taxes at his principal seat. In this case the distant manor became part of his chosen county. Holwell is wholly Dorset today with no sign of "detachment". The church is down one lane, with no way beyond, and the village stores on another. The churchyard is maintained in first-class condition by the voluntary labour of the parishioners on what I gathered was some sort of rota system. Plough land is almost completely absent, and there is one tiny detached outcrop of limestone near Holwell House.

The other Oxford Clay villages of Melbury Osmond, Chetnole, Leigh, Lydlinch and Buckhorn Weston follow the same pattern, or lack of pattern. They are all on the clay but are sometimes influenced by the nearness of limestone, just as Holwell House was built near that outcrop. This is especially the case at Melbury Osmond where the great house—the seat of the earls of Ilchester—is on limestone outside the village. Such a house must dominate any village if it is still inhabited by the family. As I write this is doubtful in future at Melbury where a new earl has the title but not the estates.

Chetnole and Leigh are both clay but sheltered on the north by a curious spit of cornbrash limestone which juts out for a couple of miles from the main formation at Ryme Intrinsica. This was once cider-drinking country with orchards attached to every farm, and at Leigh some of the cider was first class. Leigh suffers a little from a picturesque angle because before the war two of the biggest farmers had a fancy for pigs. Keeping these animals has nothing to do with soil in the sense of cows being found in wet vales and sheep on dry hills. Pigs are purely personal preference. Their influence on Leigh was a fairly high proportion of corrugated iron—the only cheap building material before 1939.

Lydlinch to me is remarkable for the farm gates being marked with a Y, its deer park, and its common. The Y was the bracing of the gate and the initial of the squire, whose name was Yeatman. The deer park belongs to him and it still has a considerable herd inside the high metal fencing of the park. It is very poor wet land only one stage better than the adjoining common. This was never ploughed during the war because it is heavily bushed and undrained. Possibly it could be remade with modern drainage, and I know one or two men who would like to try. Fortunately or unfortunately it is not easy to plough common land in peace time, so Lydlinch Common remains utterly wild. It is one of the few places where gypsy caravans seem to be allowed to remain for weeks unmolested, and which respectable motor caravans have not discovered.

Near Lydlinch is Bagber, a place which has named a bridge and a common, but is hardly a village. Its only claim to fame is that it was the birthplace of our greatest Dorset poet, William Barnes.

All the principal villages and towns in this part of the Vale are on the limestone belt between the Kimmeridge and Oxford Clay. Of these Sturminster Newton can fairly claim to be the capital of the Vale. It has an extremely prosperous livestock market, and in this land of small dairies the custom is still reasonably well maintained of the wife going with her husband for shopping on market day. Larger towns at a distance such as Yeovil and Bournemouth may have attracted some shoppers, but there is a tendency for this trend to be reversed. The market is within a hundred yards of the square and parking is not wildly impossible.

The minster of Stour Minster has completely vanished but the parish church is well worth a visit. Hardy called the town Stourcastle in *Tess* and there are fragments of a castle to justify the name. For me the charm of the place is the approach over an old Gothic bridge leading off the main road, and the quiet market square. This is definitely a town which should be visited twice, once on market day and once on any day except Monday. In my youth the mill near the bridge was an imposing sight especially in flood time.

Sturminster Newton is as little changed as any place in Dorset, yet in the surrounding rural district the R.D.C. had a wonderful record for building houses after the last war. Dorset has rather a knack of appearing sleepy whilst remaining very much alive.

This is another district where the Pitt-Rivers family are large landowners. They have a manor at nearby Hinton St. Mary. In view of the Farnham Museum and the interest old General Pitt-Rivers took in archaeology it is interesting that a notable Roman pavement has recently been discovered at Hinton St. Mary. It is claimed that this pavement contains a mosaic of Christ, made soon after Christianity became the official religion of the Roman Empire. It came to light in September, 1963, in a field belonging to Mr. W. J. White, an agricultural engineer and blacksmith. There seems to be little doubt that the date of the pavement is Roman-Christian. Whether the bust is meant to represent Our Lord is open to argument by experts. If it is, then this is the earliest representation of Christ so far discovered in Britain.

On the same limestone ridge north of Hinton St. Mary is Marnhull—the birthplace of Tess. This is one of the most prosperous villages in Dorset. The soil is very good, and the stone-built farm houses speak of good times which were never swamped in the depression. Marnhull is very definitely a place to which Blackmore Vale people have elected to retire. Treves disliked the "Camberwell type" houses, but I find the stone mellowing nicely, and the dwellings very pleasantly solid. The church is superb, with a magnificent tower. It is on the highest point of the low ridge and is a landmark for most of the Vale.

Further north still are Fifehead Magdalen and the Stour villages of Stour Provost, East Stour and West Stour. All have some land on the clay but the villages are stone built on the limestone. A quarry at Todber by the roadside beyond Marnhull shows this corallian limestone very well. It explains why walls have replaced hedges in a few places and why the soil is of such a rich red colour.

Both Stour Provost and Fifehead Magdalen are just off the main road and, as usual, well above the river. Stour Provost is largely owned by the Dorset County Council, and let in small holdings of under 50 acres. This has happily not led to the destruction of one of the most charming village streets in Dorset. As far as I remember this street does not lead anywhere and this may have saved it from being shaken by heavy traffic.

The second town in the floor of Blackmore Vale is Gillingham. This was the centre of the Royal Forest of Gillingham. I have been shown a few ditches and mounds on the farm of a friend, on the Lodden, just outside the town which are said to mark the site of a Norman hunting lodge or palace. The name King's Court still survives and it is reasonably sure that Henry I, John and Edward I all used it. The district was de-afforested by Charles I, and it is now all good farming land with few woods and little more than a normal amount of hedgerow timber. It is a little unusual for such potentially good grazing to have been a forest, although Epping near London is another example. Gillingham Forest stresses the fact that the south was much visited by royalty between Norman and Tudor times.

Of this long history and royal connection there is little to be seen in these modern days. Gillingham is a very small industrial town, built to a large extent of the local red brick. There are other industrial towns in the south-west of England which are highly picturesque. Some of the old cloth factories in the Cotswold valleys have massive stone buildings by fast flowing streams, which used to drive waterwheels. Gillingham has a very pleasant corn mill in the very centre of the town, but this is the only attractive commercial building. In my younger days the bacon factory, the fertiliser works, the brick kilns and the milk factory brought prosperity to the town but not beauty. Gillingham has the most charming pastoral Dorset countryside all round, but it has set its mind on a commercial future.

North of Gillingham the county border is only a couple of miles away. In this region the line of the boundary is even stranger than usual. The chalk ridge would seem to be a natural place to have put it, which would have made Mere and Zeals part of Dorset, where they obviously belong. Instead they are both in Wiltshire. Silton, in Dorset, is hidden away from main roads in very pleasant parklike surroundings. The church is on a limestone knoll but the Kimmeridge Clay is very near on the north. It is easy to get the impression that "the village has vanished". Personally I doubt if there ever was a village in the sense of a compact collection of houses. It is the old story of the clay lands giving a scattering of isolated farms with no centre. Bourton, just beyond Silton, is on one of the main roads to the west and everyone thinks it is in Somerset. In my youth and middle age it had a flourishing foundry making boilers, and may have had visions of joining Gillingham in an industrial future. Once it had a linen factory and during the Kaiser's war I remember a considerable munitions industry. To-day the milk factory is all that remains, and that depends on the fields.

West of Gillingham, Kington Magna and Buckhorn Weston are both on the border of the limestone with the Oxford Clay. Both names witness to a connection with the royal forest of Gillingham, both are mainly built on the drier limestone ridge, and flow down the slope to the flat, wet clay. The limestone ridges curve round into Somerset and enclose this flat impervious vale with fairly steep hills. A very short burst of heavy rain causes flooding. It is said locally that if anyone empties a bucket at Templecombe there will be a flood at Nyland. Certainly this collection of isolated farms near Kington Magna is under water fairly frequently. The A30 main road here, just west of West Stour, is notorious in wet weather.

In some ways the end of the Oxford Clay belt is the end of Blackmore Vale, but there is still a good deal of relatively low land in the north of the county following a soil layout which is easy to trace. The stiff blue Oxford Clay is immediately next to a very rubbly limestone rock called cornbrash. It gives a red strong soil which is famous for wheat. Under permanent grass the dandelion is a persistent weed, presumably because its roots can go down deeply into the broken rock. It is easy to spot the very narrow strip of cornbrash in spring by the large number of dandelions in the pastures. Usually this formation gives a very distinct ridge along the edge of the clay with villages almost touching each other along it. A very good place to see this effect is just past the church at Stalbridge by the Lodge gates. The gates are in a high stone wall surrounding a large park, but the mansion inside the park has utterly vanished. Only the gate posts surmounted by stone heraldic heads remain as evidence that this was once a mansion capable of entertaining kings. Inside the wall there is the pleasant farm house of the home farm, and all the land of the park is now used for agriculture. The height of the wall suggests that at one time fallow deer might have been run here.

Just across the road from the park gates, any gap in the hedge will show the land falling away to the flat clay vale, with only one or two groups of farm buildings until there is the opposite limestone ridge at Marnhull.

Stalbridge has no market and is little more than a big village with one main street. There is a graceful stone cross in this street, which is in considerable danger from traffic. The church has suffered greatly from restoration. I get the impression that it was a village where a great many farm workers once lived when the great house was still in the park. Obviously the estate once spent a good deal of money on putting up solid stone farm houses on the land round Stalbridge. Cook's Farm, for instance, is big enough for a small manor. It may be that many milkers and cheese-makers lived in, but married employees had cottages on the dry land in the village.

Golden Cap from Thorncombe Beacon

Today there are far fewer farm workers and Stalbridge has not successfully followed Gillingham in becoming industrial. The train service on the old Somerset and Dorset railway has now vanished, but since well before the war there has been a good bus service to Yeovil. Stalbridge is largely a dormitory as far as young people are concerned. It is a dormitory in very pleasant surroundings, although with only a few odd corners to speak of age and beauty.

The other villages along the low cornbrash ridge are all small. Most of them have a number of pleasant quaint houses which speak of the local stone. Garden walls are stone, and roofs are frequently thatch, although inevitably there are new colonies of council houses which still look raw. Stalbridge Weston, Stourton Caundle, Bishops Caundle, Folke, Long Burton, Yetminster and Ryme Intrinsica all have Oxford Clay to the south of them, and thus edge the Blackmore Vale. To the north they have a belt of curious soils on Fullers Earth or Forest Marble. These are usually heavy clay in need of drainage, but not by any means as flat as the Oxford Clay. This is very much more broken country than the true Blackmore Vale with sudden hills such as the ridge crossed by the Dorchester road just before it reaches Sherborne.

For some reason this group of villages on cornbrash has been almost entirely neglected by the guide books and is therefore the more worth exploring. Mention is usually confined to Yetminster and Ryme Intrinsica. Yetminster is the biggest village and the nearest Dorset equivalent to the stone building of the Cotswold country. Many cottages date from Queen Anne with more than a few from Tudor days. Ryme is noted because of its name. Apparently "Intrinsica" means inside in opposition to Extrinsica, and "ryme" usually indicates a settlement in a sheltered place. Ryme Extrinsica would thus have the same meaning as when Holwell was described as "Somerset detached". Ryme Intrinsica is right on the county border and could well be called "Ryme Within". It has less old houses than Yetminster, but solid buildings in mellow stone are of the same pattern.

The appearance of stone walls in place of hedges in this district marks the very sharp soil changes on either side of the villages. Almost certainly this land was so stony that it paid to pick up the flat pieces to save wear and tear on plough shares. There was no difficulty about growing hedges, the wall was simply a way of getting rid of unwanted stones.

Chesil Beach

In the clay belt on the Fullers Earth and Forest Marble, north of the cornbrash ridge the houses are once more fairly scattered. In fact there are only two villages entirely on this formation in Dorset. Both Halstock and Lillington have no very compact village centre. Lillington is off main roads and is very small. Halstock equally off main roads is larger and has its quota of village shops and an inn. The inn is "The Quiet Woman" and she is depicted on the sign with her head under her arm, as opposed to "The Silent Woman" near Wareham who is shown as an angel.

Across the clay valley another strip of limestone, Inferior Oolite, gives another ridge and another series of towns and villages. Of these Sherborne is by far the most important. It was the Saxon capital of that part of Western Wessex which was overrun well after Hampshire had been occupied. In addition it was a cathedral city from A.D. 705 until after the Norman Conquest. Throughout the centuries of Danish raiding and invasion the bishops of Sherborne were warriors as well as priests. St. Aldhelm, the first bishop, built a church at Sherborne and founded a seat of learning. The present glorious abbey church is on the site of St. Aldhelm's Saxon building, and Sherborne School can claim direct succession from his day.

My first sight of Sherborne Abbey, years ago, was coming down the hill from Dorchester on a sunny autumn afternoon. The leaves on the trees were still dark green and the golden light emphasised the warm tint of the local Ham Hill stone. Inside the church the colour was intensified. There is nothing cold and grey about the building inside or out. Much of the original Norman work remains in massive pillars and arches, but these now support the wonderful delicate fan tracery of the roof. It would seem to be impossible for any man to enter this church for the first time without a feeling of overpowering awe. It is glorious beyond words.

Sherborne Castle was erected in Norman times but probably on the site of Saxon fortifications. It was in fact built where the palace of the Saxon bishops of Sherborne had stood, and this must have been a strong point. It was held at various times by bishops and the Crown until Queen Elizabeth gave it to Sir Walter Raleigh, with a large estate. Near here is one of the many places in the southwest where Raleigh smoked a pipe, and had a bucket of water thrown over him by his servant who thought he was on fire. The castle was twice besieged in the Civil War and was finally "slighted" by Parliament. A few relics remain including the gatehouse tower, and enough wall to show how strong these castles still remained even after the invention of gunpowder. The modern castle dates from Tudor times and William of Orange stayed here on his way to London to expel James II.

Every corner of Sherborne is full of beautiful and historic buildings. The Saxon school was refounded by Royal Charter in 1550. Through the generosity of the Digby family, the local landowners, many of the old abbey buildings were made available for the school. These include the Abbot's Hall, the Abbot's Lodgings, and the abbey kitchens. Compared with the utter destruction of the abbey of Shaftesbury, Sherborne has been extremely fortunate.

The town owes part of its prosperity to its schools. There is a public school for girls, two schools of what used to be called grammar school type, one for boys and one for girls, and a Catholic convent school. Education and sanctity have not been always entirely successful in preserving Sherborne's good name. It is also famous for its Pack Monday Fair held in October. It has been claimed that the fair got its name because the workmen had a spree when they "packed up" in preparation for leaving the town after finishing the abbey church. More probably the name refers to the packmen who attended all the old fairs in the countryside. During my lifetime the pleasure fair lasted for a week but the cattle, sheep and horse sale was on Monday. The proceedings opened at midnight on Sunday when a noisy procession paraded through the town making "rough music". In the reign of King Henry VIII it was complained that labourers and artificers used their "riotous expenses and unlawful games to the great trouble and inquieting of the inhabitants next thereto adjoining". It sounds like an accurate description of the midnight opening of the fair. Unfortunately in 1962 and 1963 hooliganism and silly damage were added to the noise, and in 1964 the Chief Constable of Dorset turned up with one hundred policemen and suppressed the traditional procession.

On the same ridge are two charming villages, Oborne on the west and Bradford Abbas south-west. Bradford was the seat of the Horsey family for many centuries, but their great house at Clifton Maybank is now reduced to one wing. The name comes from the Norman Maubanks whose heiress married a Horsey. The family were not swamped by the new rich at the Reformation, in fact Sir John Horsey was sufficiently in touch with the changing times to get the abbey, the ground about it, the valuable metal of the bells, and the lead roof from the king. He sold the lot to the townsmen of Sherborne for £300.

North of Sherborne there is one more major change of soil which we shall encounter more extensively in West Dorset. The soils of the Lias may be extremely deep and rich or fairly heavy clay. In this Dorset promontory jutting into Somerset they are well-drained and very fertile. The villages of Nether Compton, Trent and Sandford are not part of Blackmore Vale, they are cut off from the rest of the county not only by the sudden soil change but by the great London–Exeter highway.

Sandford Orcas has a fine manor house but the most interesting of these villages is Trent. It has a stone church steeple which is unusual in Dorset and some lovely stone cottages. On this really wonderful soil it naturally has a feeling of prosperity, but its claim to fame is in the dramatic story of a fugitive king. Trent Manor was the home of Colonel Wyndham, and Charles II came here in a desperate condition after losing the Battle of Worcester. It took him fourteen days to reach Trent from Worcester always with a huge price on his head, and his enemies very near. He hid in a secret room while the church bells of Trent rejoiced at the news of his defeat. After more than a fortnight he set out for Charmouth in the hope of getting a ship for France. The story then moves to a ship's captain being either frightened or restrained by his wife. At any rate there was no ship, and Charles set out on a return journey to Trent. At Charmouth a smith had noticed that a horse in the party had been shod in Worcester style and the hunt was on. I like the comment of the local minister to the landlady of the inn. "Charles Stuart lay last night in your house and kissed you at his departure, so that now you cannot but be a maid of honour." To which the landlady had the pluck to reply, "If it was the king I would think the better of my lips all the days of my life."

Every Dorset writer has repeated this story and I hope it is true. In the meantime Charles was in Bridport disguised as a man-servant in the George Inn. This was opposite the present Greyhound Hotel and in my youth was a chemist's shop, with a great reputation for "Poor Man's Friend" ointment. Charles must have thought he had no friends for the inn yard was full of Parliamentary troops. He slipped out of the town on the Dorchester road but immediately heard the sound of pursuit. He then turned down a lane just out of the town, and made across country through very narrow lanes to the north. This lane carries a stone commemorating the event. As night fell he reached Broadwindsor and stayed the night at the George Inn, burnt down in the last century. Here the king was upstairs with hostile troops in the room below. Their attention was distracted by the fact that a camp follower chose this occasion to have a baby in the bar, so no drunken lout stumbled upstairs to molest the travellers. Next morning Trent Manor was reached once more and here the king was hidden successfully for another eleven days. On October 5th, 1651, the king left for the hamlet of Brighton and escaped successfully from Shoreham.

It is stretching several points to class Trent with Blackmore Vale, but it is pleasant to end a chapter on the royal hunting forest of the White Hart with the escape of a hunted king.

VIII

WEST DORSET

WITH the changes in underlying rock occurring in wild confusion, West Dorset is even more varied than the rest of the county. There is a main road to the west near the coast, and another just out of the county to the north. Everything else is of local importance only, with the Crewkerne–Bridport highway as the only one with much feeling of purpose. This is a wholly delightful land and the lack of signposts is no serious drawback. Every lane leads to a pleasant spot, even if it is not the one you are seeking.

It is fitting to start at South Perrott because there is a trace of fantasy about the fact that it should obviously be outside the county. It is hard to imagine why it became part of Dorset. It is at the foot of a long hill which drops from the chalk ridge at Winyard's Gap, and all its trading contacts are in Somerset. The soil is widely varied with some of the mixed clays of Halstock and of the Vale below Sherborne, but it is near enough limestone to have some old solid houses. The church is run in conjunction with Mosterton—two miles away—and with Chedington, a long two miles up the hill. It is sad to find these small villages without a resident priest, but comforting that the churches are in good repair ànd well tended.

Mosterton church is curiously bare, and much more like a Nonconformist chapel. It was "rebuilt and enlarged" in 1855, and provided with a gallery. It is difficult to understand the need for enlargement. The village is no more than a straggle of houses on the Crewkerne–Beaminster road, with an inn opposite the church. The enlarged church is still small and the village has not altered in my memory of fifty years, and I cannot recall any stories of past prosperity. The inn has been restored more pleasantly than the church, and old windows have been replaced in a genuine Tudor style with warm stone.

Seaborough is strange even for Dorset. It is possible to get there by half a dozen twisting lanes, but it is not on the way to anywhere. It shelters under a long and very steep hill which is the county border. The great house of Seaborough Court stands in a huge park, which is not shut in behind high walls or fences, and it is unusual in another respect. A feature of nearly all parks is the noble and ornamental trees which were planted a century and a half ago. Many of these trees are now showing signs of age, some are going back and slowly dying. At Seaborough there are young trees dotted about in the pasture of the park. Possibly they lower the value of the grazing, but someone has obviously planned beauty for future generations.

There are good stone farm houses at Seaborough. One, near the church, is very large and might well be four hundred years old. It has an astonishing range of farm buildings, which vary from solid stone to modern concrete, with an occasional trace of the bad patching of the grim years of our fathers and grandfathers.

The church here is delightful. It is small, and little of the building is ancient. The walls look as if they were rebuilt in the last century, on top of two feet or so of old masonry. Even these fairly modern walls needed a couple of buttresses later on. The porch has a round arch which almost touched my head. It cannot be more than 6 foot 1 inch high, and would remove the hat of any man of average height. Inside the church there is one ancient memorial. It is the effigy of a crusader and is in a rather battered condition. Apparently this man who died in 1219 distinguished himself very greatly in the Crusade. He was the armed man which the manor was required to send on the king's demand. On his return he was given a substantial estate at Seaborough by Ralph de Vallebus, the Norman lord of the manor.

It is extremely easy to get lost when leaving Seaborough for Beaminster, but with luck it is possible to find Broadwindsor. Beaminster is the centre of the tumbled West Dorset countryside, and Broadwindsor is one of a ring of encircling villages. Today it is likely that Yeovil or Bridport attract the shoppers, but Beaminster was "town" for many centuries. It was a manufacturing centre for linen and woollens. Villages such as Broadwindsor had many sheep on their hills, and a certain number of fertile fields which suited the flax crop. The size of its church, with Norman and early English portions, speaks of a fairly large and prosperous community. In fact these West Dorset villages had far more in the way of cottage industry than the corn-growing areas of the chalk. I can remember when growing flax came into this category of industry. A flax grower and his family would take a small arable field from a farmer for one year only. They sowed the flax and hand weeded it. Then at harvest time it had to be hand pulled and tied into sheaves. Pulling machines only came into common use about 1939. In the winter the flax was stored in a barn and the family carried out all the processes to the point of selling the fibre to linen factories. The seed of the flax, known as linseed, has always been valuable, and saving the seed was one of the first jobs. The other major operation was to separate the fibre from the other plant materials which make up the stem. Very roughly this involved rotting the softer parts of the stem and leaving the tough fibre. Sometimes this rotting, or "retting", was done in the dew and sometimes by immersing the flax in a stream. Later the fragments of decayed stem were beaten and combed from the fibre under extremely dusty conditions.

Presumably the flax growers were fully occupied by working flax in winter, but were available in spring and early summer for sheep shearing, turnip hoeing and haymaking. All these jobs can well be done on piecework, and as a result West Dorset has a strong tradition of independence. The old factories in Beaminster were large solid buildings of three or four storeys, built in the eighteenth and early nineteenth century. At that time the town had twice its present population, and there were a lot of fairly large houses. There are very good examples of Tudor, Queen Anne, Georgian and early Victorian in the streets and lanes of the town. The ancient grammar school is now part of the State education system and has been given new modern buildings. When I was at school there in the First War it was called "The Beaminster and Netherbury Grammar School". The Beaminster part went back to the sixteenth century and to the usual provision for a schoolmaster to have £10 per annum for teaching poor boys. I believe they originally met in the church. The Netherbury endowment was even older and went back to before 1500.

As evidence of the old importance of the town it had an enormous number of pubs. In my schooldays we claimed that there were seventeen, but this has been sadly reduced. The "White Hart", just out of the square, is a most imposing building for a small town, especially a town five miles from a railway. The coach from Crewkerne to Bridport used to stop there, but this is not a coaching route in the grand manner of the London–Bath road.

The church tower is the glory of Beaminster, partly because of its proportions, and partly because of the warmth of the colour of the stone. In my youth the church bells played many verses of "O Worship the King" every three hours day and night. The inside of the church has suffered at the hands of the restorers, and even more from the memorials of the eighteenth century. The Strode family were an admirable lot, but there is no real need for them to appear, in Roman dress, more than life size. They should have known better, because Lower Strode, near Netherbury, is a charming house, and must have been part of Strode Manor.

Beaminster is entirely surrounded by hills, like a basin, except for a narrow winding river valley towards Netherbury. This valley is difficult to spot from the rim of the heights. A footpath worth finding follows this stream and gives a view of the great house of Parnham which is completely hidden from the Beaminster–Bridport road. The path crosses an avenue of tall trees running from Parnham to the hill top, where there is a private cemetery, and then goes straight to Netherbury church situated on a ledge on an extremely steep hillside. The village at the foot of the hill was connected with the flax industry as there used to be a flax mill down the river at Slape.

Returning to Beaminster, the best place to see the town is on the road along the hills at Beaminster Down. The Down was common land in my schooldays, covered in low gorse bushes, but it was ploughed and cropped during the last war and is still under cultivation. The road beyond here is running on a ridge with Beaminster on the south and the Axe valley on the north. Even the tilt of the land in the west is different. Beaminster's little stream goes into the sea at Bridport, and the Axe into Devon. Those essentially Dorset rivers—the Frome, the Piddle and the Stour—are over the hill and flowing eastward. The road across the Down goes on to Mosterton, but there is a fork, down a passable lane to Broadwindsor, which is worth exploring. It is claimed to be part of the Hard or Harrow Way, a pre-Roman track, which crosses England from Kent to Axmouth. Just above Beaminster it runs over the top of a road tunnel on the main Beaminster–Crewkerne road, and thus the first British road crosses the peak in development of the mail coach age when Beaminster tunnel was made.

Looking down on Beaminster from this spot it is possible to see how the new building estates are separate from the old town. It is a familiar pattern but not often is it possible to get an almost aerial view of a settlement. From this place the church tower dominates the scene, as it usually does in small communities, but there is one jarring addition to the view. The former milk factory chimney would pass unnoticed among other factory chimneys, but Beaminster's industries were all based on water power. Without any doubt that chimney is ugly, and it is entirely beside the point to say that the prosperity of the town and the surrounding district depended largely on milk. To my personal knowledge the inhabitants of the town and the owners of the factory have been writing letters to *The Western Gazette* on this subject for fifty years, without the slightest result.

Of Beaminster's satellite villages I have mentioned Broadwindsor and Netherbury, without stating that this is famous country for cider-making. At Netherbury the natural advantages of the soil have been brought up-to-date in a wholly admirable way. There is no great cider factory here, but at least two farmers have sought advice from the National Fruit and Cider Institute, and now make farm cider at home by the best methods.

Nearby, on the Bridport–Beaminster road is the hamlet of Melplash which is part of Netherbury parish. The Victorian–Norman church adjoins the school, and then comes the pub. The school has now been closed, which spoils the ancient joke that here we have Salvation, Education and Damnation side by side.

Another village within two miles of the town is Stoke Abbot. This is a beautiful place of deep lanes, orchards and old houses, with a church of quiet charm. The hills crowd round it and the hills themselves are as widely different in shape as the houses in the village. Whaddon Hill is steep-sided and limestone, with a flat top. Beyond it, across the fields, is a round knoll which used to be called Rifle Pits, and in the other direction towards Broadwindsor is Lewesdon. This is a noble place, crowned with trees, and only slightly lower than the bare top of its neighbour Pilsdon Pen, which at 909 feet is the highest hill in Dorset. Pilsdon is capped by ancient earthworks. An old saying seems to imply that Lewesdon and Pilsdon are much alike—"As much akin as Lewesdon Hill and Pilsdon Pen". Personally I think this is meant to stress the differences between kinsmen, for these hills are utterly different. Lewesdon is wooded and Pilsdon quite bare. Lewesdon's shape is rounded and roughly conical. Pilsdon rises like a cliff from the Vale, and then has a long

level tip which drops gently towards Somerset. They are not alike
in any particular except in being two pleasant hills which are land-
marks for half the county.

It may seem strange that in writing of the villages in this district
I should continually return to Beaminster. Actually there is a good
reason. The hills here are in such chaos that sometimes the roads
between villages are very bad. All ways lead to Beaminster but
it is not easy to get from, say, Stoke Abbot to Netherbury, although
they are only two miles apart. I do not think there is any metalled
road between them. Much of my memories of this district are of
schoolboy rambles across country, which may well be forbidden
in these more crowded days. From Melplash, for instance, just after
passing the beautiful old manor house, there is a lane on the other
side of the road which climbs to the top of South Warren Hill.
There is a story that plague victims were taken along this lane and
trees planted over their grave so that the soil should not be disturbed
for hundreds of years. In my youth it used to be possible to get
across the limestone ridge to Mapperton Farm, and from there the
possibilities were endless. There was Loscombe, which was certainly
a combe and very definitely lost. From there an exceedingly narrow
and very muddy lane went to Poorton, where the land in the bottom
is much better than the name implies. From here other lanes went
over the hill to Powerstock, sheltering under the mighty ramparts
of Eggardon Hill. A gracious village of gardens and orchards set in
a chaos of lanes running through sandstone cliffs. Or from Mapperton Farm one could turn back to Mapperton village and the loveliest
manor house in Dorset.

In a sense there is no village of Mapperton. Mapperton Farm is
nearly a mile south-west of the church and Marsh Farm half a mile
north. There is a lovely little church at the end of the drive, immediately next to the gem of a manor. The few cottages nearby were
obviously erected for the squire's servants. The house is of two
storeys only, with dormer windows in the roof, and is built of a
yellow stone which is golden in sunlight. It dates from the reign
of Henry VIII and is a perfect example of domestic building in an
age which had abandoned the idea of a house being a castle. Unlike
Melplash Court it never degenerated to being a farm house, and
therefore escaped strange adventures of restoration as a manor.

All these delightful places can be reached by road—even Loscombe—but I am glad I found them first down footpaths and lanes.

I have included Powerstock in the Beaminster villages, but it was on a branch railway line to Bridport which had certainly led to a change of allegiance in the past hundred years. This village and neighbouring Loders certainly look towards Bridport as "town". Loders has more than its share of soil variations but most of them are good soils. The result is a village of fertile fields but with an amazing difference in levels. Some of the lanes were certainly pack-horse trails and are too steep for wheeled traffic. The church is beautiful and has a curious small chamber over the porch which was a priest's room. The provision of such a room has a connection with the history of the village. Henry I gave the manor to the earl of Devon who came from Caen. The Abbey of St. Marie of Monte-bourg in the Cotentin was in another lordship of the earl, and the abbey was in financial difficulties. So the earl gave it to the manors of Loders, of Axmouth in Devon, and of Wick in the Isle of Wight. To administer this property the abbot of Montebourg established a Priory at Loders in 1130, or possibly earlier. At this time it was not at all unusual for Norman nobles and French religious houses to have estates in both countries, but it led to endless trouble in the following centuries when England and France were often at war. The English king would forbid dues being paid to mother monasteries in France, and collect them himself. Then when peace came the French abbot would demand not only current tribute but the back money. In 1414 Henry V dissolved all foreign monasteries and Loders priory ceased to exist as a religious house. Whilst Loders was still owned by the priory there was the difficulty of caring for the needs of the villagers by foreign monks. To get over this they allotted a small portion of their tithes for the support of a native priest whom they called their vicar. He was a single man, of course, and the priest room over the church porch gave him a comfortable lodging.

I am indebted for this summarised bit of history to a booklet by the late Sir Edward Le Breton who owned the priory build-ings. The church is much as it was in the old days, but Loders Court retains little of the original structure except for one wall thirteen feet thick. It was turned into a Georgian manor house in 1799.

Upstream from Loders is Askerswell. This is partly a chalk village and it ends on the eastward side in a typical chalk cul-de-sac in the hills. To the north it is dominated by Eggardon Hill. Near the foot

of the hill but still well above the old church is an ancient inn which
has been "restored and enlarged" recently with much greater success
than Victorian church restorers achieved. From this inn it is possible
to see many of the roads and lanes from the coast at Swyre, and
this probably accounts for the unofficial name which has always been
"Spyway". The official sign was "Three Horse Shoes". There is very
little doubt that this was once a centre for the smuggling trade. A
mile south of Askerswell the traffic is endless on the Dorchester–
Exeter road, but in the village the principal influx of visitors will
be people looking for Spyway. It is one of the growing number of
secluded English inns which specialise in good food.

The town of Bridport might possibly have been included in the
chapter on the Dorset coast, but it is two miles from the sea. It has
its port of West Bay, but from the centre of the town every view
is of encircling hills. In the best possible meaning of the word Bridport has always been an industrial town, and its industries always
had a connection with the countryside and the sea. The name of
Bridport is known literally all over the world for nets. It was a town
in Saxon times and had its first Charter from Henry III. By the
time of the first Elizabeth it was claimed that all the queen's ships
were rigged with Bridport ropes. Flax and hempen lines were once
made from materials grown in the surrounding fields, but this has
not been the case for many years, and synthetic nylon has now joined
the list of materials used in the old trade. Once many nets were
made at home. This is now confined to small orders of unusual shape
which do not justify new settings for machines. In the town factories
it is possible to see every type of net from lacy-looking sardine nets,
to immensely strong nets for sharks.

The trade for cordage, twine, ropes and nets has always been a
skilled job, and always with a steady demand. Bridport has not had
any industrial revolution. It has not blasted the countryside, and it
has escaped the worst depressions. Perhaps this accounts for the fact
that it has always been famous for good food and drink.

The main street running east and west is very wide and has very
wide pavements. This is said to be connected with the old rope walks
which needed plenty of room. From the centre of the town, by the
Georgian Town Hall, the hilly fields seem very near. One hill to
the westward has the curious conical shape of the sandstone, and is
surmounted by an exceedingly unnatural-looking clump of trees.
These trees are not old, but they are suffering from exposure and

they have dwindled in my lifetime. The usual story is told that this hill, remote from the town, was used to bury plague victims, and the trees planted to stop disturbing the soil. It may be true of some past trees but not of the present set. I believe their presence is due to the fact that the owner of Symondsbury had an old print showing the hill crowned with a tuft of trees. In his time—some seventy years ago—it was bare, so he replanted it. This sounds highly reasonable.

Most of Bridport's main street is not older than Georgian, but it has the charm of no two houses being alike. It has escaped the worst ravages of the multiple stores, possibly because it was considered just too small for their operations. There are much older buildings in the wide street which runs south to the sea. Here. is the parish church, which dates from the fourteenth century and, like Loders, has a priest room, in this case over the south porch. This building fits the character of the town. It is solid, prosperous but not pretentious.

The remainder of West Dorset, apart from the coast, has a more simple pattern than the tumbled Beaminster-Bridport country. There is one isolated parish jutting into Devon, but the centre of this area is Marshwood Vale. The Vale itself is a basin of blue impervious clay of Lower Lias. It is surrounded on every side by steep hills, except where the tiny Char river winds to the sea. The steeper hills are capped with greensand rock, as at Pilsdon, which is reminiscent of the shape of the land at Shaftesbury. Other hills are of Middle and Upper Lias, giving fertile soils, with small farms clustering along the slopes above the wet bottom of the Vale. Marshwood Vale is a wonderful example of the way our forefathers avoided settlements on impervious clay. There are isolated farms in the Vale, some of which suffer from lack of water. Although a horse can be bogged down after hounds in crossing some pastures in winter, this is only surface wet. There is often no underground supply of pure well water, and wells are frequently tainted with unpleasant tasting natural salts. All churches are on the edge of the clay. Pilsdon is right at the foot of the hills, Marshwood right on top, whilst Bettiscombe is on the lower slopes. The only inn in the true Vale is in the centre, where a maze of lanes meet. Here at Shave Cross it is usual to find frustrated motorists who have been unable to discover a way out. All directions to farms in the Vale start with the words "Go to Shave Cross and enquire at the inn". This is excellent advice.

Unfortunately having found Cutty Stubbs, or Mandeville Stoke, or Bluntshay, the only instructions for getting home start in the same way—"Go to Shave Cross."

Of the names on a map inside the ring of hills, Broad Oak sounds as if it might be a village, but it is no more than a few houses on the way from Dottery to Shave Cross, with half a dozen farms down side lanes. The Oak, on a "T" road, which presumably gave the place its name, has been dying for thirty years, but still had leaves on one branch when I last saw it. On its trunk was an advertisement for Bingo. Soon it must die and the place lose some of its meaning. No one will replant because the road is due for widening. Already this has happened on the ridge just out of the Vale where the trees at Four Ashes have been swept from the cross-road.

Pilsdon on the floor of the Vale is supplied with drinking water from the ridge. It grows the earliest of wild daffodils, and has a tiny church and a manor house. The manor is no longer a private dwelling and there is no village in the proper sense of the word. Bettiscombe church is larger and the manor is the home of a local land-owning family, but once more there is no collection of shops with an inn or two to mark a community centre.

Marshwood is right out of its Vale, with a singularly ugly Victorian church on the skyline and a long straggle of undistinguished houses along the ridge. The redeeming feature is an inn on a five-course way with a grand view. It has the pleasant name of Birdsmoorgate.

The nearest thing to a real village in the Vale is Whitchurch Canonicorum, but it is only partially on the solid blue clay. Much of the village is on the steep hillsides bordering the Char brook. The name arises from the fact that the tithes were divided between the canons of Salisbury and Wells. The church is wonderful, with several Norman arches and early English work of a quality to humble modern visitors. In my youth many superstitions lingered in this remote valley, even under the shadow of this glorious church. Many were of white magic and concerned with charms for curing humans and animals. A few came from darker beliefs in witchcraft and the evil eye. In bright sunny weather this is an amazingly beautiful district. It is a different story after months of hopeless winter rain. Step off the modern tarred road for a few yards and you can guess what these lanes were like as recently as my boyhood. Impassable did not merely mean difficult. The little farms across the fields were cut off in desperate poverty and loneliness, with the sad old gods hemming them in.

The neighbouring village of Wootton Fitzpaine has always seemed much more civilised. It is not in the Vale at all but on Middle Lias, or Greensand, which gives drier land and good water. It has had an unchanged squire of the best type ever since I can remember and the farmers have always been more prosperous than most. This does not mean huge capitalistic enterprises, but working farmers who could still send their sons to the local grammar schools even in bad times. When I was last there the village had no pub, but a licensed club, which is an excellent idea for the visitor who becomes a guest.

Beyond Wootton is one of the few places in Dorset I have never visited, except to look down on it from the surrounding hills. Monkton Wyld is a hamlet with a small modern church, and it is entirely surrounded by steep wooded hillsides. Recently a good deal of felling has been done which gives a certain appearance of desolation. A lot of replanting has taken place so that now new trees clothe the hill sides.

For the last village in Dorset we must go back along the ridge to the west of the Vale and travel in Devon for a few miles. The highest hill on this ridge is Lambert's Castle which is crowned with a large hill fort. This used to be the scene of horse racing, not under the control of the Jockey Club or any other authority. What happened at Lambert's Castle races seems to be nobody's business.

Turning north at Birdsmoorgate the village of Thorncombe juts out into Devon. Once it was part of Devon, as witness the inscription on a memorial in the church to "Sir Thomas Brook, 1419, and his wife, 1437, of Thorncombe in the County of Devon". It is indeed reminiscent of Devon in that the village is built on a very steep hillside with springs gushing out by the road. The lanes are narrow in the Devon fashion and Axminster is the main market town. For shopping, however, Chard in Somerset is more likely to be visited. Yet in some ways Thorncombe is stubbornly Dorset, with its own extremely loyal branch of the Dorset Farmers' Union.

The name would seem to be associated with the holy thorn of Glastonbury, of which several specimens exist in the village. These may have some connection with nearby Forde Abbey which is on the River Axe and right on the county border. It was founded in 1148 and greatly improved just before the Dissolution. Very happily

The sea is beyond the Chesil
Beach across the Fleet and
Portland is on the horizon

the new work early in the 1500s was not destroyed when the building passed into private hands, indeed the chapel is much older and so are most of the outer walls. Even the interior alterations to change a monastic building into a mansion are superb in their own right. Inigo Jones was responsible for the alteration in Stuart times and most of his work survives unchanged. This is probably the best example of domestic monastic building surviving in England. It is still in private hands as a dwelling, and may be visited on the usual terms for "stately homes". All West Dorset is lovely and this last outpost is the most wonderful building in the most delightful setting in all England.

Old waterfront and harbour, Weymouth

IX

THE COAST

THE coast of Devon from Exmouth eastward is colourful and at times spectacular. As the main road from Seaton approaches the Dorset border, however, there is a fairly dull patch. The sea is out of sight and the highway runs through poorish upland country of no great distinction. Then, suddenly, it turns a corner above Lyme Regis to the best sea view in England. The little town is far below—actually only 500 feet below, but this is a big drop for a main road in half a mile. Straight ahead is the most wonderful coastline, stretching for twenty miles to Portland Bill. The great cliffs are broken by half a dozen little coombes, and no two cliffs are of the same colour. The highest of them all, 617 feet, is Golden Cap, and in the sunlight its cap is bright gold. Nearer the town of Lyme, and just east of it, the cliffs are in layers like chocolate cake. The sinister part of this is the blue, almost black clay of the Lower Lias. This is the formation which gave the wet land of Marshwood. It is quite impervious to water, and when it occurs in a cliff the other strata are almost sure to slip. Some of the houses in Lyme have suffered from earth movement, and there are a few on the front which are distinctly out of true. On a larger scale the cliffs to the eastward have slipped on many occasions. The present main road now goes due north before attempting to return to the coast at Charmouth. On my first motor-cycle, in 1924, I remember following a completely different route near the cliff edge. I believe it is possible to walk the old road still, but some of it is hanging in fragments and could not be used by a car.

Lyme's one river is a fast flowing brook which cannot be much more than a mile long. Its length is fixed by the distance to the encircling hills in which there is no break. Lyme has the sea to the south, the hills come to the very edge of it, and these hills vary from steep, to very steep, to precipices. The main road comes down a one in five gradient from Devon to the edge of the sea and immediately takes a sharp turn to climb up an equally steep hill out of the town. The river runs through old houses which overhang it in places, and finally tunnels beneath houses to the sea. In one spot the river bed is a road along which I have driven a car. This is a fascinating part of the town which brings memories of all the stories one has ever heard of press gangs and pirates.

This beautiful and ancient borough owes its first charter to Edward I but long before this it had a Dorset connection. The Saxon abbots of Sherborne had the right of salt-boiling on a piece of land near the stream. The patronage of Edward I led to the name Regis, and also to the attempt to make Lyme a harbour. There was no natural shelter on this important part of the south coast from Weymouth to Torbay. The estuaries at Axmouth, Exmouth and Teignmouth were indifferent harbours in bad weather. Thus there was good reason in the days of sail for trying to make an artificial haven. The result was the Cobb, a massive sea wall which also acts as a jetty. In those far off days no one could have known that a wall jutting out from a naturally unbroken cliff would lead to curious swirling of the tides. Not only was the wall exposed to the occasional hurricane, but it led to the deposit of sand and gravel inside the haven it was designed to form. Goodness knows how often Lyme's Cobb has been breached by the sea, but it has been stubbornly repaired. The town sent two ships against the Armada but it is doubtful if these small craft could now shelter in the silted harbour. This is a place for summer yachtsmen and lobster fishermen. As a port it has no future, but no one could imagine a more pleasant town in which to live, or in which to spend a relaxed holiday.

Perhaps Lyme's greatest moment in history was when the Duke of Monmouth landed there in his attempt to wrest the throne of England from James II. Apparently that attempt got nearer to success than many historians suggest. It certainly started well in Lyme, where volunteers flocked in, and the duke left the town with 2,000 infantry and 3,000 mounted men.

The holiday boatmen of Lyme always have a few fossils in their pockets to offer visitors, sometimes under the description of lucky charms. The Blue Lias Clay is very rich in such things, and not all of vest pocket size. In 1811, presumably after one of Lyme's many cliff slips, a local girl found the first known remains of an ichthyosaurus. This prehistoric creature was accepted at the South Kensington

History Museum, and the girl qualified for a window in Lyme Regis church.

Unlike Lyme the next break in the cliffs has a stream which winds for miles inland and drains the whole of Marshwood Vale. Yet Charmouth has very little to do with its river. Most of the village lines the steep hill on the way to Lyme. From this street there is a wonderful impression of the sudden hills and deep valleys of the coast and of Marshwood. Building has naturally increased on the few twisting lanes in the quarter mile south to the sea, but the beach itself is still reasonably free from "development". There is no harbour, no sand, and for some months of the year it is possible to be alone with the restless sea and the ever-moving pebbles.

Charmouth village has a few pleasant old houses, and the setting is superb, but on the whole no one would visit it for its buildings. Just inland the same might be said of the village of Catherston Leweston. Here the Bullen family reigned until recently, and they did much to save the coast and skyline from indiscriminate building, probably to their own considerable financial loss. It is to be hoped that Town and Country Planning will now do as good a job. For preservation I have more faith in individual land owners than committees.

The main road eastward from Charmouth is lovely enough, but to see the coast properly it is essential to take a lane on the right at the very bottom of the valley. This is quite passable for cars and climbs to the top of a hill nearly 500 feet high. At the top the road ceases, but a right of way goes on across grassy downs. Far below on the right there is a very lonely farm called Westhay. Beyond this the cliffs are low and there are places where it is possible to reach the edge of the sea. This lonely land is part of the lost village of Stanton St. Gabriel. Further eastward in this National Trust Golden Cap Estate are the remains of Stanton St. Gabriel church. Rather strangely, although the old church has been derelict for more than a century, and there is no sign of a village near it, there is an extensive new settlement inland along the main road. This is called Morcombelake and originated as a place of retirement for the elderly in the first quarter of this century. It has an inn, and a small factory making a well-known biscuit called Dorset Knobs. Morcombelake is mainly under the shoulder of Hardown Hill which is nearly 700 feet high. The situation gives shelter from the north and pleasant sea views southward. It is a small "development", and not much of an eyesore. As long as it is not allowed to sprawl it will do little harm, apart from narrowing a very busy highway.

The next gap in the cliffs houses Chideock—forget the "e" in pronouncing the name. The setting here is rather like Lyme Regis in that the circle of hills around the village is unbroken. The little stream rises just behind the village and cuts across the beach to the sea. There is not even a motor road through the hills to the north; one does start hopefully northward just past Chideock Manor but dies soon after the settlement at North Chideock. Many of the houses line the main road hillside much as at Charmouth, but there are more old cottages and less Victorian holiday buildings. Here again the countryside has been saved to a large extent by an old land-owning family, the Welds. They are a Catholic family and have already been mentioned in connection with Bindon Abbey at Wool.

The road from the village to the coast is about half a mile long and at its end the last house on the beach is an inn. The handful of houses on this road carry the rather grand name of Seatown, but there is happily nothing resembling a town. The flat beach cannot be more than a few hundred yards long. Westward is the cliff of Golden Cap, and eastward Doghouse Hill and Thorncombe Beacon are almost equally high. These hills and the whole of the coast from east of Charmouth to Eype Mouth, apart from Seatown, are owned by the National Trust.

East of Chideock, beyond Thorncombe Beacon, a very narrow valley takes a trickle of fresh water to the sea. Eype Mouth must be amongst the smallest beaches in England to have its own motor road winding down a combe to the sea. I am not sure if Eype is a civil parish; it has a church and an hotel so may well be classed as a village. The hotel has joined the modern trend of specialising in good food and attracting an all-the-year-motoring trade for meals. There is room for a book on "eating out" by the English, and its influence not only on country pubs but on what were once seasonal holiday hotels.

East of Eype Mouth the cliffs are lower than the giants of Lyme, Charmouth and Chideock. West Cliff at West Bay, the port of Bridport, is only about 100 feet high. In my youth part of the cliff was of yellow sandstone but all this portion has slipped into the sea so the cliff edge must be yards further inland than it was in

1914. This must cause some concern to the dwellers in the housing estate, sheltering on the flank of West Cliff. These homes were built mainly between the wars in the 1919–30 period at a time when cars were beginning to make it possible to live out of town. Before then West Bay consisted of a few old houses and cottages connected with the sea. In Victorian times there had been a ship-building yard, and there was a trade in selling shingle from the beach until quite recently. The harbour could never have been profitable. Like Lyme's Cobb it is wholly artificial, but instead of one giant curving wall it has two piers sticking out into the sea. The entrance between these piers is very narrow and impossible of approach in even a moderate sea. The biggest craft the harbour could accommodate would be the sort of paddle pleasure steamers which used to be a feature of the seaside of my youth.

The River Brit flows between the piers to the sea, and has to be controlled by hatches to make sure that river silt shall be swept straight through and not dropped in the harbour. In addition there is the problem we met at Lyme whereby any obstruction in the flow of the tide must cause swirling and the deposit of sand or shingle. Here the coast is naturally more smooth and unobstructed than at Lyme, so that these utterly irrelevant piers must be even more annoying to the ocean. West Bay harbour has a bar just off its mouth. The piers have been smashed by gales on many occasions, including several within middle-aged memory. I can remember when a substantial restaurant was entirely removed from the angle between the west pier and the esplanade. The cost must have run into tens of thousands of pounds. At first sight one wonders why the citizens of Bridport should attempt to maintain a wholly un-economic harbour under impossible conditions. Certainly no port dues or mooring charges for yachts can ever show a profit. The trouble is that having inherited this picturesque folly from the Middle Ages it is more and more impossible every year to get rid of it. There are houses at West Bay to be protected. There is a new church and three hotels. One way to the housing estate on the West Cliff already mentioned is along the quayside. In the shelter of the piers to the east there is a most amazing row of houses, four storeys high, which looks as if it was the beginning of a new Victorian town. It is a pleasant terrace and would have been almost at home on Brighton front, but has nothing whatever to do with Dorset. Then there is a very new caravan park only just above sea level, on the banks of the river. If the piers were allowed to remain smashed it must be remembered that the river still has to get out or it will flood the whole area. In addition the rich meadows stretching into the heart of Bridport would be liable to flooding on every high tide. This harbour is now part of coast protection and has to be maintained whatever the cost. Personally I find this a completely satisfactory state of affairs—not being a Bridport ratepayer—since West Bay is utterly different from every other English port.

The East Cliff is a delightful yellow wall of sandstone which runs at an even height to the next break at Burton Bradstock. Here the Bride river breaks through, which rises at Bridehead and runs down through Long Bredy and Litton Cheney. The mouth of the stream is a caravan camp but the cleft through the cliffs is so narrow that the camp is almost hidden. Every now and then high tides with a gale behind them will flood Burton Bradstock, which hides behind the coast ridge and is invisible from the sea. A friend of mine lives in the old manor farm house only feet above sea level. All the doors are fitted with sliding hatches, rather like those sometimes seen on roadside cottage doors to stop children from straying into the street. Here, however, the object is to keep the water out rather than to keep children in. It could not work if the water was up for long because it would soak under the old walls, but a tide may only be a danger for a few hours. Burton also has a small beach with a car park just out of the village on the east. Here one becomes conscious of the utterly unbroken nature of this coast which was disguised at West Bay by the man-made harbour. This is part of the Chesil Bank which runs without the shadow of a break to the point of Portland Bill.

East of Burton Bradstock one road runs up the Bride Valley and the other skirts the coast over the coastal ridge. The best way to follow this road is westward into the sunset from the top of Abbotsbury Hill. From here the great cliffs of the Bridport-Lyme Regis region merge with the Devon coast as far as Start Point. There are amazing colours, curious lights and shadows, veils of mist which leave Golden Cap floating insubstantial as a dream island. In a thousand journeys you will never see this land twice the same. It is Merlin's magic earth, a precious stone, the walls of England and the fields of home. On our present occasion, though, travelling eastward, it is easier to look about and chat in safety.

This coastal strip has a strange mixed geology, but always on the south is the smooth line of the Chesil Bank, edged with foam. The road is always in sight of the sea but for eight miles from Burton it climbs fairly steadily and runs parallel with the sea about 600 yards inland. Two old villages are on or just off this road. In the sensible fashion of our fathers they are both hidden away from the sea gales in little folds of the hills. Swyre comes first and then Puncknowle—pronounced Punnell.

Swyre has a modern addition which seeks the coast. West Bexington was a 1919-39 development which has had a reasonably happy ending. It had a charming old farm house near the coast, and another further along with the frightening name of Labour-in-Vain. Both were on an untarred road and much of their land had gone derelict. It was good wheat land in the Crimean War, but was difficult to cultivate and many old drains were choked. Between the wars a swimming pool was built just behind the Chesil beach. This is now dry. At the same time many small houses were erected, or building plots sold. In the depression some of the new owners found themselves unable to keep up payments they had undertaken very optimistically. For years the only road was a long string of potholes and the water supply was indifferent. There seemed reason to fear that West Bexington would develop into the sort of new slum which was not uncommon before the days of Planning and Control. Fortunately this did not happen. No great number of houses were built, the site by the open sea was superb, although windy, and the surviving new-comers have made their houses fit into the country-side. I liked this desolate stretch of almost derelict land in its old state, but neighbouring fields have been changed almost as much in being reclaimed for farming. It would be churlish to suggest that a dozen little houses have had any great influence on the view from the coast road.

Old Swyre has a rebuilt modern pub on the coast road, but otherwise hides down a by-way. There are old stone cottages and a good farm house, but neighbouring Puncknowle is more interesting, although progress has taken away one of its attractions. In the middle of the village there was a grotto, containing a pipe from which clear water gushed perpetually. This is now dry and has been replaced by taps in the village houses, no doubt to the delight of the inhabitants.

I refuse to look up Puncknowle in any reference book of place names. If it does not mean Puck's Knoll then it should, because this is enchanted land. Twenty years ago there were old ladies here who had often seen fairies. They told me so. The village shelters behind a curious circular hill called the Knoll, nearly 600 feet above the nearby sea. On the top of this knoll a prehistoric grave was found in the last war. Tumuli line the coastal ridge and very near is the ancient castle, the hill fort above Abbotsbury. Punnell men know the old songs. They are an independent lot, and they have a habit of falling out with the lord of the manor.

Due north, up a narrow road, is a village within sight of the sea which should have come in the chalk chapter. Chilcombe is worth a visit if only because of its absolute isolation. There is the farm house, now in private ownership, the partly Norman church and two cottages.

Back on the coast road the village of Abbotsbury is possibly the most interesting in Dorset. It has had two owners only in a thousand years, the abbey and the Fox Strangways family, the earls of Ilchester. In 1964 the title passed out of the direct male line, and the property was inherited by the daughter of the late earl. This has not broken with the old traditions. For instance, the Strangways have maintained the Swannery in the lagoon behind the Chesil which used to belong to the abbot. They have also kept up the duck "decoys" which are fairly well known in Norfolk but not in Dorset. Ducks are enticed into curving "pipes" of netting which narrow into a trap. The abbot used them as a source of winter meat, but they are now employed as a means of ringing wild fowl to find out more of their journeyings. Fred Lexster was in charge of the Swannery and the decoys, a very knowledgeable naturalist with a gift of speech, and his family have been swanherds for generations. John Fair took over in 1980.

Near the Swannery are reed beds which are regularly irrigated and cut for thatching. This is unusual in Dorset and it may account for the way thatching has persisted in the cottages of the village. With occasional ridging reed will last for a century against the twenty years of straw thatch. The great tithe barn at Abbotsbury is reed-thatched, and this explains its preservation.

The village consists of little more than one long street of stone houses, many of which have fragments of stone from the abbey built into their walls. It is only too easy to imagine how this wonderful site might have been "developed". The hills shelter the

village on every side and there is a patch of limestone soil which
will grow vegetables as early as Penzance. A sub-tropical garden
has been laid out near the sea and can be visited on most days in
summer. This garden is on the road which runs down to the
beach. Opposite is what was obviously the wall round another garden, which is above the Chesil bank with an unbroken view from
Portland to Start Point. In my youth a large house was built in
this garden for one of the Ilchesters. Unfortunately it could not be
made weather-proof and was never inhabited. The panelling and
fireplaces were removed, and the whole house sold as building
material. Very unfortunate for the family, but a rough justice
when you remember how their ancestors used the abbey as a stone
quarry.

From a distance the most outstanding feature of Abbotsbury is
St. Catherine's Chapel, set on a rounded hill between the village
and the sea. There is no road to the chapel for vehicles and presumably the stone for the building was quarried on the spot from
the Corallian Limestone on which it stands. Like many chapels to
St. Catherine this one is associated with sailors. It must have been
a day mark for shipping and probably carried a beacon light. St. Catherine was also approached by spinsters. The Dorset dialect jingle
asks for a husband, and finishes by hoping for a good one, but
anyone better than never a one. "Arn-a-one's better than Narn-a-
one."

Abbotsbury beach has a reasonable road behind it which allows
motorists to find free parking for several miles along the beach,
and in dry weather I have gone as far west as Bexington. The bathing here is not safe for children or for non-swimmers; there is a
very steep slope and the shifting pebbles make it easy to fall. For
swimmers it is pleasant to be able to jump into deep water without
wading more than two steps. Waves crash on the ridge in a highly
spectacular manner, and there is sometimes a dangerous undertow,
but usually it is possible to dive out through the waves. Coming in
again needs a little experience in riding the breakers, but there is only
danger when conditions are such that only a fool would dream of
bathing. This is quite a different set of conditions from those on the
north Cornwall coast where the sea is highly dangerous at certain
states of the tide without appearing to be so. Abbotsbury beach looks
worse than it is.

The main attraction for visitors to the beach is the fishing. Abbotsbury mackerel have always been famous, and at one time a large proportion of the farm workers in the village went fishing on summer evenings. Indeed agricultural work was abandoned at any time of the day if word came from the beach that fish were shoaling close inshore. The method used is the familiar seine net. A boat is rowed in a semicircle several hundred yards from the shore and the net thrown out. Some three or four men on each end of the net then haul it in laboriously. It takes about fifteen minutes for each shot and almost anything can happen. I have seen thousands caught in one go, and left covered with sacking on the pebbles whilst the net was repacked and the boat relaunched with all possible speed. A couple of hundred mackerel seems to justify another immediate effort, but frequently there is nothing, or a few jellyfish. I have seen a seal tear huge holes through a net and once a lordly salmon be hauled in. These salmon belong to the lord of the manor, a right inherited from the abbot, but "red mackerel" is not unknown on Abbotsbury tea tables.

Evening on this beach is never twice the same. It may be that the line of foam stretches from Portland to Devon, with a lurid sky and a wind which it is hard to face. It can be a quiet misty sunset with the little waves moving the pebbles very gently. In summer the terns—sea swallows—swoop down when the nets come in, and will catch any small fish you care to toss in the air. In the twilight the fishermen carry half-bushel baskets of fish over the ridge to the waiting lorries. Those bowed plodding figures, crossing the skyline with their harvest, have not changed in a thousand years. Gulls drift across the face of the moon over the sea, or it may be two swans break the silence with the swish of their wings. You can see a triangle of duck, or perhaps as many as a dozen cormorants making for home. In tempest or in calm it is very easy to be utterly alone after dark, which is strange on a beach freely available for cars. The reason is that there are no hotels, no teashops, no camping, no ice-creams, but there is now a public lavatory. Long may the Ilchester tradition remain.

The brackish lagoon—the Fleet—behind the beach stretches to Portland but the Ilchesters appear to have rights over all of it. Fishermen cross to the beach from inland villages such as Langton Herring or from the region round the Moonfleet Hotel, but I do not remember any motor-boats or even sailing craft. The Abbotsbury end of the ridge carries a Ternery, which is strictly protected, but the solitude is preserved more by that eight miles of pebble ridge than by notice boards. None the less the quiet here could have been unintentionally destroyed without the long ownership of one family. For instance the Moonfleet Hotel could rightly claim to be doing no damage if they had a few motor-boats in the Fleet, and, possibly, some bathing huts on the Chesil. Yet the eerie loneliness which is the south of the Chesil would be gone, and it would only be a matter of months for new hotels to be offering the same facilities. The fact that there is no coastal amusement fringe has left a large stretch of country south of the ridgeway from Abbotsbury to Preston almost undiscovered. The road to Weymouth from Abbotsbury runs through it, and for a while there was a railway line from Abbotsbury to Upwey crossing a narrow vale of Kimmeridge Clay. There is a road to the deserted Halt near Coryates, but some of the farms in the district take a bit of finding. Until the last war there were half a dozen gates across the road to Friar Waddon, and the way to Friar Waddon Dairy House was only for the adventurous. Corton Dairy House is equally isolated and, on the south side of the road, it is none too easy to find Rodden. On the outskirts of Weymouth Chickerell is a bleak village on a ridge which presents the worst of itself to the main road. There is little to be said for Chickerell unless you explore the footpaths southward to the East Fleet, or the farms inland towards Buckland Ripers.

The real country to seek between Abbotsbury and Weymouth is on the ridge from Abbotsbury Castle to White Nothe. Some can only be reached by footpaths but a car is useful for reaching starting points. The main road eastward goes inland to Portesham, which is a pleasant village, with an unfailing clear stream rushing through boulders by the side of its main street. This was the home of Thomas Masterman Hardy, Nelson's flag captain at Trafalgar, in whose arms the admiral is said to have died.

A road to Gorwell turns up the hill in Abbotsbury opposite the Ilchester Arms. The surface is good but in many places it is too narrow for cars to pass. This road gets quickly on the ridge, leaving Portesham far below, and provides wonderful hill and coastal views. There are by-ways to unknown farms in deep coombes. Some are on private roads which must be treated as footpaths, such as at Gorwell, or to the strange valley of the stones between Gorwell and Little Bredy. Eventually the narrow road along the ridge reaches Blackdown and the Hardy Monument.

This is one of the most famous places in Dorset as a spot from which amazing views can be obtained without getting out of a car. Westward the coast curves to Devon, with Lamberts Castle, Pilsdon and Lewesdon as ramparts inland on the Dorset border. Northward the whole of the rolling chalk country stretches away, fold after fold to Cranborne Chase. Eastward is all Purbeck, the great Heath, and a blue distance which might be the New Forest. Far below on the south is the pleasure town of Weymouth and the great fortress rock of Portland Bill.

There is a very rough track along the ridge from the Monument to the Dorchester–Weymouth road. I have driven a car along it, but possibly illegally, and it is certainly a journey which should be taken on foot. With a slightly lower pass to let the Weymouth–Wareham road through, the same ridge of chalk goes to White Nothe, Durdle Door and Lulworth. It should be explored, a bit at a time by the elderly, the whole of its length. There is no finer ridgeway in England

To reach the coast at Weymouth it is as well to take by-roads off the ridge through Bincombe. The main road through Upwey is a rather sad example of ribbon development. Even the clear springs near Upwey's little church have been "developed" as a Wishing Well. None the less for nine months of the year even this is a charming and quiet spot, set in the confusion of steep hills. Bincombe is one mile off the tourist route, and is completely agricultural although only four miles from Weymouth. This could only happen in Dorset. The farm houses, church and cottages are all under the shelter of the great curve of the ridgeway, here known as Bincombe Hill. This hill is of chalk, but the underlying rocks change so rapidly that limestone walls have been built instead of planting hedges. They sweep over the hill top, mainly as a division between farms rather than as fences for fields, and the only other thing to break the smooth skyline is a host of burial mounds.

Weymouth itself now has its border on the ridgeway, four miles inland. The sea front faces due east which is a disadvantage as far as attempting to turn it into a winter resort, but a great asset in summer. The beach is completely untroubled by westerly, south-westerly and southerly gales. These are the main cause of giant seas, and whilst they rage outside, the sea at Weymouth remains smooth and calm. The sandy beach has a gentle slope, and is perfectly safe for children and non-swimmers.

At one time there were two adjoining rival boroughs in this pleasant bay. Both Weymouth and Melcombe Regis sent members to Parliament although they shared the same harbour. The port was important in Roman times, and revived again after the Norman conquest. For seventy miles westward it was the only safe haven for sailing ships, and the same was true for twenty miles eastward. Today the port trade is by no means negligible as it deals with all the sea-borne passenger traffic to the Channel Islands, plus most of the vegetable and flower trade. The harbour part of the town, with an unfenced railway along the quayside is a fascinating place of narrow streets and innumerable taverns. The sea front is a noble curve of Georgian houses almost wholly concerned with the summer visitor trade. Weymouth owes the start of this side of her activity to George III. His Majesty's doctor had revolutionary ideas on cold water, and Weymouth is believed to be the first place where a British monarch took a sea bathe. Whilst he did so a brass band concealed in a bathing machine on wheels played "God Save the King". I remember those communal "machines", one for each sex, which were on railway lines, and consisted inside of a number of small cubicles. The more affluent could have an individual machine on wheels which was pulled out to sea by a horse, so that the modest could plunge into deep water without being spied upon from the beach. They all had a curious salty smell which I have never met anywhere else, but would recognise at once if I met it again.

Weymouth expressed its thanks to George III by erecting a statue to him at the top of the two principal shopping streets. It is described in a guide book as "unique both in size and design". This is the most tactful thing which could ever be said about a most monstrous piece of work. The town also carved a figure representing the king on a white horse on the hillside at Osmington. The white horse is not old, in fact it was carved after the king's first bathing visit, and the addition of the rider was not a happy afterthought since he is trotting away from Weymouth.

South of Weymouth a short bridge crosses the Fleet running behind the Chesil Beach to Abbotsbury. At this point the Chesil curves a little towards the south and the road which leads to Portland run straight for nearly a mile in the shelter of its eastern side. Over this mile there is no tree, no bush and no hollow in the ground. There is nothing but the windswept road, and the utterly bare Chesil bank It is not difficult to block this only way out of Portland, and this presumably adds to the security of the grim convict prison and Borstal.

The first impression of Portland is of a very hard and bleak place. From a distance it looks like pictures of the rock of Gibraltar, since the cliffs on the north are nearly 500 feet high, and were once a fortress. The Verne always used to be garrisoned by a battalion of infantry in my youth, yet nothing could be seen of their presence from outside. The barrack square and living quarters were surrounded by high mounds, and approached across moats and through tunnels in the rock. In Victorian times it must have been impregnable, but a death trap in the days of bombers. On the same level, and entirely without shelter from any wind is the Borstal Institution which was once the convict prison. In Victorian days the convicts built the great breakwater which encloses Portland harbour, one of the largest and safest naval bases in the world. Here the might of the British navy could be seen when it was the unchallenged ruler of the sea. Today it is still a naval base with a helicopter station, but the naval hospital has been switched to civilian use and there is talk of attempting to use the harbour for commerce. The railway to the mainland has now been taken up.

It would be a mistake to think, however, that the departure of the military and the sad shrinkage of the navy has been a death blow to Portland. In a way they came from outside and were not native to the island. The business of Portland is stone, of which it has an inexhaustible supply, and it is the best building stone in the world. The United Nations Building in New York came here for its stone, and the natives will still show you a hole in the ground from which they say St. Paul's was taken. Present quarrying and stone cutting is done with modern tools—I was shown a circular saw with diamonds as the cutting edge—but the old skills are as necessary as ever.

Unfortunately quarrying is a rather untidy business, especially when it has been practised for many centuries. There is useless rock to be moved from the surface and various forms of spoil. Frequently in the past it was got rid of by pushing it over the cliffs to form loose banks of boulders. As a result there is only one reasonably soft little bay, at Church Hope Cove, and I rather think this is the only place on the island with trees, although this may not be completely accurate. It is also the site of the castle built by William Rufus.

In spite of having the best building stone in the world Portland has not built much of beauty on the island. To my mind by far the best building is the church at Easton which was finished quite recently. Very seldom does modern Gothic recapture the lightness and elegance of the past, but this has been achieved at Easton.

For the rest, Portland is roughly pear-shaped, being about $1\frac{3}{4}$ miles across at the widest part and running $4\frac{1}{2}$ miles southward to a point at the Bill. All the northern cliffs are high but at the Bill they drop to only a dozen feet, and the general slope is fairly even from north to south. There are quarries nearly everywhere but in the centre and south some land is still cultivated. Before the war almost all of it was farmed on the medieval strip system in open fields, with only tiny stone-walled paddocks for animals. During the war the Dorset War Agricultural Executive Committee took over blocks of land and farmed it, with some damage to ancient boundary stones. Possession in many cases had to be taken by erecting notices on the land because the ownership was so intricate. Portland had never accepted the normal plan of land passing from father to eldest son. The custom was to divide it between the whole family, although one member might take on the actual farming. A one-acre strip in some cases had sixty-four owners and was cultivated by no one. The point was that farming a one-acre strip was quite unprofitable before the war, but at any moment the big quarrying company might move in, when the mineral rights on even one sixty-fourth of an acre would be worth something. I have no idea how the Government untangled the puzzle when the time came to hand back the land they had ploughed. The ancient Court Leet of the Royal Manor of Portland will probably have some problems for many years to come.

Back on the ridgeway, north of Weymouth and east of the railway tunnel, it is worth dropping off to find the coast at Osmington. There is a narrow road down from Came Wood to Sutton Poyntz and Preston which gives pleasant glimpses of the bay, although great fields packed with caravans do not improve the view. The village of Sutton Poyntz is still charming, with some extremely strong springs gushing out of the sheltering hills. Osmington village is well inland, and is a pleasant place with a fair proportion of suburban houses, but it has not been overwhelmed. The tripper attraction is to Osmington Mills where a narrow gorge cuts down to a rocky beach. It is a little difficult to understand why Osmington Mills

Pack Horse Bridge, Fifehead Neville
Bridge over the River Stour at
Sturminster Newton

should have been so popular for so long. Possibly it started because it was in comfortable horse-brake distance of Weymouth and gave a complete change. Instead of a sandy beach there was clambering over rocks and good shrimping where the tide flowed between boulders. The only other attraction is that the inn, within a stone's throw of the sea, has always made a speciality of lobster teas, from really fresh local lobsters.

The next break in the cliffs is at Ringstead Bay where at some stages of the tide there can be golden sands, and at others only beds of pebbles. There was a radar station here and a perfectly good road drops to the beach from the ridgeway. Apparently, however, it is still a private road although there is a G.P.O. pillar box on the beach and a dozen or so modern villas. A car-parking fee is charged during holiday season. The track along the ridge is tarred for a third of the way and passes between a farm and a duck pond, thereafter it is still a right of way but is rough and only passable in fine weather. Straight inland from White Nothe it meets another rough track coming south from Holworth Farm, and then continues east as a green track to a small group of houses on the top of White Nothe. Southwards towards Ringstead beach there are a few private roads to houses on the steep hillsides. There is too a footpath which leads to a curious little wooden chapel of St. Catherine, and then drops down the steep, tumbled, Burning Cliff where landslips have obviously taken place. The length of the cliffs from Ringstead to White Nothe is another National Trust acquisition brought about through the efforts of Enterprise Neptune.

The path from White Nothe to Durdle Door along the chalk ridge is very lonely and extremely beautiful. At one point there is a rounded chalk coombe going almost down to the sea where the cliffs are no more than twenty feet high. In my youth a gully in the cliff went down to the beach. It had a hairpin bend in the middle and was much too steep to climb except with the aid of a wire rope which fishermen, or possibly smugglers, had thoughtfully provided. Meade Falkner describes this smugglers' escape route in *Moonfleet*.

Lulworth Cove is the sort of harbour which a child artist might draw from the imagination after a first visit to the sea. It has everything a haven should have, but only on a scale for fishing boats, and it is strangely unreal. The entrance channel between high cliffs is very narrow which is just what a harbour entrance should be. The completely calm bay inside is perfectly circular and surrounded

Corfe Castle

by towering cliffs, with only one narrow path from inland which of course is bordered by a tiny stream. On fine winter days it is wholly lovely, but during the holiday season it should be avoided whether you like crowds or not. The very nature of the narrow coombe winding down to the bay means a physical limit to the number of cars which can be parked. Every available space has been utilised but there are days when it is no longer possible to get to Lulworth Cove through sheer pressure of crowds. Fortunately there has not been a great deal of "development" in the way of teashops —possibly not enough for some tastes—and out-of-season this beautiful place returns to quiet sanity.

The cliff walk eastward from Lulworth Cove is now closed before it drops to the tiny bay at Arish Mel. Before the war this little beach was almost unknown; it is now part of the military firing range and even more solitary. This is generally regarded as the beginning of the "Isle" of Purbeck, which is only an island if you accept the barren heaths between Arish Mel and Wareham as cutting off this corner of Dorset as effectively as the sea.

Inland from Arish Mel the village of East Lulworth has miraculously escaped the pressure of the battle range on one side and an Army Camp plus Lulworth Cove on the other. Once more the answer is probably long-continued private ownership. The Welds have held Lulworth since 1641, and although they could not entirely save Lulworth Cove and West Lulworth, they have kept East Lulworth almost untouched. The great stone castle in a wooded park was erected by a Weld, and is a curious mixture of castle and residence. It is square in shape with massive, battlemented towers on either corner, and its walls could probably have withstood the cannon of the seventeenth century. Nevertheless it was obviously meant to be lived in as a manor house, and it has no natural defence advantages such as the hill at Corfe. Unfortunately Lulworth Castle was completely gutted by fire in 1929, although from a distance the mighty walls look untouched, and it still gives the impression of a picturebook castle.

The road from East Lulworth over the great Purbeck Ridge is often open on Sundays, but it is fenced on each side with barbed wire and carries frequent notices that live ammunition may be in the fields. It is pleasant to be able to give credit to the men who had to fence this road in that they used real imagination. There is a car park on the peak of the ridge which makes it possible to view the promised land. It is something to be able to look down on the deserted church and farms of Tyneham, and to see Worbarrow Bay, which I remember as the best bathing on the Dorset coast. This valley is not quite derelict, because grazing animals have been allowed to use it. The army shoot from the north into the first ridge of Purbeck. The valley southward and the coastal ridge have only been cleared because some extremely badly aimed shells might go over the first ridge, a chance which seems very remote. The grazing keeps the abandoned farms fairly green, but they have probably not been fertilised, and there is no ploughing. Apart altogether from the barbed wire and the notices, it is easy to see where the range ends and the free village of Kimmeridge begins by the prosperous fertile colour of the fields.

Kimmeridge beach can be reached by a toll road and it is very popular in summer, although rocks make the bathing difficult. Here the mighty cliffs south of Tyneham suddenly give place to a much lower level. This is Kimmeridge Clay which weathers to blue-black and could not possibly form a cliff at all except that it is regularly interlayered with stone. During the ages the sea has washed away the clay but the stone layers have fallen like a natural breakwater, so that the waves now never reach the very vulnerable cliffs. In the actual bay of Kimmeridge the blue clay cliffs have been almost completely removed by the sea, leaving the floor of the bay paved with ledges of stone. At low water it is possible to play games of bowls with pebbles along these flat floors of rock.

There is the remains of a jetty and a few lines from a forgotten railway at Kimmeridge. Many attempts have been made to find an industrial use for the material in these curious clay cliffs. Alum was once extracted and glass was made some centuries ago. More recently a French company attempted to extract oil from the local shale. Unfortunately the oil contained much too much free sulphur and gave an abominable stink when burnt in lamps. Crude oil has actually been extracted since 1959 from wells at Kimmeridge and Wareham, fortunately without making the area into an industrial complex. In the mean time Kimmeridge is wholly rural and completely charming. There are old stone cottages with stone roofs in the Cotswold style, sheltering a mile from the sea under the hill. The houses by the sea are of Victorian coastguard type but there are very few of them.

The clay influences the coast for several miles further east of Kimmeridge, at first by stone ledges running out to sea and then, where the soft stuff has been washed away, another bay has been formed. Chapman's Pool has no houses by the shore and no carriageway to the beach. You must clamber down the last few hundred yards having paid a toll on a private road to get so far. The bathing is only fair, but the walk is enough to stop many people, so there is room to breathe here on the busiest August week-end. Immediately west of Chapman's Pool is Encombe House, the seat of the owners of this part of the coast. They are to be thanked for keeping Chapman's Pool unspoiled and can hardly be blamed for keeping strictly private the grounds of the house, called the Golden Valley. Treves, in his classic book, claims it was closed "owing to the atrocious conduct of trippers", who must have been horse-brake parties from Swanage. I saw it as a guest after giving a talk to a Women's Institute meeting at the great house. The reward was worth the price.

The roads to Encombe and to Chapman's Pool arise in the village of Kingston. This is on the ridge south of that central valley of Purbeck which I described earlier as the Weald of Sussex and Kent in miniature. There are two churches at Kingston quite close together, of which the older is by no means ruinous, and it is difficult to know why the modern one was needed. The village is small and one can only imagine some story of feud between lord and local priest. The new Victorian building is very ornate inside, but it is especially interesting in providing a lavish display of Purbeck marble, probably the last which was widely used in a church.

Kingston is also on the road to Worth Matravers and to the great headland of St. Aldhelm's Head. Like all sensible old seaside settlements Worth Matravers stays well away from the rush and noise and bluster of the sea. From the village pub you can look down the path to Winspit, a narrow cut in the cliffs where a tall ship was once lost in the days of sail, or follow a path by the radar station to Renscombe Farm and to the windswept cliffs of the Headland. Here a very low, solid Norman Chapel once carried a signal light for the shipping off this perilous coast. This tiny St. Aldhelm's chapel must be as nearly unaltered as any old building in England. It has no ornamentation, and no vanities to reduce the strength of thick walls and mighty buttresses. In a way it is fitting that this beacon should be so near the radar station which was a guard in 1939.

Worth Matravers is largely an all-stone village, with a church which contains Saxon fragments. The latter might be expected so near St. Aldhelm's Head but it is unusual to find the good Dorset farming name of Jesty cropping up on a memorial in a rather unusual way. I am prepared to back the memorial and to maintain stoutly that Benjamin Jesty of Worth was the first man to experiment with cowpox as a preventive of smallpox, in spite of all medical claims for Jenner in this connection.

Much of this coast can only be explored on foot or farm track. It is all wild and unspoilt from Winspit, past the curious little break at Dancing Ledge, to Anvil Point. Here we are on the outskirts of Swanage, where the 261-acre Durlston Country Park was opened by the County Council in 1973 as part of their policy of "Conservation for public enjoyment". Rubbish has been removed, most overhead cables have been put underground, car parks and lavatories, picnic facilities and an information centre have been provided. In order to protect the plants, birds and animals of this stretch of coast the cliffs from Durlston Head to Tilly Whim Caves are now a wild life sanctuary. Plenty of paths encourage exploration on foot, and between some of the unusual signposts are texts and exhortations, the work of a Victorian eccentric who helped make modern Swanage. Tilly Whim Caves are old stone quarries; the lighthouse is easily accessible, the Great Globe of Portland stone still weighs forty tons, and the nineteenth-century Durlston Head Castle now serves refreshments.

Swanage was the centre for the stone trade from Purbeck to London. On the quayside there are old railway lines from which great blocks of stone were unloaded into ships. Earlier still it must have been a skilful and cruelly hard job to get blocks of the unkind stuff into small sailing barges. Bits of old Swanage remain in the mill with its duck pond, but almost all the town was created in Victorian times by one or two men who were determined to make it a resort. They had the advantage of a bracing climate, and a sheltered sandy beach. Personally I think they did a very good job for those of us who like the facilities of town hotels within easy reach of lonely country and uncrowded sea.

Near Swanage the quarrying business seems to have turned mainly to road stone, with a sideline of sundials, bird baths and little stone rabbits for the garden. The days of the old "Queen Anne's men" seems to have faded in our time. They appear to have been a guild of quarrymen who had to be the sons of quarrymen born in wedlock, and not too soon after wedlock either. They had the right to go anywhere in certain parishes for stone, rather like the Free Coal Miners in the Forest of Dean. The story given me was that the French attempted a landing at Swanage during Queen Anne's reign, were driven off by quarrymen, and as a reward they were given a charter and a variety of rights. This may be partially true, but almost certainly the charter confirmed very much older rights, for quarrying was the trade of Swanage in Roman times.

As fighting men the combination of stoneworkers and seamen must have been fairly tough. Certainly the Danes found them so when King Alfred's fleet met them off Peveril Point and started the long tale of English naval victories.

Over the chalk hill of Ballard Down the Dorset coast goes on to Studland and Poole but these I mentioned on the straightforward soils of the Heath. Of the immensely varied coastal strip there remains the valley of Purbeck.

The valley is Wealden Clay and stretches from Swanage to Tyneham. It is a yellowish retentive clay, yielding rather wet pastures. Because the Purbeck stone, the chalk and the greensand are all so close, there are often queer mixtures of surface soil, and a tendency for springs to break out in unexpected places. In addition because the stone is so near there was a tendency to use it for houses, which has given a high percentage of solid and beautiful cottages and farms.

There are strangely sudden differences between the big arable fields on the Purbeck stone and the small wet pastures in such villages as Langton Matravers. Most of the houses here are on the stone of the hillside, and the actual vale between Swanage and Corfe has the usual clay character of isolated farm houses only, except for modern building. Beyond Corfe there are three villages in the vale, Church Knowle, Steeple and Tyneham, but here the vale is narrow and most of the houses are not on clay. Tyneham, for instance, on which we looked down, has its church on the chalk, and its biggest farm quite isolated on the clay. Steeple church is on a low hill, and Church Knowle is obviously a knoll. The prefix "Church" suggests that it had a church early in its history and in fact there was a priest here in Domesday Book which implies a church.

These three villages are all very small, and the size of the churches seems a little remarkable, especially since the parishes of Tyneham and Steeple were united as long ago as 1721. Rather unexpectedly Steeple parish goes over the great north ridge of Purbeck to Creech

Grange. The curate of Steeple had to cross the ridge to conduct services in the chapel-of-ease at Creech, which came very near mountaineering. On the top of the hill is one of the most curious bits of landscaping in Dorset. From the old mansion at Creech the very steep hill is thickly wooded to the skyline. Looking up from the Grange there is only one break in the woods which is closed by what seems to be a lodge gate in the wall of the park. It stands out against the sky exactly as the gate and lodge keeper's lodgings might be expected to appear. Yet it is all a fake. There never was an estate wall on the ridge, the gateway never had a gate and the lodge keeper's lodgings are solid masonry. It is utterly without purpose except to look imposing from the house, a good enough reason for a wealthy landowner in the 1740s.

Steeple has a particular interest for American visitors since in the fourteenth century the Lawrences who owned the village intermarried with the Washingtons. The arms of the Washingtons are quartered with those of the Lawrences, and take the form of three stars, over two horizontal stripes. This is claimed to be the origin of the flag of the United States, and shields with these arms quartered can still be seen in the church, the best dating from 1616.

Church Knowle is a village with every type of roofing but all the older houses have walls of stone. Presumably those old grey roofs of slab stone were sometimes too heavy even for low walls three feet thick. Certainly where they remain they have become sunken and twisted in a curious way. Early owners substituted thatch which needs the lightest of roof timbers—little more than ash poles. Later grim slates came in when the railways had made transport easy, and finally various "artistic" tiles were used, some of which are wholly synthetic. The church managed to survive terrific restoration in 1833–41 without losing its stone roof. Inside I like the ornate stone tomb of a gentleman who died in 1609 but who had ordered the monument in 1572, which is thirty-seven years before his death.

Wareham bridge is claimed as the gateway of Purbeck, but the first four miles southward are over barren heath. The entrance to the fertile vale and to the coast is at Corfe, which is always called Corfe Castle because this one narrow pass through the hills is entirely dominated by the castle. I have found the name a little confusing in referring to the history of Dorset. It is easy to say that Elfrida murdered her stepson King Edward at Corfe Castle, and immediately a picture arises of the old bridge at the entrance, and of the mighty walls above. In fact the castle is Norman and all that existed in Elfrida's time was a Saxon hunting lodge. Even this must have been a strong place, since the bare knoll of Corfe was difficult to climb, before the Normans built the tremendous walls and the soaring keep. Its story needs a book to itself, and I must leave it with only two references. It was a prison as well as a castle and King John sent here the sister of that Arthur whom he murdered, and whose story Shakespeare told with the romantic addition of Hubert being persuaded to spare the lad's eyes.

Finally the castle was held for the king in the Civil War of 1643 by Lady Bankes, and defended with complete success against all the military arts then known. Unfortunately in a second siege two years later the fortress was betrayed by one of the defenders, and within a month Parliament had ordered its destruction. It is remarkable that mining, gunpowder and every effort of the military engineers still left more of Corfe standing than remains of most old abbeys. It was built for strength rather than beauty and it still gives the impression of rugged power.

Below the dizzy heights of the ruins the little town crowds round the castle gate as it has done all through the centuries. All the old houses are of stone with low grey walls and stone roofs. In the little square there are no brick houses and no variation from curving roofs, and doorways made for men of 5 feet 6 inches. Even the hotel, which came with the railway, is not too wildly bad an imitation on the outside of the old Greyhound Inn opposite. There are many antique and giftie shops, but only a few enlarged windows are glaringly commercial. Presumably a man who has something to sell must have a window big enough to display his goods. The banks selling money are not very intrusive, but this may not be a fair comparison.

Down a back street there is one bit of red brick on top of an older wall of stone. It is very old red brick and very mellow, and this small building is labelled both "Town Hall" and "Museum". Further away from the castle are early council houses of complete utility, and making no effort to blend with the past. Some private efforts in stone are equally glaring but a few are in the tradition of good craftsmanship. Almost out of the town a modern council estate in stone struck me as well worth the extra money it must have cost.

This question of picturesque old houses, down narrow passages, raises many difficulties. They are beautiful, but if an attempt was made to preserve them uninhabited as museum pieces they would be almost meaningless. I can understand the local councillor who asked me how I would like to live in them.

Corfe church is old and beautiful. Its font has the most ornate lid I have ever seen, covered in weird carving and much gilding. It can only be raised by means of a pulley arrangement, and an infant would seem to be in peril if the rope broke during a christening.

To me there is something sensible about the way the builders of the church decided on a solid, low tower. They must have looked up at the mighty keep of the castle and decided not to compete. Very seldom in any ancient town is the church other than the greatest and most spectacular building.

Both church and castle were the work of the stoneworkers of Purbeck, and for centuries they have come here on Shrove Tuesday to have their sons entered on the records. One old custom involved the entered apprentice dashing across the road carrying a mug of ale, whilst his mates tried to stop him. There was also a fee of one pound of pepper for keeping open the old track to Ower Quay, and a tradition of kicking a football along this right of way. Old customs linger in Dorset and Corfe is possibly the least changed inhabited place in the county, even if Wareham is a little older.

Possibly it is fitting to end this book with Corfe, with its rich variety of men, after looking at this land of immensely varied soil and scenery. Here you can find families who have worked stone for a thousand years, or burrowed in threes and fours for china clay. There are dairy farmers from the wet pastures of the vale, cultivators from the large fields of the chalk, and smallholders from tiny cottages lost in the heath. Sailors from the coves of Purbeck still earn a hard living for nine months of the year, and an easy one in the holiday season. Men come back to Corfe to sleep from the factories of Poole or the Atomic Research Station. Just as Dorset is England in miniature, so does this small, ancient town hold examples of much of Dorset's beauty and character. The unofficial county motto is "Who's afeard", and Corfe gives the impression of quiet, abiding strength.

Ralph Wightman would have rejoiced with Dorset and the nation as a whole at the news that Henry Ralph Bankes of Kingston Lacy House, who died on 19 August 1981, left the whole of his estate —some 25 square miles of Dorset's finest scenery, including Corfe Castle and village—to the National Trust which accepted officially this greatest ever bequest on 15 April 1982.

INDEX

Abbotsbury, 19, 20, 48, 85, 167, 169, 170, 171, 172
Abbotsbury Swannery, 19, 169
Ackling Dyke, 60
Affpuddle, 25, 70, 71, 72
Agglestone, 43
Alderholt, 53
Allen, River, 37, 38, 56, 57, 63
Almer, 66
Alton Pancras, 104, 105, 106
Ansty, 110
Antell family, 77
Anvil Point, 181
Arish Mell, 20, 28, 45, 178
Arne, 32, 43, 44, 45,
Ashley family, 62, 63
Ashmore, 14, 59, 61, 124, 125
Askerswell, 156
Athelhampton, 73, 74, 75
Avon, River, 61
Axe, River, 160

Badbury Rings, 55, 56, 57, 60, 120
Bagber, 141
Ballard Down, 20, 42, 45, 182
Ballard Point, 45
Bankes family, 42, 55, 56, 57, 184, 185
Barnes, William, 85, 141
Bastard, John, 114
Batcombe, 16, 17, 101
Batcombe Down, 14, 59
Beaminster, 9, 95, 100, 106, 151–4, 155
Belchalwell, 16, 134, 137
Benfield, Eric, 82, 83
Benville Lane, 95
Bere Regis, 9, 11, 37, 46, 48, 50, 53, 59, 65, 66–8, 69, 112
Bettiscombe, 158, 159
Bexington, 168, 170
Bincombe, 18, 173

Bindon Abbey, 48, 58, 67
Bindon Hill, 45
Bingham family, 109
Birdsmoorgate, 160
Bishops Caundle, 18, 145
Blackdown, 172
Blackmore Vale, 10, 14, 15, 16, 17, 34, 97, 106, 107, 128, 129, 142, 149
Blandford, 59, 79, 112, 113–14, 129
Blandford St. Mary, 113, 115
Bloxworth, 53
Blue Pool, 24, 46
Bockhampton, Lower, 77
    Upper, 78
Bokerly Dyke, 122, 123
Bonsley Common, 115
Borstal Institution, 175
Bourton, 143
Bovington, 25, 26, 28, 29, 34, 42, 44, 47, 58, 69
Bradford Abbas, 18, 147
Bradford Peverell, 90, 91, 93
Branscombe Hill, 45
Briantspuddle, 25, 69, 70, 71
Bride, River, 167
Bridport, 9, 18, 19, 20, 28, 30, 89, 100, 152, 156, 157–8, 167
Brit, River, 166
Broad Oak, 159
Broadwey, 19
Broadwindsor, 149, 151, 153, 154
Brownsea Island, 32–4
Bryanston, 113, 115
Brymer family, 75
Buckhorn Weston, 17, 139, 140, 143
Buckland Newton, 16, 138
Buckland Ripers, 172
Bulbarrow Hill, 14, 59, 136, 138
Bullen family, 164
Burleston, 73

Burton Bradstock, 19, 167, 168
Buzbury, 120

Came Wood, 176
Canford Magna, 30, 31, 40, 52, 62
Cann, 130
Cashmore Inn, 121, 122
Casterbridge, 77
Castle Hill, Cranborne, 60
Castleman, Major, 121
Catherston Leweston, 164
Cattistock, 16, 90, 94, 95
Cecil family, 60, 61
Cerne, River, 103, 129
Cerne Abbas, 48, 96, 97, 98–101, 104
Chalbury, 58
Chantmarle, 95
Chapmans Pool, 29, 180
Charborough, 53, 54
Charlton Marshall, 113
Charminster, 27, 97, 103, 104, 106, 115
Charmouth, 30, 162, 164
Char River, 158
Chedington, 16, 96, 150
Chesil Beach, 19, 20, 167, 168, 169, 170, 172, 174
Chesilborne, 107, 108, 115
Chesterton, G. K., 98
Chetnole, 17, 18, 140
Chettle, 120, 121, 122
Chideock, 30, 165
Chilcombe, 169
Childe Okeford, 16, 134, 135, 136
Church Hope Cove, 175
Churchill, John, 140
  Sir Winston, 31, 101
Church Knowle, 20, 37, 45, 182, 183
Clare, Angel, 86
Clayesmore, 133
Clegg, A. Lindsay, 39
Clifton Maybank, 147
Clouds Hill, Bovington, 49
Cobb, Lyme Regis, 163, 166
Cobbett, William, 10
Compton Abbas, 16, 132
Compton Valence, 90

Corfe Castle, 20, 36, 37, 43, 44, 45, 67, 131, 182, 183–5
Corfe Mullen, 11, 40, 50, 53, 55
Corscombe, 14, 16, 90, 96
Corton, 172
Coryates, 172
Cowgrove, 53, 56
Cranborne, 11, 53, 59–62, 64, 106, 123
Cranborne Chase, 14, 117, 121, 122, 123, 124, 125, 127
Cranborne Common, 23
Crane, River, 121
Creech Barrow, 20, 46
Creech Grange, 28, 45, 182, 183
Crichel, Long, 120
Crichel, More, 63, 64
Crichel Down, 64
Cruxton, 92
Culpeppers Dish, 25

Daggons Road, 61
Damer, Joseph, 111
Dancing Ledge, 181
Debenham, Sir Ernest, 70, 71, 112
Devil's Nine Stones, Winterborne Abbas, 80, 86
Dewlish, 108, 109, 110
Dibben, Mr., 123
Digby family, 101
Dodington, G. B., 118
Doghouse Hill, 165
Dorchester, 27, 30, 35, 56, 59, 77, 79, 82, 84, 85, 86–9, 91, 97, 103, 104, 145
Dorset County Council, 26
Dorset County Council Farm Institute, 77
Dorset County Guide, 35
Dorset County Handbook, 35
Dorsetshire Gap, 107
Drag North, 94
Drax, Admiral Sir R. A. R. Plunkett-Ernle-Erle, 54
Durdle Door, 173, 177
Durweston, 113, 115, 116, 135

Eastbury, 117, 118

East Compton, 133
East Creech, 24, 45
East Holme, 37, 46
East Lulworth, 18, 20, 28, 178
East Stour, 17, 142
Edmonsham, 53
Egdon Heath, 10, 23
Eggardon Hill, 10, 80, 89, 155, 156
Egmont Point, 21
Encombe Glen, 29
Encombe House, 180
Eton College, 104, 105
Evershot, 16
Eypes Mouth, 165

Fair, John, 169
Farm Institute, Stinsford, 77
Farnham, 14, 59, 125, 126
Farnham Museum, 141
Farquharson, Ronald, 118
Farquharson family, 117
Ferndown, 51
Fifehead Magdalen, 17, 142
Fifehead Neville, 17
Fleet, 20
    The, 171, 172
Folke, 18, 145
Folly, Plush, 106, 107
Fontmell Magna, 16, 132, 133
Forde Abbey, 48, 96, 160
Fordington, Dorchester, 87, 88, 89,
    103
Fox Strangways family, 169
Frampton, 90, 91, 92, 93
Frampton family, 49
Friar Whaddon, 172
Frome, River, 11, 23, 45, 46, 47, 49,
    50, 77, 79, 80, 83, 84, 85, 86, 90,
    91, 94, 95, 102, 103, 104, 113,
    129, 153
Frome St. Quintin, 16
Frome Vauchurch, 90, 91, 92
Furzebrook, 24, 45, 46

Gaunts, 57
"General Allenby", The, 66
George Inn, The, Bridport, 148
George Inn, The, Broadwindsor, 149

Giant's Head, 100
Gillingham, 17, 139, 142, 143, 145
Glanvilles Wootton, 17, 139
Godlington, 44
Godmanstone, 102
Golden Cap, 19, 162, 165, 167
Golden Valley, 29, 180
Gold Hill, Shaftesbury, 132
    Shillingstone, 135
Gorwell, 172
Greyhound Hotel, The, Bridport,
    148
Greyhound Inn, Corfe Castle, 184
Gussage All Saints, 63, 121, 122
Gussage St. Andrew, 121
Gussage St. Michael, 121, 122

Halfway Inn, Purbeck, 44
Halstock, 96, 146, 150
Hambledon Hill, 134
Hambro family, 110
Hammoon, 17, 135
Hampreston, 11, 40, 51, 129
Hamworthy, 30
Handley, 59, 60, 122, 123
Handley Common, 123, 124
Hardown Hill, 164
Hardy, Thomas, 10, 14, 15, 23, 48,
    66, 67, 77, 78, 141
    Thomas Masterman, 172
Hardy Monument, 172, 173
Harrow Way, 153
Hartfoot Lane, 110
Haydon, 18
Hazelbury Bryan, 17, 139
Hermitage, 17, 139
Higher Kingcombe, 94
Higher Kingston, 77
Highhall, 56
Highways and Byways in Dorset, 35
Hilfield, 16, 97
Hillbutts, 56
Hilton, 14, 16, 110, 111
Hinton Martell, 53, 57
Hinton St. Mary, 17, 141
History of Dorset (Hutchins), 92
History of Wimborne Minster and
    District, 39

Hod Hill, 79, 113, 134
Holme Bridge, 46, 47
Holme Lane, 46, 47
Holmes Common, 127
Holnest, 18, 139
Holt, 22, 40, 53, 57, 58, 64
Holwell, 17, 140, 145
Honeybrook, 56
Hooke, 94
    River, 90, 93, 94, 95, 129
Hooper family, 63
Horsey family, 147
Horton, 53, 57, 58
Horton Inn, 57
Hundred Barrow Hill, Bere Regis,
    67, 68

Ibberton, 16, 134, 137
"Ilchester Arms, The", Abbotsbury,
    172
Ilchester family, 140, 169, 170, 171
Iwerne Courtney, 16, 132
Iwerne Minster, 14, 16, 132, 133, 134

Jeffreys, Lord Justice, 89
Jesty, Benjamin, 181

Kimmeridge, 9, 20, 21, 28, 179
Kingcombe, 94
King's Stag, 139
Kingston, 180
Kingston Lacey, 11, 53, 55, 56, 57
Kingston Russell, 18
Kington Magna, 17, 143, 144
Knighton Farm, Canford, 52

Lamberts Castle, 160
Langton Herring, 171
Langton Long, 113, 115
Langton Matravers, 182
Larmer Grounds, 124
Larmer Tree, 126, 139
Lawrence of Arabia, 36, 49
Le Breton, Sir Edward, 156
Leigh, 17, 18, 140
Leigh, Nr. Wimborne, 40
Lewesdon Hill, 154

Leweston, 18
Lexster, Fred, 169
Lillington, 18, 146
Little Bredy, 172
Little Piddle, 70
Litton Cheney, 167
Lodden, 142
Loders, 19, 156
Longbrody, 167
Long Burton, 18, 145
Long Crichel, 120
Longham, 11, 40
Loscombe, 94, 155
Loveless, George, 72, 73
Lulworth, 19, 28, 47, 173
Lulworth Castle, 179
Lulworth Cove, 177, 178
Lydlinch, 17, 140
Lydlinch Common, 18, 141
Lyme Regis, 19, 28, 30, 31, 162–4
Lytchett Matravers, 53, 54
Lytchett Minster, 54

Maiden Castle, 14, 80, 82, 83, 84, 99
Maiden Newton, 90, 91, 93, 95, 96,
    99
Manston, 17, 139
Mapperton, 155
Mappowder, 17, 106, 139
Margaret Marsh, 139
Marnhull, 17, 142, 144
Marshwood, 159
Marshwood Vale, 19, 158, 162
Martin family, 74
Martinstown, see Winterborne St.
    Martin
Maumbury Rings, 89
Mayor of Casterbridge, The, 87
Melbury Abbas, 16, 124, 129, 130,
    132
Melbury Bubb, 18
Melbury Down, 11
Melbury Osmond, 18, 140
Melbury Sampford, 18
Melcombe Bingham, 16, 109, 110
Melcombe Horsey, 16, 109
Melcombe Regis, 174
Melplash, 154, 155

"Mellstock", 77
Middlebere, 32, 43, 44, 45
Middlemarsh, 18
Milborne St. Andrew, 71, 112
Mill Street, Dorchester, 87
Milton, Gillingham, 17
Milton Abbas, 59, 109, 110, 111, 112
Milton Abbey, 48
Minterne Magna, 14, 16, 101
Minterne Parva, 101
Monkton Wyld, 160
Monmouth, 58
Moonfleet Hotel, 171, 172
Moors River, 11, 57
Morcombelake, 164
Morden, 53, 54
More Crichel, 63, 64
Moreton, 23, 26, 49, 50
Morning Well, 106
Morton, Cardinal John, 53, 67
Mosterton, 150, 153
Motcombe, 17
Mount Pleasant, 94
Muckleford, 91, 93

National Trust, 185
Netherbury, 153, 154, 155
Nether Cerne, 102
Nether Compton, 148
Nettlecombe Tout, 106, 107
Newton Heath, 44
Nine Barrow Down, 45
North Poorton, 94
North Wootton, 18

Oborne, 18, 147
Okeford Fitzpaine, 16, 134, 136, 137
Osmington, 174, 176
Osmington Mills, 28
Osmond, Stanley, 26
Ower, 32, 185

Pack Monday Fair, 147
Page, Harry, 31
Parnham, 153
Paul, Noel, 23, 26
Pentridge, 60, 122
Perceval, Professor John, 10

Peveril Point, 21, 182
Piddle, River, 11, 23, 46, 50, 65, 66, 68, 70, 77, 102, 104, 113, 129, 1 35
Piddlehinton, 70, 77, 81, 104, 105, 106, 115
Piddletrenthide, 70, 77, 104, 105, 106, 107, 108, 110
Pilsdon, 158
Pilsdon Pen, 19, 154, 158
Pimperne, 117
Pitt Rivers family, 126, 141
Plush, 106, 107
Poole, 10, 28, 29–32, 34, 36, 37, 41, 42, 43, 44, 51, 52, 56, 57, 126, 182
Poorton, 155
Portesham, 18, 172
Portland, 10, 18, 20, 162, 167, 170, 171, 174–6
Portland Bill, 19, 28
Portman family, 115
Poundbury, 83, 91
Povington, 28, 45, 47
Powerstock, 94, 155, 156
Poxwell, 18
Preston, 29, 172, 176
Puckstone, 43
Puddletown, 11, 25, 59, 68, 70, 73, 74, 75–7, 81
Pulham, 17, 18, 139
Puncknowle, 168, 169
Purbeck, 10, 17, 19, 20, 36, 47
Purse Caundle, 18
Pydel, Baron, 70, 74

Quatre Bras, 93
"Quiet Woman, The", Halstock, 146

Raleigh, Sir Walter, 146
Rampisham, 16, 90, 95
Rawlesbury Camp, 138
Redcliff, 36
Rempstone, 44
Ridgeway Hill, Purbeck, 45
Rings Hill, 45
Ringstead, 177
Rodden, 172
Roosevelt, F. D., 31

Ryme Intrinsica, 18, 140, 145

St. Aldhelm's Head, 20, 42, 146, 180, 181
St. Catherine's Chapel, Abbotsbury, 19, 170
  Ringstead, 177
St. James Common, 23
"St. Peter's Finger", 54
Sandbanks, 32, 43
Sandford Orcas, 148
Seaborough, 151
Seatown, 165
Sedgemoor, 58
Shaftesbury, 16, 30, 35, 36, 130–2
Shapwick, 55, 59, 64, 65, 113
Shave Cross, 158
Shaw, T. E., 36
Sherborne, 18, 30, 48, 97, 145, 146–7, 148
Shillingstone, 16, 79, 134, 135, 136, 137
Shroton, 132, 134
"Silent Woman, The", near Wareham, 146
Silton, 17, 143
Sixpenny Handley, 59, 60, 122, 123
Slape, 153
Sleep, 43, 44
Southover Heath, 25
South Perrott, 150
South Warren Hill, 155
Spetisbury, 113
Spread Eagle Hill, 128, 129
Spyway, 157
Stalbridge, 16, 18, 144, 145
Stalbridge Weston, 145
Steeple, 20, 182, 183
Stinsford, 53, 58, 77
Stoborough, 24, 43, 45, 46
Stock Gaylard, 17
Stoke Abbott, 154, 155
Stoke Wake, 16, 138
Stonebarrow Hill, 19
Stour, River, 11, 17, 23, 30, 37, 49, 50, 51, 52, 53, 61, 64, 65, 66, 79, 102, 113, 120, 129, 135, 153

Stourpaine, 113, 115, 116
Stour Provost, 17, 142
Stourton Caundle, 18, 145
Stratton, 93
Studland, 18, 20, 28, 29, 36, 42, 43, 44, 182
Sturminster Marshall, 54, 64, 65, 113
Sturminster Newton, 17, 114, 129, 141
Sutton Poyntz, 176
Sutton Waldron, 16, 132, 133
Swanage, 20, 28, 36, 46, 181–2
Swyre, 157, 168
Sydling St. Nicholas, 91, 96, 97, 98
Symondsbury, 158

Tarrant Crawford, 120
Tarrant Gunville, 14, 117, 120, 127
Tarrant Hinton, 118, 119, 120
Tarrant Keynston, 57, 120
Tarrant Launceston, 118
Tarrant Monkton, 118, 119
Tarrant Rawston, 119, 120
Tarrant Rushton, 119, 120
Tess of the D'Urbervilles, 48, 67, 86, 142
Thorncombe, 160, 165
"Three Horse Shoes, The", Spyway, 157
Throop Clump, 69
Tilly Whim Caves, 181
Todber, 17
Tollard Royal, 59, 124
Toller Down Gate, 9, 95
Toller Fratrum, 90, 93
Toller Porcorum, 90, 93, 94
Toller Whelme, 96
Tolpuddle, 70, 72, 73
Tolpuddle Martyrs, 49, 64, 72–3
Trent, 18, 19, 148, 149
Treves, Sir Frederick, 35, 40, 41, 46, 47, 54, 63, 69, 70, 71, 121, 142, 180
Turberville family, 48, 67
Turnerspuddle, 25, 68, 69, 70
Turnworth, 115, 136
Tyneham, 20, 28, 47, 179, 182

Uddens Water, 57
United Kingdom Atomic Energy Research Establishment, Winfrith, 25, 26, 28, 42, 46, 47
Upcerne, 101
Upper Bockhampton, 78
Up Sylding, 106, 108
Upwey, 172, 173
Upwey Wishing Well, 81

Vanbrugh, Sir John, 118
Verwood, 52, 61
Verwood Common, 23

Waddock Cross, 68
Wareham, 9, 10, 11, 27, 30, 31, 32, 34–7, 42, 43, 44, 45, 46, 58, 68, 183, 185
"Weatherbury", 77
Weld family, 48, 165, 178
West Bay, 19, 157, 165, 166, 167
West Bexington, 168
Western Gazette, The, 154
West Holme, 28, 48
West Lulworth, 18, 45, 178
West Moors, 52, 61
West Orchard, 17, 139
West Parley, 11, 52
West Stafford, 49, 80, 86
West Stour, 17, 142, 144
Weymouth, 10, 19, 28, 82, 85, 172, 173–4
Whaddon Hill, 154
Whitchurch Canonicorum, 159
Whitcombe, 85, 86
White, Mr. W. J., 142
"White Hart, The", Beaminster, 152
White Nothe, 21, 172, 173, 177
White Sheet Hill, 94
Wightman family, 95
Wimborne, 11, 34, 37–41, 42, 48, 49, 50, 51, 54, 55, 56, 57, 58
Wimborne Family, 52
Wimborne St. Giles, 59, 62, 63, 64, 103

Winchester College, 97, 105
Winfrith Heath, 69; see also United Kingdom Atomic Energy Research Establishment, Winfrith
Winspit, 180
Winterborne Abbas, 79, 81, 86, 89
Winterborne Came, 80, 86
Winterborne Clenstone, 66, 112
Winterborne Herringston, 80, 85, 86
Winterborne Houghton, 66, 112
Winterborne Kingston, 65, 66
Winterborne Monkton, 80, 82, 85
Winterborne St. Martin, 79, 80, 81
Winterborne Steepleton, 59, 79, 81
Winterborne Stickland, 66, 112
Winterborne Thomson, 65, 66
Winterborne Whitchurch, 66, 112
Winterborne Zelston, 59, 65, 66, 112
Winyard's Gap, 96, 107, 129, 150
Witchampton, 56, 59, 63, 64
Wolfe, General, 134
Wolfeton House, 103
Woodbury Hill Fair, 9, 66, 67, 134
Woodcutts, 124, 125, 126, 127
Woodcutts Common, 127
Woodsford, 49, 50
Woodyates, 122, 123
Wool, 25, 26, 46, 47–8, 50, 68
Woolbridge Manor, 67
Woolland, 16, 134, 137, 138
Wootton Fitzpaine, 160
Wootton Glanvilles, 17, 139
Worbarrow Bay, 21, 28, 45, 179
Worgret Heath, 37, 58
"World's End, The", 66
Worth Matravers, 180, 181
Wraxall, 16, 90, 95, 97, 106
Wren, Christopher, 114
Wyke Regis, 20
Wynford Eagle, 90
Wytch, 32, 44

Yeatman, 140
Yetminster, 18, 22, 145